EAT MESQUITE AND MORE

A Cookbook
for Sonoran Desert
Foods and Living

by Desert Harvesters

DesertHarvesters.org
Tucson, AZ

A TASTE OF DESERT HARVESTERS EVENTS

Gathering of harvesters at Desert Harvesters' hammermill training

Photo: Jim Harris

Page 3 captions in clockwise direction beginning at top left:

1. *Prickly pear fruit-harvesting workshop*   Photo: Brad Lancaster

2. *Planting future abundance in public right-of-way*   Photo: Brad Lancaster

3. *Community native, wild foods tasting*   Photo: Ian Fritz

4. *Community mesquite milling*   Photo: Brad Lancaster

5. *Sampling the diverse flavors of pods picked from different mesquite trees*   Photo: Brad Lancaster

6. *Processing barrel cactus fruit in hands-on workshop*   Photo: Jill Lorenzini

COVER IMAGE CAPTIONS

Front cover captions in clockwise direction beginning at top:

1. *Salt-Cured Cholla Buds*   Photo: Jill Lorenzini

2. *Chiltepin Beet Hummus, Olive-Mesquite Tapenade, Sky Island Pesto, Cholla Pickles, Southwest Focaccia*   Photo: Christian Timmerman

3. *Three-Bean Salad with ironwood blossom garnish, palo verde and cholla bud salsapacho, and green foothills palo verde seedpods on side*   Photo: Brad Lancaster

4. *Salad of amaranth greens, pincushion cactus fruit, hierba del venado, wolfberries, and desert lavender flowers*   Photo: Jill Lorenzini

5. *Chiltepin Flan with wolfberry garnish*   Photo Christian Timmerman

6. *Toasted desert hackberries*   Photo: Jill Lorenzini

7. *Mesquite Beer*   Photo: Christian Timmerman

Inside front cover photo captions in clockwise direction starting at top left:

1. *Savory Mesquite Muffins*   Photo: Christian Timmerman

2. *Vegetable and Cholla Bud Skewers*   Photo: Christian Timmerman

3. *Saguaro fruit and desert ironwood seed harvest time*   Photo: Jill Lorenzini

4. *Chocolate-Dipped Juñ (dried saguaro fruit) with chia seeds*   Photo: Jill Lorenzini

5. *Desert Dry Rub on salmon*   Photo: Christian Timmerman

6. *Prickly pear fruit harvest by cargo bicycle*   Photo: Brad Lancaster

Inside back cover photo captions in clockwise direction starting at top left:

1. *Emory oak acorns and meal*   Photo: Jill Lorenzini

2. *Mesquite Ice Cream, Mesquite Toffee, prickly pear ice cream with Prickly Pear Syrup*   Photo: Christian Timmerman

3. *Salad of wild and garden greens with chuparosa and palo verde blossom garnish*   Photo: Brad Lancaster

4. *Mesqcafé Olé and Muff's Mesquite Biscotti*   Photo: Christian Timmerman

5. *Verdolagas Fritters with Verdolagas Salsa*   Photo: Jill Lorenzini

6. *Prickly Pear Lemonade*   Photo: Christian Timmerman

Back cover photo captions in clockwise direction starting at top left:

1. *Saguaro fruit*   Photo: Barbara Rose

2. *Mandala of velvet and screwbean mesquite pods; desert ironwood, palo verde, and barrel cactus seeds; and dried cholla buds*   Photo: Jill Lorenzini

3. *Barrel cactus fruit*   Photo: Jill Lorenzini

4. *Desert ironwood blossoms*   Photo: Jill Lorenzini

TESTIMONIALS

I've been a huge fan of Desert Harvesters for years and this beautifully designed book is truly a must if you want to explore the culinary heritage and flavors of the Sonoran Desert.
- Pascal Baudar, author of
The New Wildcrafted Cuisine and *The Wildcrafting Brewer*

Eat Mesquite and More is a book of recipes and plant lore we may all really need someday, but it's also a book to enjoy right now with its interesting blend of native desert plants and recipes keyed to our habitual tastes and new, adventurous tastes as well.
- Deborah Madison, author of *Vegetable Literacy* and *In My Kitchen*

This fantastic book will become the first reference for every forager in the Sonoran Desert region and a cherished manifesto even for those living far from the saguaro's shadow.
- Samuel Thayer, author of *The Forager's Harvest, Nature's Garden,* and *Incredible Wild Edibles*

We need to celebrate food, weaving it into every part of our being, our sense of place.
Eat Mesquite and More helps us do that as it honors the plants (and a few animals!), the cultures, and this magnificent desert region. I love this book!
- Wendy C. Hodgson, author of *Food Plants of the Sonoran Desert,*
Sr. research botanist and herbarium curator Desert Botanical Garden

The recipes in this book will inspire residents of the Southwest desert regions (and beyond) to new uses for the wonderful flavors of mesquite, cacti, and other abundant indigenous plants.
- Sandor Ellix Katz, author of *Wild Fermentation* and *The Art of Fermentation*

… the definitive resource for Baja Arizonans who care about eating locally and caring for this place we call home.
- Megan Kimble, managing editor, and Doug Biggers,
editor and publisher, *Edible Baja Arizona* magazine

Chock full of interesting recipes, it showcases the creativity of so many cooks.
…useful for both the experienced forager and beginners alike.
- Carolyn Niethammer, author of *The Prickly Pear Cookbook* and *Cooking the Wild Southwest*

Eat Mesquite and More is a place-based guide to health and wellbeing that connects us to the bounty of the southwestern drylands.
- Daphne Miller, M.D., author of *Farmacology* and *The Jungle Effect*

I can almost taste this book, one that brings to life the flavors of this magical land while honoring the cultural traditions of the region and advocating for regenerative land management practices.
- Courtney White, author and co-founder of the Quivira Coalition

---

For more testimonials see the *Eat Mesquite and More* page at DesertHarvesters.org.

green press
INITIATIVE

Desert Harvesters is committed to preserving ancient forests and natural resources. We elected to print this title on 100% post consumer recycled paper, processed chlorine free. As a result, for this printing, we have saved:

78 Trees (40' tall and 6-8" diameter)
36,343 Gallons of Wastewater
34 million BTU's of Total Energy
2,433 Pounds of Solid Waste
6,701 Pounds of Greenhouse Gases

Desert Harvesters chose printer, Thomson-Shore, Inc., because they stock this paper, and are a member of Green Press Initiative, a nonprofit program dedicated to supporting authors, publishers, and suppliers in their efforts to reduce their use of fiber obtained from endangered forests.

For more information, visit www.greenpressinitiative.org

Environmental impact estimates were made using the Environmental Defense Paper Calculator. For more information visit: www.papercalculator.org.

Printed and bound in the United States of America on acid- and chlorine-free, *100% post-consumer* recycled paper

Cover and book design: Teri Reindl Bingham

Illustrations: Jill Lorenzini (LorenziniWorks.com),
Joe Marshall (PorkChopPress.com), Bill Mackey (WorkerIncorporated.com), Kay Sather, Marina Cornelius

Photographs: Christian Timmerman (ThroughHikers.com), Jill Lorenzini (LorenziniWorks.com),
Ian Fritz (IanFritz.com), Brad Lancaster (HarvestingRainwater.com), Barbara Rose (BeanTreeFarm.com),
Kimi Eisele (KimiEisele.com), Kathleen Dreier (KathleenDreier.com), Jim Martin Harris (JMartinHarris.com),
Josh Schachter (JoshPhotos.com), Ben Johnson (BenJohnsonArt.com), Doris Evans (Flickr.com/Photos/DorisEvans/Albums), Steven Meckler (MecklerPhotography.com), Phil Medica (U.S. Geological Society),
Charles van Riper III, Wade Sherbrooke, and Desert Harvesters volunteers

Desert Harvesters
Eat Mesquite and More: A Cookbook for Sonoran Desert Foods and Living
ISBN: 978-0-692-93874-4

1. Cooking (wild foods). 2. Southwest cooking. 3. Cooking with mesquite, saguaro, desert ironwood, acorn, prickly pear, devil's claw, wolfberry, hackberry, chiltepin, barrel cactus, cholla, desert chia, palo verde, desert flowers, wild greens and desert herbs, wild meats and insects. 4. Solar cooking. 5. Planting, harvesting, processing, and celebrating wild, native Sonoran Desert foods. 7. Locavore. 8. Foraging. 9. Food forests. 10. Rainwater harvesting. 11. Food and water security. 12. Green infrastructure. 13. Dryland agroforestry.

Library of Congress Control Number (LCCN): 2017952735

TABLE OF
CONTENTS

DEVIL'S CLAW (WET SUMMER)

WOLFBERRY (WET SUMMER | SPRING)

HACKBERRY (FALL)

CHILTEPIN (FALL)

BARREL CACTUS (FALL | WINTER)

NOPAL AKA PRICKLY PEAR PAD (SPRING)

MEATS & INSECTS

PART III: LIVING AND EATING IN PLACE

ATTRIBUTES ARE IDENTIFIED FOR RECIPES, when applicable. These attributes include:

 Gluten-free   Solar-cooked   Raw   Vegan

PART I

MANIFEASTO

Chiltepin Beet Hummus, Olive-Mesquite Tapenade, Sky Island Pesto, Cholla Pickles, Southwest Focaccia

Desert Harvesters Manifeasto

Nature is a system of abundance, cycles, and efficiency. We can mimic that.
Increase the fecundity of plants and their companions.
Leave and invest fallen pods, leaves, and cut-up prunings as fertile mulch for animals, soil life, and trees.
Say "thank you" for your harvest with generous actions.
Turn landscapes into lifescapes and lushscapes.
Give back. REINVEST.

We live in a land of precious water.
Use local, free, and gravity-fed water, rather than imported, costly, and mechanically pumped waters.
Therefore PLANT THE RAIN.

Capture rainwater by digging basins and other earthworks.
Catch rainwater runoff from roofs.
Divert public street runoff into public right-of-way rain gardens.
When you grow and harvest rain-irrigated desert food you ENHANCE our local ecosystem.

HARVEST nearby.
Look for wild native-food sources in your backyard, rights-of-way, and urban trails.
If they don't exist there, PLANT them.
Re-plant and re-wild the urban and suburban core.
If you live in rural areas, look around! Learn what surrounds you.
See the abundance? Savor it.

DELIGHT your taste buds.
Be a culinary cupid. Introduce new flavors to one another.
Find new combinations of traditional, wild foods. INNOVATE.
Prickly pear borscht, anyone? Mesquite muesli?
Practice place-based, place-appropriate, place-inspired fusion.
We're not in Kansas anymore.

Be here now. CELEBRATE.
Give thanks to the ancestors.
Make offerings for the future.
Contribute to food, fertility, and water security, here, now, and for
your children, their children, and their children.

Expand your COMMUNITY.
Meet your fellow desert dwellers.
Those that have roots and flowers.
Those that crawl and flutter.
Get to know other humans who harvest.
There is so much to observe, so much to love.
Invite. Involve. Include.

FEASTING

Mesquite bark, dirt, pollen and water.
The flavors of their aroma mingle
at the back of my mouth
calling on my senses.

The taste of green is
so strong it colors my
tongue like a gumball.

The flavor of dirt
is more than that.
I can feel the grit scrape my palate.
The imagined grains grind between my teeth.

The dust of pollen rests
on the hairs of my nostrils like
they would on the delicate abdomen of a bee.
I taste through smell.
I imagine nectar seeping through me.

The holiness of the moisture of clouds is gourmet.
I gorge on the summer and winter
rains of the desert.
I savor the goodness of wetness
it has the longest aftertaste.
The taste lasts a lifetime moving me to recall it
a reminder of my humanness.
I feast, but I eat nothing.

- Ofelia Zepeda

Ofelia Zepeda is a member of the Tohono O'odham Nation. She holds a PhD in linguistics from the University of Arizona and is the author of a grammar of the Tohono O'odham language, A Papago Grammar *(1983) as well as the poetry collections* Ocean Power: Poems from the Desert *(1995) and* Jewed'l-hoi/Earth Movements, O'odham Poems *(1996). Zepeda was awarded a MacArthur Fellowship in 1999.*

FOREWORD

Eat Mesquite and More is not merely a book containing delicious multi-cultural recipes that incorporate the desert's bounty. It is a celebration of how to personally know and wisely utilize desert resources such as mesquite, wild fruits, cholla cactus buds, *quelites*, and hundreds of other edible desert plants that nourish us and connect us to this bounty. It is also an invitation to live in the Sonoran Desert fully engaged with this remarkable but vulnerable place that is like no other on the planet.

More than any other grassroots organization to emerge from the Sonoran Desert over the last century, Desert Harvesters takes seriously the call for us to be inspired stewards, but in a way that is filled with fun, flavor, feast, and frolic. They exemplify a paradigm shift in the history of the conservation movement, away from being engaged with the desert *only with our minds* (policy, politics, protest, and polemics) to being engaged through our hearts and souls, minds and bodies, senses and sensibilities.

In short, the desert is good to eat, good to gather in, good to garden in, and good to glorify. If that sounds suspiciously like a religious affirmation, well, just remember the root meaning of *religio* in Latin—re: "(to do) again" and *ligare*: "to bind" or "to connect." RECONNECT! To re-mind and re-bind us to where and who we are.

That—with a broad brushstroke—is what Desert Harvesters hopes every recipe, story, and every commentary in this precious book will help you to do. As well as inspire you to harvest and give back to the desert, thus:

- Reminding us of where we live and how to live with dignity and delectability.

- Re-binding us directly to the plants and indirectly to the animals with whom we share this place.

- Allowing us to socially coalesce with one another through foraging forays, communal foresting and gardening, rainwater harvesting, feasts, and festivals, which teach us how to be better citizens and stewards.

- Reconnecting our sense of taste to a sense of place through helping us experience the unique *terroir* of the foods, beverages, herbs, and culinary expressions that are native or endemic to this Stinkin' Hot Desert.

• Helping us innovate means of gaining the food we need for our well-being in ways that use less water and fossil fuel, two scarce and poorly managed resources.

Without this kind of reconnection, most desert residents lose sight and sense of where they live. Without a deep sense of natural and cultural history, we cannot shape a sustainable future. Without such means of gaining nourishment becoming common behavior in our community, we risk watching our own communities, and the larger natural communities that support us, deteriorate. Desert Harvesters' inquiries, outreach events, publications, and communal practices are so valuable because they help us root *ourselves in place* in the face of ignorance, climate change, economic recessions, and geopolitical uncertainty.

Grassroots planting, foraging, cooking, and feasting efforts fostered by Desert Harvesters are one of the many reasons Tucson has been honored as the first designated UNESCO City of Gastronomy in the United States. This designation values the agricultural and culinary contributions of *all* cultures in our region, their traditions *and* innovations. It also gives activists here a mandate and momentum for dealing with the still-persisting problems of food insecurity and food injustice in our borderlands region. We live along a border marked by a great disparity in access to affordable healthy food. The solutions that Desert Harvesters has advanced can work on either side of the geopolitical divide, while mischievously challenging agribusiness-as-usual.

So bask in the blessed ferment, fun, and feasting this new cookbook offers. Eat mesquite, eat more than mesquite, reconnect to where you live. And enjoy it!

- Gary Paul Nabhan

Gary Paul Nabhan is a nature writer, agrarian activist, and ethnobiologist who works on conserving the links between biodiversity and cultural diversity. He has been honored as a pioneer and creative force in the "local food movement" and seed saving community by Utne Reader, Mother Earth News, New York Times, Bioneers, *and* Time *magazine. As the W. K. Kellogg Endowed Chair in Sustainable Food Systems at the University of Arizona's Southwest Center, he serves as founding director of the Center for Regional Food Studies.*

INTRODUCTION

In 2011, Desert Harvesters published *Eat Mesquite!: A Cookbook* containing over 80 recipes featuring mesquite, most often as a flour ground from the pods of either native velvet, screwbean, or honey mesquite trees. The project was both a celebration of the desert's abundance and a way to gauge and grow public interest in a single, wild, indigenous food source.

The recipes in that cookbook were culled from over 150 community contributions from people devoted to supporting a local food system, eating healthy, and upholding regional food traditions. We also included some from the out-of-print little cookbook called *Mesquite Meal Recipes* published by the San Pedro Mesquite Company, which graciously gave us permission to reprint whatever we chose.

We viewed mesquite as a "gateway food," a way of inviting people to see and engage with not only mesquite but also 400 or more other wild foods indigenous to the Sonoran Desert. *Eat Mesquite and More* celebrates this abundance, focusing on mesquite and including 15 additional wild desert foods. It contains some of the recipes from our first cookbook as well as new additions solicited from community members and vetted by a team of volunteer cooks and reviewers.

This cookbook is a community affair, more of a potluck than a fancy banquet. All of the recipes are a little different in style and approach. While our volunteers tested and tasted as many as possible, our process was not quite as exact as that of a *Cook's Illustrated* test kitchen. Still, we worked to make the written entries as consistent as possible, while maintaining the individual flavor and personality of the contributors.

We encourage you to practice with the recipes—especially before throwing a dinner party—to gain confidence in what works best for your kitchen and equipment. We also encourage a spirit of playfulness and experimentation so you can innovate new flavors and make substitutions as needed.

The cookbook includes a "Meet the Ingredient" introduction to each food to help you identify, understand, and appreciate the food source more deeply. Written by seasoned desert harvester Jill Lorenzini with help from other harvesters, these introductions include basic information on seasonality, harvesting, nutrition, planting, and more. We hope you develop your own relationship with each of these foods, understanding them within the context of the desert ecosystem as well as that of your backyard and kitchen. Jill also created the beautiful black-and-white icons identifying each food.

While many of these foods have long been part of Southwest culinary practices, much of that heritage has not been codified in writing but passed along via story and demonstration. We celebrate that intangible heritage in the stories that accompany each section of the cookbook about notable harvesters from the Sonoran Desert (and beyond). These stories feature people and organizations that have influenced generations of harvesters, use particularly creative culinary approaches, have brought wild foods into their businesses, or are doing important work to share best practices of harvesting and eating desert foods with wide audiences. We hope you find their stories as inspiring as we do!

This book collects just a sampling of flavors and practices. We consider the harvesting, cooking, and sharing of wild food ingredients an ongoing process of discovery and learning. You might discover new combinations of flavors or develop more efficient ways of preparing or harvesting these foods. Submit reviews of the recipes as well as variations, changes, and entirely new recipes to our Recipe Database at DesertHarvesters.org. As you deepen your relationship with the desert, please share what you discover with us and with your neighbors and friends.

See you out there. Or at the dinner table!

- Desert Harvesters

ABOUT
DESERT HARVESTERS

Desert Harvesters is a non-profit, grassroots organization in Tucson, Arizona, born of a desire to grow, connect with, and contribute to a more delicious life in the place where we live, work, and play.

Our mission is to promote and enhance the planting, awareness, and use of native wild food sources, which can thrive on harvested rainfall and runoff without the additional irrigation that depletes both groundwater and creeks and rivers. We offer workshops in how to harvest and prepare mesquite and other native foods, hold community events to celebrate local harvests, and plant native food-bearing trees and understory plantings throughout Tucson and beyond. By fostering a reciprocal relationship between native plants and local people, we believe we can strengthen local food security, reconnect people with the ecosystem, and build a more dynamic and sustainable community.

Our effort began in 1996 with an annual tree planting in the Dunbar/Spring neighborhood north of downtown Tucson. Neighbors came together to plant hardy, endemic, food-bearing trees such as desert ironwood, velvet mesquite, and foothills palo verde, as well as diverse understory plantings. Over the next decade, we created a resilient neighborhood forest—one that could double as a living pantry, a pharmacy, a flood control system, a natural air conditioner, a habitat for native wildlife, and an auditorium of native bird song.

We learned to "plant the rain," in deep, mulched basins. From indigenous teachers with long traditions of reciprocity with desert foods, we learned how to harvest and prepare what the plants provided. We learned how to mill mesquite pods into tasty and nutritious flour and eventually bought a Meadows Mills #5 hammermill with a grant from an organization called PRO Neighborhoods.

We held our first public milling in 2003 where we milled pods from neighborhood trees into flour to make mesquite pancakes with prickly pear syrup. Our goal was to show people the whole system, inspiring them to spread the ideas and practices. By 2013, we needed three hammermills to keep up with all the milling. That year we served over 1,500 pancakes in our community garden/food forest against a backdrop of live music and wild food demonstrations. We held community bake sales and "tasting parties" giving people a chance to experiment and innovate. And in 2011, we created *Eat Mesquite!: A Cookbook*, drawing on the culinary traditions and innovation in our community to share the secrets of mesquite with a wider audience.

Over the years, we've expanded our offerings. We now offer near-monthly introductory wild food demonstrations and hands-on harvesting and processing workshops as well as our annual mesquite millings through a partnership with the Community Food Bank of Southern Arizona and its Santa Cruz River Farmers' Market and Las Milpitas Farm. We collaborate with Neighborhood Foresters to continue planting and caring for native wild food forests at home, along our streets, and in schoolyards and parks. We consult with local restaurants, breweries, and bars, helping them introduce seasonal local wild foods and drinks throughout the year. We encourage growing native foods on-site, irrigated solely with free rainwater, greywater, and condensate when possible. We work to build on the many traditions and efforts that resulted in Tucson being named the first UNESCO World City of Gastronomy in the United States in 2015.

At Desert Harvesters, our idea of fun is spending time planting and harvesting desert foods, preparing that food into beautiful meals, and sharing it in community with others. We'd love to have you at our table. Join us at DesertHarvesters.org.

PLANTING, HARVESTING, PROCESSING, AND ENJOYING LOCAL ABUNDANCE

1a. Planting rain in newly installed neighborhood traffic circle Photo: Brad Lancaster

1b. Planting wild food plants in traffic circle Photo: Brad Lancaster

1c. Harvesting from now-grown wild food plants in traffic circle Photo: Brad Lancaster

2. Barrel cactus flowers and buds Photo: Jill Lorenzini

3. Green foothills palo verde seed pods Photo: Jill Lorenzini

4. Processing ironwood pods and seeds Photo: Jill Lorenzini

5. Prickly Pear Wine, Acorn Saguaro Seed Bread, wild and garden greens salad,
palo verde and chuparosa blossom garnishes Photo: Christian Timmerman

PART II
RECIPES

Verdolagas Fritters, Verdolagas Salsa, and Verdolagas Potato Salad

Photo: Jill Lorenzini

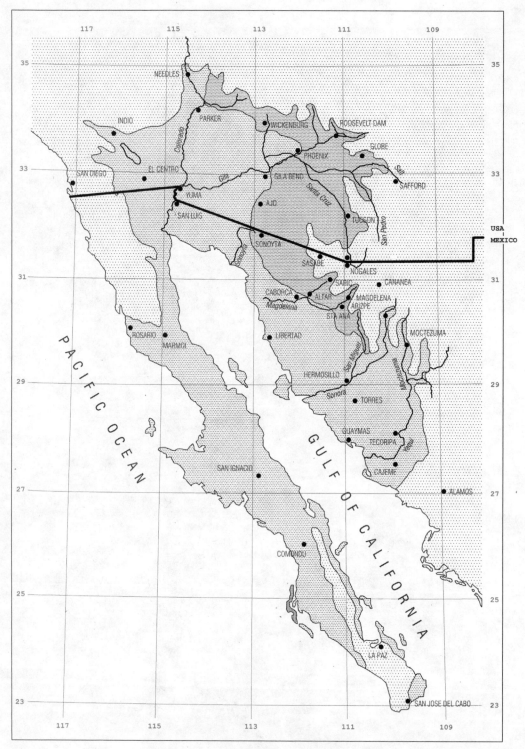

MAP OF SONORAN DESERT

SONORAN DESERT
ARIZONA UPLAND SUBZONE OF SONORAN DESERT

Map: Bill Mackey

ABOUT
THE RECIPES

Welcome to your Sonoran Desert culinary adventure! The recipes in this book honor the deceiving abundance of our desert region. That dry, dusty landscape full of spiky shrubs and thorny cactus? Look again. See the blooms and buds and seeds and fruits? The desert is truly a rich food forest. And you are about to enter it.

THE RECIPES

The recipes in this book are organized by the season in which their primary desert ingredients are most often harvested (see Wild Foods Harvest Calendar, p. 28). Sometimes an ingredient crosses into several seasons or has a second harvest. Also, many desert foods can be processed and stored for use throughout the year.

The cookbook begins with summer, the season that represents the cusp of endings and beginnings in the Sonoran Desert. As the dry heat gives way to the life-giving rains, summer is a time of renewal and is marked by the Tohono O'odham—and many other desert dwellers—as the new year.

This book emphasizes ingredients of food plants native to the Sonoran Desert (see map, p. 24), highlighting its Arizona Upland subdivision, the home of Desert Harvesters. Many of these food plants, or close relatives of them, can also be found or grown in the other eleven deserts of North America and also in the deserts of South America. As such, this book can be a resource and a template throughout the Americas.

We also encourage harvesters to explore neighboring elevations and microclimates. Our inclusion of acorns is an invitation to do just that. Acorns are typically found growing in transition zones and in elevations above the Sonoran Desert, in the mountains known as "Sky Islands" (see p. 142).

The seasons in the book are as follows:

DRY SUMMER: May, June

WET SUMMER: Late June, July, August, Early September

FALL: Mid-September, October, November

WINTER: December, January, February

SPRING: Late February, March, April

While many dishes incorporate several wild desert ingredients, we have chosen a primary ingredient category for its placement. For example, the recipe for Jill's EZ Mesquite Vegan Pancakes is listed under "Mesquite Breakfasts," though the recipe calls for the optional additions of saguaro, barrel cactus, desert chia, wolfberry, and hackberry. You will find cross-listings for recipes uding other wild desert foods in the indices in the back of the book.

Additional attributes are also identified for recipes, when applicable. These attributes include:

(GF) Gluten-free

(S) Solar-cooked

(R) Raw

(V) Vegan

Since the majority of the recipes in this book are meatless (except those in the Meats & Insects section), we've opted to only list "Vegan" as an attribute. Of course, many of the recipes can be modified to become vegan or gluten-free or even solar-cooked, if you are familiar with substitutions and solar ovens. You can also use the indices in the back of the book to find recipes by these specific attributes.

THE INGREDIENTS

Some or all of the ingredients celebrated in these pages may be new to you. Be sure to read the "Meet the Ingredient" introduction to each desert food as each unveils a holistic portrait of each ingredient.

Each of the ingredients in this book has specific and special nutritional, medicinal, and gustatory properties. Cactus foods tend to be cooling. Seeds are nutrient-rich. Mesquite, prickly pear, and acorn help regulate blood-sugar levels. Chia, mustard, peppergrass, and plantago seeds are hygroscopic, meaning they readily take up water. We think of many of these ingredients as "tonic foods," medicines that invigorate or strengthen the body and mind.

Desert foods can be potent! Many desert plants regularly and abundantly produce food, despite being born of harsh and dry conditions. Even in drought, they can share bounty.

We recommend sampling small amounts of desert foods first to see how your body and palate react to the tastes and textures. As you find your way, discerning what suits you, you can add more quantities. We also suggest pairing this cookbook with the many resources at the back of this book (p. 329) that offer more in-depth information about both indigenous and contemporary uses of these ingredients. This kind of knowledge will help guide your cooking and eating adventures.

We also encourage creativity. Experiment with these recipes. Find ways to use desert foods in your favorite tried-and-true dishes for fantastic fusion feasting!

THE ETHICAL HARVEST

We hope the recipes in this cookbook inspire you to harvest your own ingredients. We encourage an ethic and practice of *increasing* rather than *depleting* the bounty, a relationship that is reciprocal rather than extractive.

Many lives and ecological systems depend on these foods. Birds, bats, and insects pollinate desert flowers, resulting in fruits and seeds that many animals consume. Seeds are then distributed in droppings, which grow and produce future harvests. It is important to leave enough for these other creatures.

Some guidelines suggest harvesting only 10 to 30 percent of a single plant's bounty. But consider that others might precede or follow you, thus collectively depleting the bounty. Another adage is "Only pick what is within reach," which might make sense with a tall tree, where most of the fruit and seed remains out of reach. But in smaller plants, picking everything in reach might again deplete the bounty. These are things to consider as you shape your conscious practice or seek vendors from whom to purchase. Be wise and generous.

Of course, you can easily increase the bounty by planting more of it. We encourage you to include native food-bearing plants in your landscaping efforts (see Planting Rain, p. 310, and the Planting Tips in the Basics section of each wild food chapter). Then you'll have easy access to delicious desert foods right outside your door.

A NOTE ABOUT PHOTOGRAPHS: *Throughout the book, dish names included in recipe listings are capitalized in photograph captions. Additional dishes are not.*

RECIPE FOR SONORAN DESERT
ABUNDANCE

Contributed by Jill Lorenzini

This recipe combines the best of traditional knowledge with new ideas and practices. It yields a food-wealthy community that cares about natural resources and finds ways to connect with people and build community at every turn.

INGREDIENTS:

Indigenous knowledge of the desert and native plants for food and medicine

Intact native ecosystems as templates for planting and replanting native food forests

Permaculture principles and design strategies based on understandings of how local ecosystems naturally thrive

Rainwater harvesting concepts and design

Organizations that teach about and promote the benefits of perennial native desert plant foods

Plant nurseries that provide native food plants and other resources

Mulch and compost, site-generated or local, if possible

Seasonal rains, winter and summer

City, county, and state allies who promote programs and incentives that encourage water conservation and enhancement through rainwater harvesting, greywater harvesting, stormwater harvesting curb cuts, urban agriculture, compost toilets, right-of-way plantings, mulching, wild native food forests, and food security resources.

INSTRUCTIONS:

Preheat community consciousness to a degree that inspires action, participation, resiliency, and cooperation. Combine indigenous wisdom and food traditions with permaculture and rainwater harvesting principles. Mix well. Dig deep basins for collecting rain and runoff. Line basins with rocks where needed to prevent erosion. Study intact native plant guilds to guide planting. Plant native food forests in and around basins, increasing food and water security. Add mulch from pruning for fertility security. Add wet rainy ingredients to dry mulchy ingredients. Curb cuts and cores recommended if available. Season with proactive, community legislation that promotes green infrastructure and replicates and evolves successful and sustainable projects. Sprinkle with water-harvesting, traffic-calming chicanes, rain gardens, and traffic circles. When "well done," use best harvest practices to collect native desert foods in every season. Extend and enhance the harvest by recruiting, training, and rewarding stewards of the food forests. Create celebrations to share and honor the traditions, nutrition, flavors, and connection to place these foods provide.

MAKES ENOUGH FOR ALL!

SONORAN DESERT WILD FOODS
HARVEST CALENDAR

WARM SEASON

MAY JUNE
APRIL — DRY SUMMER — JULY
SPRING WET SUMMER AUGUST
MARCH

EARLY SPRING

FEBRUARY

WINTER

JANUARY

DECEMBER NOVEMBER OCTOBER SEPTEMBER

AUTUMN

COOL SEASON

Yellow Month Desert in Bloom
Month of Hunger
Month to Gather Beans
Month to Gather Saguaro Fruit
Month of Rains
Month of Short Planting
Green Season Plants Come Up
Deer Mating Month
Month to Depend on Stored Fruit
Month of Big Cold
Month of Pleasant Cold
Month to Plant Squash to Withstand Frost
Month of Dry Grass

COLOR ME!

© 2017 JILL LORENZINI   MONTH NAMES FROM TOHONO O'ODHAM

MEET
MESQUITE

Prosopis spp.

O'ODHAM	*kui chepelk* or *wihog*
SPANISH	*péchita, mezquite* (velvet/honey)
	tornillo (screwbean)

Want to meet one of the Sonoran Desert's most beautiful, bountiful, beneficial bean trees? Meet mesquite! Mesquite is one of three native edible legume trees that flourish in this region (the others are palo verde and ironwood). Heat and drought-tolerant, it creates cool micro-climates with its shade, consistently produces nutritious food, drops rich mulch, offers habitat for native plants and animals, and gives form and structure to the desert landscape. What a tree!

Three native mesquite trees—velvet (*Prosopis velutina*), screwbean (*Prosopis pubescens*), and honey (*Prosopis glandulosa* var. *torreyana*)—produce sweet, edible pods in the hot months of summer. Before that, in late spring, their long, yellow flower clusters draw bees and other pollinators, which depend on the flowers for forage and, in turn, help make possible the delicious pods.

The summer monsoon begins brewing in late June, introducing moisture into hot desert air, forcing the buildup of giant cumulus clouds, ripe with rain. Mesquite trees heavy with pods bend and blow in these winds, sometimes dropping ripe pods filled with seeds to the ground, where they lay perfectly positioned for germination when storm clouds finally release their rain.

A staple food for indigenous people for thousands of years, mesquite has been valued for its sweet taste, nourishment, storability, abundance, and ease of harvest. Mortar holes worn deep into solid rock indicate the depth and length of connection people have had with mesquite. Dry pods were processed into a meal by either pounding or grinding with a rock, in a bowl-shaped depression in the rock or on a flat rock surface. Gyration grinding methods were also developed. The naturally sweet meal was moistened and formed into small cakes and dried for eating or storing or made into gruel with other desert ingredients like saguaro seed and barrel cactus seed flours.

Today, blenders, grinders, hammermills, refrigerators, and ovens offer great tools for helping to incorporate desert foods like mesquite into our menus. A community hammermill makes it possible for harvesters to grind their gathered pods into flour for the season. Freezing or refrigerating containers of mesquite flour in labeled, baking-sized portions extends its use life. Mesquite pods also can be roasted and toasted in the oven to enhance their natural nutty and sweet flavors before grinding and using in baked goods or brewed beverages.

Make mesquite sweeter? You can simmer whole pods in water for hours on the stove or in a solar oven to break down the pods. As the broth darkens to a caramel color and the liquid reduces by half, the room fills with the syrupy smell of the concentrated flavors. Further reduce the liquid and add a sweetener to make mesquite syrup or molasses. Tossing a few pods onto coals, or using mesquite wood for fuel, imparts mesquite's sweet flavors to grilled foods.

The health benefits of mesquite are almost as sweet as the pods. Mesquite flour is gluten-free, with plenty of calcium, magnesium, iron, dietary fiber, and zinc. Unlike processed sugars, which give only temporary bursts of energy, mesquite is full of natural sugars that provide stable, sustained energy. Consuming mesquite pods and other desert foods with these healthful benefits is key to preventing or treating some diabetic conditions.

Sweet mesquite. So good to eat.

EATING AND COOKING WITH MESQUITE:

As a legume, mesquite should be introduced gradually into your diet to enhance digestibility. Some note gastric disturbances after eating it. Some who are allergic to mesquite pollen are also allergic to the flour, so use caution.

Mesquite contains no gluten and will not produce leavening. A good rule of thumb for adding and substituting mesquite flours to maintain leavening is to use a 1:3 ratio of mesquite to non-mesquite flour. Using this as a baseline, you can adjust accordingly for personal taste preferences.

Mesquite flour can clump easily, as it takes up moisture from the atmosphere. Store flour and baked goods made with mesquite in airtight containers. When using, sifting it is always a good idea. Note that screwbean mesquite pods produce coarser flour than honey and velvet varieties. Mesquite has a naturally high sugar content and is susceptible to burning. Cook with lower temperatures and watch to avoid scorching (especially with pancakes), which produces a bitter taste.

- Jill Lorenzini

MESQUITE BASICS

FLOWER BUD & BLOOM SEASON	SPRING	DRY SUMMER – April, May, June, and sometimes again in August, September.
POD HARVEST SEASON	Low desert: SUMMER	FALL – May through June and October through November. High desert: SUMMER	FALL	WINTER – June through August and November through January.
PARTS USED	Dry ripe pods, sap, flowers.
HARVESTING TIPS	Large harvest bags are helpful for carrying bulky pods. A hoe or cane can help carefully pull down otherwise out-of-reach branches and their pods.
BEST HARVESTING PRACTICES	Taste pods before harvesting to make sure they have a sweet flavor or specific desired characteristics. Each tree has its own flavor. Disagreeable ones can have a chalky, mouth-drying, or slightly caustic aftertaste. Pick dry, ripe pods from trees, not the ground. In the low desert, pick before summer rains to avoid aflatoxins. Dry pods immediately after harvest.
PRE-MILLING STORAGE TIPS	Bruchid beetles may appear once you've harvested pods. These small, mesquite-loving beetles make the small holes in the pods. Eggs already inserted in pods may hatch during storage. But not to worry! They are harmless. Give the bruchid beetles an opening and they will leave of their own accord. Small predatory wasps may even come to prey on and control the beetles for you. If you can't handle the beetles, try using heat or cold to knock them out. Put pods in the direct summer sun during the day and bring them back in before nightfall or bake them in a solar oven for an hour or two (not too long or you'll discolor them!) then store in a sealed container. Double-freeze pods (freeze for 24 hours, remove from freezer to thaw in sealed freezer bag, then freeze again) to let the cold kill the beetles, but be sure to thaw and completely dry pods (at least 3 days) before milling, or they may be too moist to mill. Note that moisture in the air will condense on cold or cool pods, so thaw them in sealed freezer bags. Once pods have warmed to ambient temperature, open the bags to make sure all is dry.
PREPPING PODS FOR MILLING IN A HAMMERMILL	Only clean, dry pods can be milled. Carefully inspect your pods to ensure they are free of any black mold, bird droppings, twigs, gravel, dirt, or any other debris that could damage the mill or contaminate the flour. Pods must also be dry enough to readily "snap" in two when you try to bend them. If they bend, rather than snap, they are too moist and will clog the mill. Learn more about this on our mesquite millings page at DesertHarvesters.org.
CAUTION	Mesquite can have sharp thorns, so use caution. Aflatoxins may be present in pods in certain conditions. Visit DesertHarvesters.org for more information on aflatoxin and how to avoid it.

MESQUITE BASICS (continued)

NUTRITION	Gluten-free, with calcium, magnesium, protein, dietary fiber, iron, zinc.
PLANTING TIPS	Plant with summer rains in terrace or bottom zone of rain garden. Seed scarification: For velvet and honey mesquite, nip the side, not the tip, of the seed coat with toenail clippers just enough to get through hard outer seed coat. For screwbean mesquite, pour boiling water over the seed. When collecting to propagate from seed or cuttings, select from trees with the best characteristics, such as best flavors, dense pod clusters (quicker, bigger harvests), and best ripening times (pre-summer rains in hot, low desert).
OTHER USES	Firewood – both pods and wood can be used for grilling and smoking foods to impart flavor. Wood for building and craft. Medicinal. Nitrogen-fixing bacteria in its roots and nitrogen in its leaf drop enhance soil fertility. Source of pigment/dye and cordage. Fodder for pollinators, myriad native songbirds, desert tortoise, chickens, goats, dogs, and cattle. Pods that fall to the ground make great mulch. Excellent climbing tree.

Velvet and screwbean mesquite pods, mesquite flour, and honey

Photo: Brad Lancaster

MESQUITE:
BREAKFASTS

Amy's Mesquite Pancakes

Photo: Josh Schachter

THE CASCABEL INSPIRATION:
DAVID AND PEARL'S MESQUITE MILL

by Brad Lancaster

The rural community of Cascabel, Arizona, sits on the banks of the San Pedro River amidst mesquite and cottonwood forests, about an hour-and-a-half drive from Tucson. The first time I went there in the late 1990s, I was in search of a way to grind mesquite pods into flour.

My neighbors and I had planted hundreds of mesquite trees in our neighborhood, and the trees were replete with nutritious pods. I knew my own personal pick-and-chew method wasn't exactly shareable, and the other techniques I'd been experimenting with—*mano y metate*, coffee grinders, blenders—were slow and tedious and did not offer an easy way to separate the flour from the chaff.

I'd heard about an innovative hammermill set up by Cascabel residents Pearl Mast and David Omick for their annual mesquite milling and pancake breakfast event. So off I went to check it out.

Hand-drawn signs directed me to a cleared lot with the sweet smell of mesquite cooking. There was a massive old hammermill! I went first to the camp stove where I met Pearl and others cooking up mesquite pancakes and waffles. Pearl handed me a plate of pancakes and pointed to a bottle of deep pink prickly pear cactus fruit syrup. I sat down to eat in the company of happy folks at the communal folding tables. We oohed and aahed over the pancakes, delighted by what we were eating.

Bellies full and satisfied, we then gathered around the genius invention to learn how the pods had been turned to flour. David had found the hammermill in a local farmer's barn, cleaned it up, and rigged it to a power supply. For the milling, he'd backed a Suzuki 4x4 Jeep onto a mobile home axle, and connected it to the hammermill with a six-inch belt.

Pearl Mast and David Omick

Photo: Brad Lancaster

That morning, Pearl got into the jeep, started up the motor to get the rear wheels moving on the axle, then cranked into second gear. The machine roared loudly, and the belt flew around the axle and mill's pulley with such force that one guy had to stand beside it with a big metal bar to keep it from flying off and decapitating someone. David began to feed mesquite pods into the mill. They turned to flour in what seemed like seconds!

Soon David was covered with white dust. The hammermill did not have a blower and a screen to separate the flour from the chaff, so some of it billowed into the air and onto David. But the bulk of the milled flour was dumped onto screens a few feet away, where a group of us gathered to help hand-sift it.

I was overjoyed. The process was so much quicker than any of my previous experiments and here I was now milling and eating mesquite in a great community of people! The whole experience

David covered in mesquite flour after milling   *Suzuki 4x4 ready to power the hammermill*

Photos: Pearl Mast and David Omick

offered a full and cyclical experience of the local food system.

The experience inspired me and others to spark a homegrown, mesquite-harvesting food revolution, which became Desert Harvesters in Tucson. With David and Pearl's help, our early years closely followed the model of that wonderful Cascabel event.

Over time, the Cascabel event moved to the Cascabel Community Center, which offered more shelter, a kitchen, and an earth oven for baking mesquite breads. Organizers acquired a better, more efficient mill. As the event grew, Desert Harvesters and Baja Arizona Sustainable Agriculture (BASA) brought additional hammermills to keep up with demand. Live musicians came to play. More cooks showed up and offered demonstrations on how to make mesquite tortillas and cook with the sun. The event merged with a local- and wild-foods potluck to showcase the natural-food abundance of the area, including saguaro fruit bars and a dish made with local white-lined sphinx moth caterpillars!

David and Pearl were the event's primary organizers for 16 years. After every event Pearl meticulously recorded how much pancake mix they used, who did what, what worked, and what didn't. So in 2015, when the Cascabel Conservation Association and others in the community took over, they were well prepared to keep up the amazing traditions.

David once told me everyone ought to have at least one true success in their lives. He and Pearl say the mesquite milling and the native wild-foods movement is their success. They are also gratified by how Desert Harvesters has progressed the movement further still with research, programming, and testing around safer and better-tasting harvesting practices, and with this cookbook, plantings, and other ventures that inspire people to positively interact with the place where they live.

With so many things wrong in the world, David and Pearl said it has felt good to be working in a life-giving direction. They don't view their work as a kind of sacrifice but as a way to celebrate connections. To that aim, Pearl recommends we keep on growing and experimenting with food that is freely available around us, and in living in ways that truly connect us with the world around us.

Visit Omick.net to learn more about David and Pearl and their off-the-grid, 128-square-foot home and their give-back, community-based lifestyle.

PEARL'S MESQUITE PANCAKES

Contributed by Pearl Mast

1 cup mesquite flour

1 cup whole wheat flour

1 cup unbleached white flour

1 tablespoon baking powder

1 1/2 teaspoons baking soda

1 teaspoon salt

1 egg

1 tablespoon oil

1 to 2 cups buttermilk,
sour milk, or fresh milk

1 tablespoon of vinegar
or lemon juice (optional,
for enhancement)

These are the famous Cascabel mesquite pancakes and the inspiration for the long-running Desert Harvesters' annual mesquite pancake event. Light in taste and texture, they are a great introduction to mesquite cooking.

In a large bowl, mix together dry ingredients. In a small bowl, whisk together egg, oil, 1 cup of milk, and vinegar or lemon juice, if using. Add wet ingredients to dry. Add more milk to thin the batter. Cook on medium heat and enjoy with your favorite syrup or toppings.

You can double, triple, or quadruple the dry part of this recipe and store it in a large gallon jar or airtight container, adding the wet ingredients in equal proportion when ready to make and eat.

MAKES ABOUT 12 PANCAKES.

AMY'S MESQUITE PANCAKES

Contributed by Amy Valdés Schwemm, Mano y Metate

This recipe varies slightly from Pearl's Mesquite Pancakes (p. 36) by using fewer ingredients and less flour. Desert Harvesters used this recipe for its annual Mesquite Pancake Breakfast for nearly five years, making hundreds of people happy.

In a large bowl mix flours, baking powder, and salt. In a separate bowl whisk together the egg, oil, and 1 cup of milk. Add wet ingredients to dry, mix well, and add up to 1 cup of water or more milk to thin batter to your desired consistency. Ladle 1/4 cup of batter onto a lightly oiled griddle on medium-low heat. Keep checking the bottom of the pancake for the desired brown color. Flip and cook until done. Serve with butter and prickly pear syrup, agave nectar, or mesquite honey.

NOTE: Dry ingredients can be mixed ahead of time, kept in an airtight container, and stored in a dry, cool place. Use about 2 cups of dry mix for the listed wet ingredients.

VARIATIONS: Omit baking powder and add 1 3/4 teaspoons of baking soda. Replace milk and water with kefir, buttermilk, or sour milk.

MAKES ABOUT 10 PANCAKES.

1 cup whole wheat pastry flour

3/4 cup mesquite flour, sifted

3 1/2 teaspoons baking powder, non-aluminum

1/4 teaspoon salt

1 egg

2 tablespoons oil

1 cup milk

Up to 1 cup water (or milk)

(V)

JILL'S EZ MESQUITE VEGAN PANCAKES

Contributed by Jill Lorenzini

1 cup blue, red, or yellow cornmeal

1 cup whole spelt pastry flour or Sonoran white wheat flour

1 cup fine mesquite flour

1 teaspoon salt

1/2 teaspoon baking soda

1/2 teaspoon baking powder

1 to 2 cups water, soy milk, or other non-dairy substitute (or more or less depending on how thick or thin you like batter)

Coconut or olive oil for skillet

OPTIONAL ADD-INS:
1/2 cup oats, seeds (barrel cactus, saguaro, desert chia, sesame, sunflower, hemp), saguaro fruit, wolfberry, hackberry, nuts, banana, grated ginger, cinnamon, etc.

This is a fast, easy-to-remember recipe for wonderful fluffy cakes with the nutty flavor of mesquite and sweet undertones of blue corn. It is vegan, so it can be mixed ahead, packs well, and all you need is liquid (milk, soy milk, or water) to mix. Many things can be added to the basic recipe to make the pancakes more seasonal, hearty, light, fruity, or nutty.

In a large bowl, mix together dry ingredients, including optional add-ins. Add liquid to desired batter consistency. In large cast-iron skillet or frying pan, heat oil on low-medium heat. Spoon pancake batter onto skillet. When you see bubbles forming, flip pancake and cook for equivalent time on other side. Serve with fruits and syrups.

MAKES ABOUT 10 PANCAKES.

MESQUITE WAFFLES

Contributed by Daniel Baker

Waffles are a fun way to introduce first-time mesquite eaters to the flavor of the flour. In this recipe, the beaten egg whites are the secret to making the waffles light and fluffy.

In a large bowl, sift together dry ingredients. In a small bowl, combine egg yolks, milk, and oil. Stir the wet mixture into dry ingredients. Fold in beaten egg whites, leaving some fluffs. Do not overmix. Pour batter into hot waffle maker, according to its size. (Follow directions suggested by waffle maker manufacturer or experiment.) Be sure to use the highest setting on your waffle iron to avoid sticking.

MAKES ABOUT 8 WAFFLES.

1 cup whole wheat flour

3/4 cup mesquite flour

3 teaspoons baking powder

1/2 teaspoon salt

2 egg yolks

1 1/4 cup goat's milk
(or other milk)

1/2 cup oil (or less if you oil
the waffle iron instead)

2 egg whites, beaten stiff

APPLE NUT MUFFINS

Contributed by Carlos Nagel

1/2 cup mesquite flour

1/2 cup whole wheat flour

1/2 cup unbleached flour

2 teaspoons baking powder

1/4 teaspoon salt

6 tablespoons sugar

1 teaspoon cinnamon

1 teaspoon ground ginger

1/2 teaspoon ground cloves

1 cup chopped or grated apple

3 eggs

1 teaspoon vanilla extract

3/4 cup milk

1/3 cup vegetable oil

1/4 cup chopped nuts

Barrel cactus seeds, desert chia seeds, or finely chopped nuts (optional)

These muffins were part of the first edition of Eat Mesquite! *and have remained a crowd favorite over time.*

Preheat oven to 350° F. Lightly grease muffin tin or use paper liners. In a large bowl, sift and combine flours, baking powder, salt, sugar, and spices, then add apple. In a separate bowl, beat eggs. Add vanilla, milk, and oil to eggs and combine well. Add wet ingredients to dry and mix only until incorporated. Gently fold in nuts. Do not overmix. Pour into muffin tin. Sprinkle chia seeds, barrel cactus seeds, or finely chopped nuts on top of muffins. Bake 20 minutes or until a toothpick comes out clean.

MAKES 12 MUFFINS.

Ⓥ

MESQUITE LEMON POPPY SEED SCONES

Contributed by Junie Hostetler

This novel scone recipe doesn't use butter, so it is lower in fat and easier than cutting butter into flour, too.

Preheat oven to 425° F. In a large bowl, mix together flours, poppy seeds, baking powder, baking soda, and salt. In a separate bowl, combine yogurt, oil, syrup, and lemon zest. Combine wet and dry mixtures and stir until just moistened. Knead on floured surface for a few seconds. Form batter into a ball. Roll out to 1 inch thick. Cut into diamonds or squares (about 1 1/2 to 2 inches wide). Bake on ungreased baking sheets for 10 minutes. Cool on wire rack.

MAKES 8 to 10 SCONES.

2 1/2 cups flour

1/2 cup mesquite flour, sifted

2 tablespoons poppy seeds

2 teaspoons baking powder

1 teaspoon baking soda

1/2 teaspoon salt

1 1/4 cups plain yogurt
(or soy or dairy-free yogurt)

1/4 cup oil

1/4 cup maple syrup
or honey

1 lemon, zest

(GF) (V)

HIGH-PROTEIN PORRIDGE WITH MESQUITE

Contributed by Carolyn Niethammer

1/3 cup quinoa

1/3 cup amaranth grain

1/4 cup mesquite flour

1 3/4 cups water

2 tablespoons raisins (optional)

The mesquite adds sweetness to this porridge featuring quinoa and amaranth, which are both high in protein.

Using a fine-mesh strainer, rinse quinoa under cold water to remove bitter coating. In a heavy-bottomed saucepan, combine all ingredients and cook over medium heat for about 20 minutes until grains are soft and water is absorbed.

VARIATION: Fresh desert hackberries can be used in place of the optional raisins.

MAKES 2 SERVINGS.

GF R V

HEALING MESQUITE BANANA MASH

Contributed by Jill Lorenzini

This is a soothing, easy-to-digest snack, which can also help strengthen the body after sickness, exertion, or fasting. For upset stomach, add a dash of cinnamon, ginger, or nutmeg.

Mash banana. Add mesquite flour and blend into banana with fork. Add spices as desired. For extra nutrition add ground chia or barrel cactus seeds.

MAKES 1 SERVING.

1 banana

2 to 3 tablespoons mesquite flour

Cinnamon, ginger, nutmeg to taste

Desert chia, barrel cactus seeds to taste

(GF) (V)

DESERT OATS

Contributed by Jill Lorenzini

1 cup oats

1/4 teaspoon salt

4 to 6 Arizona dates, pitted, cut into small chunks

2 to 3 cups liquid (non-dairy milk, water, or a combination)

1 tablespoon coconut oil

2 tablespoons mesquite flour or more (to taste)

1/2 cup chopped Arizona pecans

In a small saucepan combine oats, salt, dates, and liquid, and cook over low heat until oats are tender and liquid is absorbed. Add oil, mesquite flour, and pecans and stir to mix. Serve with non-dairy milk, yogurt, flavored agave syrup, or seasonal fruit.

MAKES 2 SERVINGS.

Ⓥ

LORI'S GRANOLA

Contributed by Lori Adkison

This granola can be made in large batches and stocked in the pantry. It is equally delicious in your morning cereal bowl or sprinkled over ice cream for a quick dessert.

Preheat oven to 300º F. In a large bowl, combine dry ingredients. In a separate bowl, mix wet ingredients together and then combine with the dry mix. Spread mixture out onto two large 1-inch-deep baking pans. Bake for approximately one hour, turning mixture every 20 minutes. Look for a light golden color to signal when it is done. Cool to room temperature and store in an airtight container.

VARIATIONS: Try different nut combinations. Add sunflower, barrel cactus, and/or pumpkin seeds. Use prickly pear or mesquite syrup in place of maple syrup. Add dried fruits, coconut, dried or candied citrus peels, cocoa nibs, or chocolate chips to baked mixture.

MAKES ABOUT 10 CUPS.

1 cup chopped roasted almonds

1 cup chopped pecans

3/4 cup sesame seeds

1/3 cup desert chia seeds (may substitute flax seeds)

2/3 cup oat bran

5 1/2 cups quick oats (may substitute rolled oats)

1/2 cup mesquite flour

1 teaspoon sea salt

1/2 teaspoon cinnamon

1 cup maple syrup

1/2 cup agave nectar (may substitute local honey)

1/2 cup oil

1 teaspoon vanilla

MUFF'S MESQUITE BISCOTTI

Contributed by Muffin Burgess (inspired by Jill Provan)

1/3 cup dried, coarsely chopped cranberries, cherries, hackberries, or wolfberries

4 teaspoons Grand Marnier or Cointreau liqueur

1/2 cup unsalted butter, very soft

1/2 cup sugar or
1/2 cup raw agave nectar

2 large eggs

1/2 teaspoon almond extract or vanilla extract, optional

2 tablespoons orange zest, grated

1 cup barley flour

1/2 cup mesquite flour

1/2 cup plus 2 tablespoons finely ground whole wheat pastry flour or unbleached white flour

1 1/2 teaspoons baking powder

Dash of cinnamon, optional

1/4 teaspoon sea salt

1 cup pine nuts

1 egg for egg wash

Preheat oven to 325° F. Line baking sheet with parchment paper or a nonstick liner. Soak cranberries or other berries in the liqueur. Cream butter by hand or in a mixer until light and creamy, about 2 minutes. Slowly add the sugar and beat until light and fluffy, about 2 minutes. Scrape down sides of bowl with a rubber spatula. Add eggs and almond or vanilla extract and beat until smooth. Beat in the zest. Sift flours together and add baking powder, cinnamon, and salt and mix till just combined. Add to wet mixture. Stir in the berries with liqueur and nuts.

On a lightly floured work surface, divide the dough into 2 equal portions. Shape each portion into a log about 12 to 14 inches long and about 2 inches in diameter, pressing ends to be flat. Gently lift the logs onto the parchment-covered baking sheet, spacing them about 2 inches apart. Press top of each log to flatten slightly. Whisk the third egg and brush it evenly over each log.

Place the cookie sheet either in the center or a little above the center rack. Bake the logs until they are set to the touch and lightly browned on top, about 25 minutes. Let the rolls cool on a wire rack for 10 minutes, then transfer to a cutting board and cut on a diagonal into slices about 1/2 inch wide, sawing slowly with a serrated knife so as not to crumble (which is next to impossible).

Gently lay slices, on sides, back onto parchment. Bake until the edges are lightly toasted (5 to 9 minutes). Turn over and bake approximately 5 minutes more until light brown. Let cool completely on a wire rack. They will cool to a firm crunch.

Store in airtight container (for up to 2 weeks). Or freeze.

VARIATIONS: Substitute tangerine or lemon zest for orange. Substitute chopped almonds or pecans for pine nuts. Increase or subtract amounts of dried fruits or nuts. Try dried apricots in place of berries. For chocoholics, add chocolate morsels.

For wheat-free recipe, substitute oat flour or rice flour for unbleached white and whole wheat flours. Ratio of mesquite flour to other flour is important: Best when no more than 1:3 mesquite flour to other flour—that is, one-fourth of the dry flour ingredients.

MAKES 24 BISCOTTI.

MESQUITE BEAN COFFEE CAKE

Contributed by Marsha Alterman and Christine L. Winters

The distinct flavor of mesquite gives this coffee cake a special desert flair. Serve with Mesqcafé Olé (p. 108) for the full experience!

Preheat oven to 375º F. In large bowl, combine white flour, salt, sugar, and 4 tablespoons of the oil. Mix until crumbly. Set aside 1/4 cup of the mixture. To the remaining flour mixture add mesquite flour, baking powder, baking soda, remaining oil, and spices. Mix thoroughly. Add milk and egg. Mix well. Pour into greased 8- x 8-inch pan. Spread reserved 1/4 cup crumble mixture over top. Bake for 25 minutes.

MAKES 12 to 16 SERVINGS.

1 cup all-purpose white flour

1/4 teaspoon salt

1/2 cup light brown sugar

1/3 cup safflower oil

1/4 cup mesquite flour

1 teaspoon baking powder

1/4 teaspoon baking soda

1/4 teaspoon cinnamon

1/8 teaspoon nutmeg

1/2 cup milk

1 egg, well beaten

MESQUITE:
BREADS / CRACKERS

Mestiza Cornbread

Photo: Ian Fritz

SAVORY MESQUITE MUFFINS

Reprinted with permission from *Mesquite Meal Recipes*
(San Pedro Mesquite Company)

1/2 cup chopped
yellow onion

1 to 2 tablespoons butter

2/3 cup mesquite flour

1 cup all-purpose flour

5 tablespoons brown sugar

2 teaspoons baking powder

3 eggs

2/3 cup milk or soy milk

1/2 cup plain yogurt

1/4 cup oil

2 tablespoons fresh thyme,
rosemary, and/or local herb
such as oreganillo

1/3 cup nuts (optional)

These muffins are a delicious blend of sweet and savory, highlighting both the flavor and versatility of mesquite. A perfect complement to soups and stews or just a great snack.

Preheat oven to 350° F. Lightly grease muffin tin or use paper liners. In a skillet over medium heat, sauté onion in butter until translucent. Set aside. In large bowl, mix all dry ingredients. Add all wet ingredients, sautéed onion, herbs, and nuts if using, and stir until just combined. Pour into muffin tin and bake for 25 to 35 minutes or until toothpick comes out clean.

MAKES 12 MUFFINS.

(S) (GF)

SOLAR-COOKED MESQUITE ZUCCHINI BREAD

Adapted from Deb Perelman at SmittenKitchen.com

This was the first recipe I ever successfully cooked in a solar oven. It's a hearty, melt-in-your-mouth, anytime bread that's sweet but not too sweet.

Place your solar oven out in the sun and adjust it so it takes in maximum sunlight. Let it heat up to between 300° F and 350° F. You may need to keep adjusting as the bread bakes in order to keep it that hot. While waiting for oven to heat up, grease and flour two 8- x 4-inch loaf pans or 24 muffin cups (or use paper liners).

In a large bowl, beat the eggs with a whisk. Mix in oil and sugar, then add zucchini and vanilla. In a medium bowl, combine flours, cinnamon, nutmeg, baking soda, baking powder, salt, and chia seeds. Stir this into the egg mixture and divide the batter into your pans or muffin cups, filling each about half full, as bread will nearly double in size as it bakes. Bake until a toothpick comes out clean: about 90 minutes for one 8- x 4-inch loaf at a pretty consistent 300° F in the solar oven. Muffins will cook faster than loaves.

VARIATION: If using a conventional oven, preheat to 350° F and bake loaves for 50 minutes, muffins for 25 minutes.

MAKES TWO 8- x 4-INCH LOAVES OR ABOUT 24 MUFFINS.

3 eggs

1/2 cup coconut oil or other oil

1 3/4 cups sugar

2 cups grated zucchini

2 teaspoons vanilla extract

1 cup mesquite flour

2 cups whole wheat pastry or gluten-free all-purpose flour

1 teaspoon cinnamon

1/4 teaspoon nutmeg

1 teaspoon baking soda

1/2 teaspoon baking powder

1 teaspoon salt

1/4 cup chia seeds

GRANNY'S GINGERBREAD

Contributed by Caitlin Stern

2 1/2 cups all-purpose flour

1 cup mesquite flour

1 1/2 teaspoons baking soda

1/2 teaspoon salt

3 teaspoons ground ginger

3 teaspoons ground cinnamon

1/2 teaspoon ground cloves

2 eggs

3/4 cup canola oil

1 1/2 cups saguaro syrup
(can substitute molasses)

1 1/2 cups hot water (not boiling)

1/3 cup diced candied ginger

This recipe originated with my grandmother, Nancy Sogge, who grew up in England but spent most of her adult life in southeast Alaska. My mother, Cecily Stern, made the recipe healthier by substituting oil for butter and molasses for refined sugar. Now I've made a Sonoran version, with mesquite flour and saguaro syrup. I hope you'll enjoy this recipe as much as my family does. With both ground and candied ginger, this tasty gingerbread delivers serious ginger spiciness!

Preheat oven to 325° F. Grease and lightly flour a 9- x 13-inch baking pan (brownie size). In a large bowl, mix flours, baking soda, salt, ground ginger, ground cinnamon, and ground cloves. In a separate bowl, mix egg and oil. Add saguaro syrup or molasses and hot water to eggs and oil mixture. Add wet ingredients to dry mixture and stir in candied ginger. Pour batter into pan. Bake 45 to 50 minutes or until toothpick comes out clean. Cool slightly before cutting. If gingerbread sticks to knife, dip knife in a glass of water between each cut.

MAKES 16 SERVINGS.

MESQUITEY DINNER ROLLS

Contributed by Native Seeds/SEARCH

These rolls tend to disappear quickly, so you might consider making a double batch!

Preheat oven to 400º F. Soften yeast in warm water and milk. Mix in sugar, salt, mesquite flour, and 2 cups of the white flour. Blend for 2 minutes with whisk. Add eggs, oil, and 1 cup of whole wheat flour. Whisk for about a minute. Stir in rest of whole wheat flour and enough white flour to make stiff dough. Knead 8 to 10 minutes on floured surface. Cover and let rest 20 minutes. Punch down and divide in half. Shape each half into 12 balls. Place on 2 greased baking sheets. Let rise about 30 minutes or until doubled in size. Bake for 15 to 20 minutes or until golden brown and hollow sounding when tapped.

MAKES 24 ROLLS.

2 tablespoons active dry yeast

1 cup warm water

2 cups milk

2 tablespoons sugar

2 teaspoons salt

1 cup mesquite flour

3 1/2 to 4 cups white flour

3 eggs

1/4 cup canola oil

2 cups whole wheat flour

SOUTHWEST FOCACCIA

Contributed by Native Seeds/SEARCH

1/2 cup olive oil, divided in half

2 cloves garlic, minced

1 to 2 teaspoons chipotle or red pepper flakes

1 package active dry yeast

1 cup warm water

2 teaspoons sugar

3/4 teaspoon salt

2 1/3 to 3 cups unbleached flour

1/3 cup mesquite flour

1/4 cup grated Parmesan cheese

Focaccia is so fun to make and this version will impress with its hint of mesquite sweetness. Add spices (fennel, oregano, or thyme) to the olive oil to enhance the flavor.

Preheat oven to 400° F. Heat 1/4 cup olive oil in small saucepan on low heat. Add garlic to oil and sauté, stirring occasionally, until soft and golden, about 10 minutes. Stir in chipotle flakes and set aside to cool. Combine yeast and water in a large bowl. Let stand 5 minutes. Stir in sugar, salt, and remaining 1/4 cup oil. Add 1 cup unbleached flour and beat with a wire whisk or spoon for 2 to 3 minutes. Stir in mesquite flour and enough of unbleached flour to make soft dough. Knead on floured surface 8 to 10 minutes. Cover and let rest 20 minutes. Punch down and roll out to fit a well-greased, 10- x 15-inch baking pan. Place dough in pan and use fingertips to spread and dimple the dough to fill pan. This helps prevent bubbles and also gives you divots to catch the oil. Drizzle with oil-garlic-chile mixture, and sprinkle with cheese. Let rise until fluffy (10 to 15 minutes). Bake 15 to 18 minutes or until golden brown.

MAKES 1 LARGE LOAF.

MESTIZA CORNBREAD
(para las mujeres locas de todas maneras!)
Contributed by Traci Faith Hamilton

Traci's Mestiza Cornbread was one of the favorite recipes at the first annual mesquite tasting event in Tucson in June 2009.

Preheat oven to 375º F. Oil a 10-inch cast iron skillet or baking dish and set aside. In a small bowl, place 2 to 3 tablespoons of water, 2 tablespoons of the calendula petals, and the chia seeds and set aside to soak. Sift together dry ingredients, making sure to remove all clumps. In a separate bowl, whip together all wet ingredients until fluffy. Drain the calendula and chia and add them to the wet mix. Combine wet and dry ingredients and blend until just incorporated, making sure not to overmix.

Con cariño pour your creation into the prepared baking vessel. Throw the remaining calendula on the top and bake for 30 to 40 minutes, until golden brown at the edges. *¡Por favor!* Check with a toothpick, making sure it comes out clean when inserted into the middle of the bread. If you are hungry eat immediately, but you may want to wait 5 or 10 minutes. Please enjoy with saguaro or prickly pear syrup! Knock yourself out, *¡Mami!*

MAKES 8 to 10 SERVINGS.

2 to 3 tablespoons water

3 to 4 tablespoons dried calendula flower petals

2 tablespoons chia seeds

1 1/2 cups blue cornmeal

3/4 cup quinoa flour
(I buy this because I haven't been able to grind it fine enough)

1/2 cup acorn flour (or more quinoa flour)

1/2 cup mesquite flour

1 1/2 teaspoons baking powder

1/2 teaspoon baking soda

3/4 teaspoon Zuni salt or sea salt

2 cups buttermilk or yogurt

2 extra-large eggs

1/4 cup oil

1/4 cup honey

GF

SAN PEDRO MESQUITE CORNBREAD

Reprinted with permission from *Mesquite Meal Recipes*
(San Pedro Mesquite Company)

1 cup cornmeal

1/2 cup all-purpose flour,
brown rice flour, or
gluten-free flour

1/2 cup mesquite flour

1 teaspoon baking powder

1 teaspoon baking soda

1 teaspoon salt

3 eggs

1 cup yogurt

1/4 honey

1/2 cup butter (melted)
or olive oil

This is an easy cornbread recipe that works well gluten-free. Yogurt and honey make for a tasty, tender crumb.

Preheat oven to 350° F. Grease an 8- x 8-inch cast iron skillet and place in oven. In medium bowl, mix cornmeal, flours, baking powder, baking soda, and salt. In separate bowl, whisk eggs and add yogurt, honey, and melted butter or oil. Add wet ingredients to dry mixture and stir until just combined. Pour batter into preheated pan. Bake for 25 to 30 minutes or until a toothpick comes out clean.

MAKES 16 SERVINGS.

(V)

MESQUITE SOURDOUGH BREAD WITH FIGS AND PECANS

Contributed by Gerard Villanueva

This delicious and versatile sourdough bread incorporates mesquite flour, dried figs, and pecans for a unique flavor. The technique is the same as the levain bread created by Chad Robertson of Tartine Bakery, but the flavors are entirely those of the American Southwest. I was inspired by the mesquite, pecans, and figs which absolutely thrive in my hometown of Austin, Texas. Even though mesquite flour, as far as I know, is not made in Central Texas, mesquite trees are found in abundance. Pecan trees are also indigenous to this area. All three types of trees are found within a couple blocks of my home, if not in my backyard. Pecans are harvested beginning in the fall. Figs, if I remember correctly, are harvested perhaps summer to fall. These three main ingredients make a very unique and delicious combination in this sourdough bread.

NOTE: This bread requires advance preparation. Expect it to take around eight hours on baking day.

TWO DAYS BEFORE BAKING:

Revive your starter.

ONE DAY BEFORE BAKING:

Make the levain. In a small bowl, dissolve the starter in the water and add the bread flour and whole wheat flour. Mix until the flours are moistened. Cover with plastic and let sit overnight on your counter to ferment. In an ambient temperature of 75º F it will take 8 to 9 hours. The levain should be bubbly. To check if the levain is ready, take a small spoonful and drop it in a bowl of water. If it floats, it is ready to use.

TOAST PECANS:

Roughly chop the pecans and place them on a baking sheet. Roast at 325º F a few minutes until they become aromatic. Careful not to burn them. Roast the pecans the day before or morning of baking the bread.

THE DAY OF BAKING:

Prepare the final dough. In a large bowl, dissolve the levain in 700 grams (24

THE LEVAIN (LEAVEN):

3/4 tablespoon sourdough starter, revived

100 grams (3 1/2 ounces) water (at 78˚ F)

50 grams (1/4 cup) bread flour

50 grams (1/4 cup) whole wheat flour

FINAL DOUGH:

All the levain

700 grams (24 ounces) water (at 80˚ F)

550 grams (2 1/3 cups) bread flour

300 grams (1 1/4 cups) whole wheat flour

150 grams (2/3 cup) mesquite flour

20 grams (5 teaspoons) salt plus 50 grams (1 3/4 ounces) water

1 1/2 heaping cups of sliced dried figs

3/4 cup roughly chopped toasted pecans

ounces) of water. Add the bread flour and whole wheat flour. Mix well until it is all moistened. Cover with plastic and let dough sit out for about 1 hour. This helps the gluten begin to form. While the dough is resting, mix together the mesquite flour and salt-and-water mixture.

At the end of the resting period, knead mesquite mixture into dough. Put the dough in the bowl of your stand mixer and mix for about 5 minutes. If you are kneading by hand, it will take longer. The dough should be smooth but still very sticky and the mesquite should be fully incorporated. Remove the dough from the mixing bowl and place it on your work counter. Gently fold in the figs and pecans.

FIRST FERMENTATION:

Place the dough in a lightly oiled bowl or container. Lightly oil the top of the dough. Cover with plastic and let it ferment for 30 minutes.

TURNING THE DOUGH:

At the end of 30 minutes, give the dough a "turn." This is done by reaching to the bottom of the dough, grabbing a handful, gently stretching it and folding the stretched portion over the top. Turn the dough 1/4 turn and repeat pulling and folding the dough. Do this two more times so that four sides of the dough have been pulled and folded. Flip the dough so that it is seam-side down, and let rest for another 30 minutes. This completes the "turn."

Turn the dough 3 more times at 30-minute intervals. This should take you 1 1/2 hours. Place the dough in a greased bowl and allow to ferment 1 1/2 to 2 hours more. It will become airier, less sticky, and increase in volume by about 20 to 25 percent. The time required will depend on the temperature of your kitchen. Check your dough every 30 minutes or so to monitor the progress.

DIVIDE INTO LOAVES:

Take the dough out of the bowl and place it on your work area. I find a marble board works best for wet dough. With a pastry cutter or knife, divide it into 2 or 3 portions. Shape each into a round shape. Lightly spray them with water and cover with plastic. Let them rest for about 20 minutes.

FINAL SHAPING:

You are now ready to do the final shaping. Take one of the portions and turn it upside down on a very lightly floured surface. Grab 1/3 of the right side of the dough, stretch it to your right a bit, and fold it over the middle. Do the same thing to the left side and then the side closest to you. Finally repeat with the side farthest from you. Now turn the whole dough portion over so that the smooth side that was touching the work surface is now on top. Repeat the process with all the portions on this side of the dough.

PROOFING:

If your dough is fairly stiff, you can place the loaves separately on parchment paper. They will hold their shape as they go through final proofing. If the dough is still wet and sticky you'll need to place them in bowls or baskets for the proofing. This prevents the loose dough from losing shape. Bannetons are the special proofing baskets used for bread. If you are using them or makeshift bowls, line them with a smooth kitchen cloth and dust the cloth generously with flour. Place each dough upside down in a basket. Lightly flour the surface of the dough, cover with plastic, and finally cover with the overhanging cloth. Proof the dough for 4 to 5 hours. The dough should increase in volume by about 30 percent and feel light to the touch. The time required will depend on the temperature of your kitchen.

About 45 minutes before you bake, preheat your oven to 500º F. Use a baking stone if you have one.

BAKING:

If using parchment paper only, score the loaves as desired and with the help of a peel (if you have one; use a flat baking sheet if you don't), slide them onto the baking stone or other baking surface. The parchment paper really makes it an easy process. Lower the temperature of the oven to 425º F. To mimic a professional steam-injected oven, spritz the loaves inside the oven with a water mister 3 times within the first 10 minutes of baking. Bake about 20 to 25 minutes until the internal temperature of the bread reaches 200º F. Rotate the dough midway to ensure even baking. Remove when done and place on a wire rack to cool completely before slicing.

If using proofing baskets, uncover the dough and remove the plastic. Cut out a piece of parchment paper slightly larger than the size of the basket. Cover the dough and basket with the parchment and then place your peel on top. Very carefully flip the whole thing over. Try not to disturb the shape of the dough. Remove the basket and then the cloth. You should be left with the dough sitting on top of the parchment paper. It is now ready to slide into the oven. Score as desired and proceed with baking and then cooling as above until done.

MAKES 2 to 3 LOAVES.

(GF)

MESQUITE OATCAKES

Contributed by Meredith A. Lane

1 and 1/3 cups Scottish or Irish oats

1/2 cup whole wheat or unbleached flour

3/4 teaspoon sugar

1/4 teaspoon salt

1/4 teaspoon baking powder

1/2 cup melted butter

1/4 to 1/3 cup hot mesquite pod slurry*

* MESQUITE POD SLURRY:

Cook broken mesquite pods in water in crock pot overnight or longer. Strain. Cook the broth down and strain again for "clarified mesquite broth." To make mesquite slurry, put some of the drained pods in a blender with a little water and blend until the remaining mesocarp is separated from the seeds and chaff. Strain through cheesecloth. Put the liquid back in the blender with another batch of pods and blend again. Repeat this process until all pods are chopped up; add only the minimum amount of water to keep the blender working. The resulting chaff and seeds can be composted or planted. The liquid is a "mesquite slurry" that can be used in this recipe, or added to soups, stews, or other concoctions.

Oatcakes are a simple, hearty cross between a cookie and a cracker, good with sharp cheese, jam or jelly, butter, or just plain!

The first time I made mesquite broth for jelly, I found myself wondering why I should discard all that biomass that was left. So I decided to blenderize the pods. I was left with mesquite slurry and started looking for ways to use it. All the recipes in the first edition of Eat Mesquite!: A Cookbook *called for either mesquite flour or mesquite broth/tea, and it was difficult to try to adapt these to use the slurry, which is really the same as mesquite flour in liquid, but the concentration is indeterminate. I love oatcakes, and had just bought a large supply of Bob's Red Mill Scottish Oats. The mesquite flavor makes them even better than the plain kind!*

Preheat oven to 325º F. In a large bowl, mix dry ingredients together. Add melted butter and mix to distribute evenly. Add enough mesquite slurry to make a soft dough. Turn out onto a cutting board scattered with additional oats. Knead gently and roll out to 1/4 inch thick. Cut in rounds or other shapes (2 to 3 inches in diameter). Transfer to greased or parchment paper-lined cookie sheet. Bake for 25 to 28 minutes. Transfer to wire rack to cool.

MAKES ABOUT 12 OATCAKES.

Ⓥ

WHOLE WHEAT MESQUITE CRACKERS

Contributed by Lori Adkison

These whole wheat, vegan crackers are perfect to serve with hummus or Mesquite Jelly (p. 80). Because they use agave syrup they are 100% vegan (unless you opt for honey).

Preheat oven to 325º F. Combine all ingredients in a medium-sized bowl and mix until dough will form a ball. Knead dough on a floured surface, adding water or flour as necessary to keep the dough from becoming too soft, sticky, or crumbly. Set dough aside to rest for 15 minutes. After resting, roll the dough into a 1/4 inch thick (or thinner if a thinner cracker is desired) rectangle. If dough starts to spring back, stop rolling and let it rest another 5 minutes. Cut the dough into desired cracker shapes with a pizza cutter or bench knife. Using a spatula, pick up crackers and place them on a parchment-lined baking sheet or pan. Spray the crackers with a cooking oil spray and sprinkle with sea salt. Bake for 10 minutes and then rotate the pan. Bake for another 8 to 10 minutes watching carefully so the crackers don't burn. They should be a deep brown color. Let crackers cool before serving. They will become crisp as they cool.

VARIATIONS: Add black sesame, barrel cactus, or chia seeds for visual interest. Add cumin seeds for a unique flavor. Instead of sunflower seeds, use pumpkin seeds ground into flour.

MAKES 1 to 2 DOZEN CRACKERS.

1 cup whole wheat flour

3/4 cup mesquite flour

1/4 cup sunflower seeds ground into flour

1/4 cup whole sesame seeds

2 tablespoons flax seeds, ground into flour

1/4 teaspoon salt

1 1/2 tablespoons agave nectar (or honey)

2 tablespoons vegetable oil

1/2 cup water

Cooking oil spray and sea salt for tops

DESERT WILD FOODS Mesquite, Desert Chia, Barrel Cactus

HARVEST SEASON Dry Summer

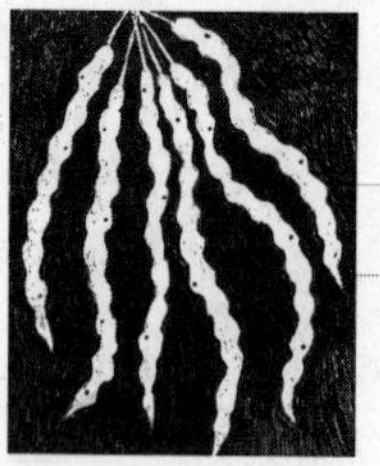

GF S V

SONORAN DESERT SEED CRACKERS

Contributed by Jill Lorenzini

2 cups cool water

4 tablespoons chia seeds

4 cups white barrel cactus pulp and seeds

1/2 cup sunflower seeds

1 teaspoon cayenne

1 teaspoon salt

1/3 cup mesquite flour

Oil to grease pans

Crunchy crispy crackers, free of gluten!

In small bowl, add water to chia seeds and let sit 10 minutes or until thick. In medium bowl, combine barrel pulp and seed, sunflower seeds, cayenne, salt, and mesquite flour. Add chia mixture. Grease two shallow baking pans. Drop cracker mixture by spoonful onto sheets. Flatten if needed to equal thickness. Dry in a low oven or warm solar oven (at about 170°F to 200° F) until chewy or crispy. Remove while warm with spatula. Let cool and serve, or store for later.

MAKES 3 to 4 DOZEN CRACKERS.

Ⓥ

MESQUITE CAROB TORTILLAS

Contributed by Chris Schmidt of the Tucsonavores

This delightful Sonoran Desert tortilla draws sweetness from mesquite and carob, then adds a spicy surprise. Sop up your soups and sauces with it or eat it as yummy stand-alone snack.

In a large bowl, mix the dry ingredients (wheat flour, mesquite flour, carob flour, amaranth, salt, and chiltepines). Add the olive oil and mix well with a fork. Gradually mix in the water, then knead the dough for about 3 minutes. Let sit for an hour, covered. Divide the dough into eight separate balls and let these sit for another half hour, covered, in the bowl. Bring a comal (or cast iron pan) to medium heat. Roll a dough ball out onto a floured cutting board until it is about 1/8 inch thick. Place tortilla on the hot comal and cook for about 20 seconds, then flip it and cook it for 20 more seconds. Repeat on both sides for 15 more seconds two more times or so. This is tedious, but it prevents the sweet flours from burning. Do this with each ball of dough.

VARIATIONS: Omit the amaranth to make the tortillas easier to fry (though you'll lose some nutritional value). Use milk instead of water for a slightly richer flavor.

MAKES 8 TORTILLAS.

1 1/2 cups whole wheat flour

1/4 cup mesquite flour

1/4 cup carob flour

1/4 cup popped amaranth

1 teaspoon salt

8 dried and crushed chiltepines

3 tablespoons plus
 1 teaspoon olive oil

1 cup water

MESQUITE:
SAVORY DISHES / SIDES

Mesquite Tamales

Photo: Christian Timmerman

TASTE FIRST:
THE LEGACY OF CLIFFORD PABLO

by Brad Lancaster

I first met Clifford Pablo, a member of the Tohono O'odham Nation, in the 1990s. His stories and struggles have long offered me a beautiful example of how to live and care for the Sonoran Desert. His life experience serves as a bounty of seeds that continue to germinate and grow in the work of Desert Harvesters and beyond. This story is based on an interview I conducted with him in late 2016.

As a child Clifford Pablo would sit behind his paternal grandfather as they rode horseback on the San Xavier reservation south of Tucson to harvest mesquite pods. Clifford learned to "taste first" as they went from tree to tree. Each tree had its own unique flavor—from hints of apple to sweet caramel—and Clifford's grandfather would only harvest from the best-tasting trees. Clifford also learned from the horses that only ate the pods within reach on tasty trees, avoiding the trees with bitter pods.

Clifford's grandfather would pick the pods in early summer then dry them in the sun. They would spread out the pods on cotton-harvesting bags then wrap them up and bring them inside at night, saving them from rodents and nighttime condensation. Once the pods were dried, they were stored in five-gallon metal cans. Clifford's maternal grandmother would grind them by hand with a stone *mano y metate* to make sweet drinks and dried cakes from the flour. Clifford's grandmother also picked green palo verde seeds, which she would pit-roast and eat warm, or dry and then grind into flour.

When the summer monsoons arrived, Clifford and his grandfather would harvest the rain by redirecting stormwater into adjoining small fields. Nutrient-rich organic matter such as mesquite leaves and rabbit droppings carried within the runoff would then be scattered by the water into the fields as free fertilizer.

Clifford Pablo (center) and fellow mesquite millers Chris Chavez (left) and Tyler Pablo.

Photo: Brad Lancaster

They never needed groundwater, imported water, or synthetic fertilizers.

They planted crops that needed more water, such as traditional O'odham melon and squash, closer to the water's inlet and placed drought-tolerant nitrogen-fixing tepary beans farther down the field. In the middle they planted corn and chiles. On the perimeter mesquite trees formed a wind- and sun-break along with fencing. Cholla cactus and its edible flower buds also grew there, providing another harvest. Native nitrogen-fixing bean trees added more nutrients, deflected winds, and shaded out some of the intense summer sun. Clifford learned the best way to start a garden is with the free fertile duff and topsoil from beneath a native mesquite tree.

During Clifford's high school years, over-pumping by the city of Tucson, surrounding mines, and nearby pecan orchards dramatically depleted groundwater levels. Many tribal wells dried up as well as a major spring, killing a forest of grand cottonwood and mesquite trees that had long lined the river on San Xavier lands. In the 1960s the construction of highway I-19 cut off the majority of water flow to the fields Clifford and his family had farmed.

In the late 1960s, the San Xavier District got some funding and asked people how they wanted to spend it. They wanted a farm. Clifford and several other community members worked for several years to coordinate this. The San Xavier Cooperative Association was formed in 1971, resulting in what today operates as the San Xavier Co-op Farm. The Association's board of directors hired outsiders to operate the farm, which primarily grew cotton up to the mid-1980s, when it shut down due to water shortages.

From 1989 to 1990, ethnobotanist Richard Felger brought a mesquite project to the District to explore the modern viability of mesquite production for food. While some were not initially interested, Clifford saw the value of the program, inspired by his childhood experiences. He advocated for the program, and was hired on. Clifford and Richard worked together to identify and propagate good trees and produce flour that could be tested. There was little to no equipment, so pods went to the Arizona-Sonora Desert Museum to be dried and were then milled into flour by a hammermill at the University of Arizona's Environmental Research Lab. Clifford did taste tests with youth and elders and found that people loved the flour and were reminded of the value of this traditional knowledge and practice.

The farm was inactive except for meetings on the Southern Arizona Water Rights Settlement Act (SAWRSA) negotiations, planning, and awaiting the promised money and rehab. Frustrated with the situation, Clifford volunteered his time to start a traditional crops garden on the farm using its last

functioning well. Elders who had told Clifford they wanted the farm "to grow the food we used to eat" were grateful. In 1994 Clifford quit his regular job, and resigned from the Cooperative board to become the farm manager. As manager, he pursued culturally relevant development and re-introduced traditional food crops, including mesquite flour. The farm began to produce and sell the flour commercially.

In 2001, Colorado River water arrived to the farm via the 3,000-plus-mile Central Arizona Project canal and its many pumps. A year later Clifford resigned from the Co-op Farm and its politics and went to work for the Tohono O'odham Farming Authority where he lobbied for traditional O'odham crops and helped Tohono O'odham Community Action (TOCA) start up a runoff farm based on traditional ways. Still wanting to inspire more young people to learn agriculture, he then went to work for the Tohono O'odham Community College's agricultural extension program to train new generations of O'odham farmers to grow and eat food healthy for the people and the land.

Clifford obtained a hammermill and, inspired by Desert Harvesters, installed it on a trailer in order to mill mesquite pods at various community events on the Tohono O'odham Nation. Interns from the college run the O'odham community millings, and the mill has come to Desert Harvesters' rescue several times during busy Tucson milling seasons.

The college interns also lead workshops for other tribal members—including at the San Xavier Co-op Farm—on how to identify and harvest high-quality mesquite pods, skills they've learned from Clifford himself, ensuring the continuation of a harvesting tradition.

What's the first thing they teach new harvesters? Taste first.

Clifford Pablo is a Tohono O'odham tribal member and an agriculture specialist. He is currently the Agriculture Extension Agent and Student Learning Farm Manager for Tohono O'odham Community College.

(V)

TOFU SNACK BITES

Reprinted with permission from *Mesquite Meal Recipes* (San Pedro Mesquite Company)

1/4 cup soy sauce

1/4 cup sesame oil

1 tablespoon vinegar

1/4 teaspoon ground black pepper

2 tablespoons ketchup

2 cloves garlic, crushed

2 12-ounce boxes firm tofu, cut into bite size pieces

1 1/4 cups sesame seeds

1/2 cup mesquite flour

1/4 cup brown sugar

These bites were a hit at our tasting gatherings. They're a fun way to prepare tofu, with the added sweetness and nutritional value of mesquite.

Preheat oven to broil. In a large bowl, mix soy sauce, oil, vinegar, pepper, ketchup, and garlic. Add tofu and marinate tofu for at least 1 hour. In a small bowl, mix sesame seeds with mesquite flour and brown sugar. Roll tofu cubes in mesquite mixture. Place on baking sheet and broil for 10 minutes. Lower heat to 350º F and continue to cook for 10 to 15 minutes. Serve on toothpicks with Prickly Pear Mustard (p. 160) or chile sauce.

MAKES 6 SERVINGS.

MESQUITE STUFFING

Contributed by Gary Nabhan and Patty West

This recipe adds a mild desert flavor to any holiday meals by adding sweet goodness to your savory stuffing.

Preheat oven to 350° F. Grease two 9- x 13-inch baking pans and set aside. If using sausage, sauté in a large skillet over medium heat for about 10 minutes or until sausage is cooked thoroughly. Remove sausage from skillet and set aside. Remove rendered fat from skillet and clean thoroughly, or alternatively, leave rendered fat in pan and combine with butter for added flavor.

In the cleaned (or not) skillet over moderate heat, melt butter and sauté leeks or onions, apples, and celery until soft. Remove from heat and add spices and cranberries (and cooked sausage, if using). In a large bowl, place the sautéed vegetables, cooked meat, bread cubes, mesquite flour, salt, and pepper, then add the stock and mix well. Place the mixture in the prepared baking dishes, moistening with more stock if necessary. Bake, covered, for 25 minutes and uncovered for final 5 minutes. Or stuff a turkey and bake according to weight.

VARIATIONS: If making recipe vegetarian, use veggie sausage or other soy-meat for added texture and flavor profile. Use spicy sausage or add roasted green chiles to give this dish more of a southwestern flair.

SERVES "Enough for a crowd!"

1 pound elk or pork sausage (optional)

1/2 cup butter

4 cups chopped onions or leeks

2 chopped apples

2 cups chopped celery

3 teaspoons poultry seasoning

1 teaspoon Sonoran oregano (or any oregano)

2 teaspoons dried, crushed rosemary

1 cup dried cranberries

10 cups dry bread cubes

1 cup mesquite flour

1 1/3 cups stock (chicken or vegetable)

Salt and pepper to taste

GF V

MESQUITE ROASTED VEGETABLES

Reprinted with permission from *Mesquite Meal Recipes*
(San Pedro Mesquite Company) with special thanks to Mercedes

2 carrots

1 stalk celery

2 large yellow potatoes

1 yam

2 zucchini

2 leeks

3 tablespoons olive oil (or less, enough to lightly coat veggies)

1 tablespoon mesquite flour (or more, to taste)

Sea salt and black pepper, to taste

Additional herbs/spices of your choice

Squeeze of lemon juice

The addition of mesquite flour will add a unique flavor and spruce up your ordinary roasted veggies. Try it at your next event for a decidedly Southwest flair.

Preheat oven to 375° F. Chop veggies and place in large mixing bowl. Add remaining ingredients, save lemon juice, and toss, thoroughly coating vegetables. Place veggies into a large baking dish and squeeze some lemon juice over the top. Bake for about 45 minutes, until vegetables are soft and golden.

MAKES 6 SERVINGS.

SONORAN LATKES

Contributed by Aaron Wright

Latkes are a Jewish rendition of potato pancakes. They are a Hanukkah tradition among Ashkenazi Jews, with the oil symbolic of the miraculously long-lasting oil used to light the Second Temple during the Maccabean Revolt against the Seleucid Empire of the 2nd century BCE. This version of latkes uses locally available ingredients that fuse a tradition and tastes of the old world desert in Israel with that of the Sonoran Desert. This recipe makes a sweet version of the traditional savory latkes thanks to the mesquite flour and prickly pear juice.

1/2 cup chia seeds

1 cup prickly pear juice

4 large russet potatoes (2 to 3 pounds), peeled and grated

3 eggs

1 teaspoon kosher salt

1/2 cup mesquite flour

1 large onion, grated (optional)

Oil (for frying)

In a small bowl, mix chia seeds and prickly pear juice. Cover and let sit until chia absorbs most of the liquid (at least 1 hour). Fill a large bowl with cold water. Grate potatoes by hand or in a food processor with a grater blade and place them in the cold water to prevent browning. In a small bowl, whisk eggs and salt. Drain the potatoes and place them in cheesecloth. Squeeze out all moisture from the potatoes and return to large bowl. Add whisked eggs, mesquite flour, and soaked chia to the potatoes (and onion if using). Mix thoroughly.

Line a baking sheet with paper towels (to absorb excess oil once the latkes are fried). Fill a large skillet with 1/2 to 1 inch of oil, and place over medium heat. Ladle 1/4 cup of potato mixture into the hot oil. Flatten the latkes to about 1/2-inch thickness. Repeat, retaining some space between latkes so they don't stick together. Fry for 3 to 5 minutes on each side, or until browned and crispy. Remove from oil and place on the paper-towel-lined baking sheet to absorb excess oil.

Latkes are traditionally topped with applesauce or sour cream. For this local variety, try topping with Mesquite Syrup (p. 80) or Prickly Pear Jelly (p. 168).

NOTE: To keep latkes warm while frying remaining mixture, preheat the to oven 200° F prior to frying. After the excess oil is drained on the paper towels, place fried latkes on a separate baking sheet and put in the oven until ready to serve.

MAKES 15 to 20 LATKES.

(GF)

SONORAN THREE SISTERS BURGERS

Contributed by Jessie Barker and Caitlin Stern

2 cups dry tepary beans

1 onion, chopped

1 large squash, chopped

1 1/2 cups frozen corn

1 egg

4 chiltepines (or about 1/4 teaspoon ground)

1/2 teaspoon salt

3/4 cup mesquite flour

3/4 cup masa harina (nixtamalized corn flour)

Olive oil for cooking onion, squash, and burgers

Water for cooking tepary beans

A quintessentially Sonoran veggie burger featuring beans, squash and corn with mesquite flour and chiltepin.

Add water to a large pot, and cook tepary beans until soft. Drain (and keep water for soup). In a large skillet over medium heat, sauté onion in plenty of olive oil until translucent. Add squash and cook until soft. In large bowl, defrost corn. Add cooked onion, squash, and beans. In small bowl, whisk egg and add to vegetables and beans. Grind chiltepines (or use pre-ground powder) and add to the mixture along with salt. Add mesquite flour and masa harina to the mixture a little at a time (e.g., 1/4 to 1/2 cup), mixing thoroughly. Form burgers. Add more masa harina as needed to help burgers keep shape. In same large skillet, heat oil over medium heat and fry burgers on both sides until brown.

MAKES 20 SMALL BURGERS.

GF

MESQUITE MOLE ENCHILADAS WITH QUELITES

Contributed by Amy Valdés Schwemm, Mano y Metate

After several attempts at mesquite mole, I was very surprised that my favorite turned out to be so simple, using the mole I already make as a base. I grind Mole Dulce with four varieties of dark chiles, handmade Oaxacan chocolate, raisins, bananas, almonds, organic corn tortilla meal, and lots of sweet and savory spices. My grandmother loved mole, and she made some unexpected foods sweet: flour tortillas, tomato sauce for meat and tortillas, etc. Mole Dulce is sweet and well rounded, but mesquite adds complexity and depth. If you like heat, add a few ground chiltepines to the sauce. Use whatever filling you like or have on hand. Chicken or turkey is traditional. My brother uses sautéed summer squash, onion, and mushroom. My friend Lori Adkison uses roasted butternut squash with roasted garlic. My grandfather liked cheese and raw onion as a filling. Sometimes I add a handful of chopped nuts to the quelites filling, like La Indita Restaurant in Tucson. Frying tortillas is messy but critical to the texture and taste. Thin, dry corn tortillas are preferred and absorb less oil.

In a saucepan, gently heat 2 tablespoons oil. Add mole powder and mesquite flour, stirring to prevent scorching. When the paste is fragrant and a shade darker in color, add broth. Stir and simmer until the sauce thickens. Thin the sauce with more broth if it becomes too thick. It should be thinner than if using as a gravy. Salt to taste. Set aside to cool slightly.

Chop the greens and fry in oil with a little diced onion. Mix in the crumbed cheese and salt to taste. Set aside to cool slightly.

In a skillet just bigger in diameter than the tortilla, put in a half inch of oil and bring to medium heat. Cook each tortilla for a few seconds, just until the tortilla becomes pliable then set aside. If left for too long, it will crisp and be difficult to roll.

Preheat oven to 375º F. After frying all of the tortillas, dip a tortilla in the sauce, coating both sides, and place in a casserole dish. Put about two tablespoons of filling in a narrow stripe across the tortilla, roll tightly, and place seam side down against the edge of the dish. Continue, and place each enchilada side by side. If using multiple fillings, garnish with a tiny bit of filling to identify. Pour any remaining sauce over all and cover the dish with a lid or baking sheet. Bake about 20 minutes. Remove the lid during the last few minutes of cooking for crispy edges, if desired. Serve with a salad, rice, and beans. If you have leftovers, heat in an oiled cast iron skillet until crispy and serve with a fried egg.

2 tablespoons cooking oil + enough to fill skillet 1/2 inch deep

1 tin Mano y Metate Mole Dulce*

2 tablespoons mesquite flour

1 1/2 cups broth (chicken or veggie)

Salt to taste

1 bunch quelites, amaranth greens, or other wild or domesticated greens

1 onion, diced (to taste)

Queso fresco or any aged or fresh farmer's cheese, crumbled

12 corn tortillas

*NOTE: Mano y Metate Mole is a product of freshly ground whole spices, nuts, seeds, and chiles. It's an easy way to use the celebrated Mexican sauces. You can buy it locally in Tucson and Southern Arizona or order it online (ManoyMetate.com).

MAKES 4 SERVINGS.

MESQUITE TAMALES

Contributed by Chef Molly Beverly, Crossroads Café, Prescott College

12 large cornhusks or 24 small ones

1 pound boneless, free range chicken thighs

Salt and pepper to taste

4 ounces medium cheddar cheese, grated

SAUCE:

3 tablespoons vegetable oil

2 tablespoons New Mexico red chile powder

1/2 teaspoon ground cumin

1 teaspoon dried oreganillo or epazote

1 teaspoon salt

1 tablespoon white or whole wheat flour

1 cup water

1 cup cooked black or white tepary beans

MASA:

2 cups toasted mesquite flour

2 cups fresh corn masa

1/2 cup soft butter

1/4 teaspoon salt

1 teaspoon baking powder

1 cup water or as needed

Tamales are a labor of love. They are special little packages of joy. These in particular are rich and delicious. Note: Most mesquite flour comes untoasted, unless otherwise noted. Toasting mesquite pods before milling is done by the Seri Indians in Desemboque, Mexico.

Place cornhusks in a bowl and cover with warm water overnight or until soft.

In a dry skillet, toast raw mesquite flour over medium heat. Stir constantly until flour turns a light brown. Watch carefully as it can burn easily. Remove from heat and from pan immediately to stop cooking.

Preheat oven to 350° F. Season chicken thighs with salt and pepper. Bake on a baking sheet for 15 to 20 minutes, until fully cooked. Let cool then shred or cut into 1/2-inch chunks.

In a small skillet, heat vegetable oil over medium heat. Add chile powder, cumin, oreganillo or epazote, salt and flour. Cook over medium heat, stirring constantly, until mixture sizzles and deepens in color to a darker red. Add water, stir, and bring to a boil. Reduce heat and simmer until slightly thick. Taste and adjust seasoning. Add beans and cooked chicken and let simmer 5 minutes. Set aside.

In a large bowl, mix toasted mesquite flour, corn masa, butter, salt, baking powder, and enough water to make a wet, but not runny, dough.

To assemble tamales, remove cornhusks from water and pat dry with a towel. Lay out husk and spread 1/4 inch of masa onto it, leaving the top 1/3 (the narrower end) uncovered. Now lay a vertical ribbon of sauce with chicken and beans on the masa. Cover with cheese. Fold the edges of the cornhusk over the filling, finishing with the pointed end. Set aside and repeat until all ingredients are used up.

To cook tamales, place them standing up, with folded side down, in a steamer. Cover and steam for 45 minutes to 1 hour. When masa pulls away from husk, they are ready. You may have to cook longer or check several times to test their readiness. Remove carefully from pot and let sit a few minutes before serving.

MAKES 12 to 24 TAMALES.

MESQUITE:
SOUPS / SPREADS / SAUCES
Mesquite Atole/Broth

Photo: Barbara Rose

GF V

MESQUITE BROTH

Contributed by Lori Adkison

6 cups mesquite chaff, from milling pods (or broken mesquite pods)

18 cups water

This broth creates a simple base for soups, syrups, and jelly.

Place the water and chaff in a large pot on the stovetop set to high and bring to a boil. Reduce heat and simmer for 1 hour then strain. Broth will be opaque and flavorful. For a clear broth, after straining, place liquid in a gallon jar and let stand in the refrigerator undisturbed for 24 hours. Gently pour liquid off the top leaving the solids on the bottom of the container. This clarified broth will have a milder mesquite flavor.

NOTE: Use a 3:1 water to chaff ratio. If you find your broth is too thick, add more water.

MAKES 4 to 5 CUPS.

GF V

ALMOST APRIL SOUP

Contributed by Barbara Rose, Bean Tree Farm

A light soup with foraged desert ingredients.

Quickly sauté mixed chopped greens in your choice of fat or oil, until tender. Ladle broth over cooked greens and simmer. Salt to taste. Ladle into soup bowls, and garnish with cilantro, chile oil, and juice or vinegar.

OPTIONAL ADDITIONS: Tortilla chips, shredded cheese, hard-boiled eggs, chopped veggies, rice noodles, etc. You could take this East too, with some ginger, lemongrass, and coconut milk.

MAKES 5 to 6 SERVINGS.

4 to 6 cups wild and cultivated greens: lamb's-quarter, mustard, radish, arugula, garlic greens, etc.

Cooking oil or fat

4 cups Mesquite Atole, p. 107

Salt to taste

1 cup cilantro, chopped

Hot chile oil

1/2 cup chickweed vinegar (or other vinegar) or one sour citrus fruit, juiced

(GF) (V)

CASCABEL STEW

*Reprinted and adapted with permission from Mesquite Meal Recipes
(San Pedro Mesquite Company) with special thanks to Mercedes*

1/2 cup + 1 tablespoon mesquite flour, divided

1/2 cup flour or brown rice flour

Salt and pepper to taste

1 pound tofu

4 tablespoons vegetable oil, divided

1 onion, chopped

2 medium potatoes, cubed

6 medium carrots, sliced

1 chopped tomato

6 green chiles

1 6-ounce can tomato paste

2 to 3 cups water

This hearty, vegetarian stew serves up a subtle mesquite sweetness and will fortify you on chilly desert evenings.

In a large bowl, mix flours (except 1 tablespoon mesquite flour), salt, and pepper. Cut tofu into 1-inch cubes. Toss cubes in the mesquite flour mixture, lightly coating each cube. In large skillet over medium-high heat, brown coated tofu cubes in oil. Set aside. In soup pot, sauté onions until translucent. Add tofu, potatoes, carrots, tomato, and chiles. Stir in tomato paste with remaining tablespoon of mesquite flour. Add water to make a broth, enough to cover tofu and veggies. Use less water for a thick stew, more for a soup. Simmer for 30 to 40 minutes, and serve.

VARIATIONS: Use any vegetables you have on hand for new flavors.

MAKES 6 SERVINGS.

Ⓥ ⒼⒻ

DESERT DRY RUB

Contributed by Jill Lorenzini

Mesquite flour is the vehicle for innovative taste combinations of different seasonal ingredients in this recipe template. The sweet rich taste combines well with spicy, nutty, hot, savory, and other desert ingredient flavors and textures to make a versatile dry rub mixture. Eat the season!

In a small bowl mix all ingredients. Store in a glass jar and use as dry rub for veggies, tofu, tempeh, meats, poultry, or fish (especially delicious on salmon!).

MAKES 6 to 8 SERVINGS.

2 cups mesquite flour

1 1/2 teaspoons salt

1 teaspoon ground black pepper

2 tablespoons ground barrel cactus seeds

1 teaspoon chile powder (chiltepin, cayenne, chipotle, ghost, or other local/seasonal powder, to taste)

1 tablespoon dried/ground seasonal herbs:

- Spring: oreganillo

- Summer: limoncillo/ cinchweed

- Fall: juniper berry

- Winter: mustard

- Other herbs: marjoram, basil, rosemary, sage, cilantro, coriander, fennel, etc.

(GF) (V)

MESQUITE SYRUP & JELLY

Contributed by Lori Adkison

3 cups clarified
Mesquite Broth (p. 76)

1/3 of 1.75-ounce package
powdered pectin (for syrup)

4 1/2 cups sugar

4 tablespoons lemon juice
(about 2 lemons' worth)

This beautiful mesquite syrup is great on its own to pour over pancakes or desserts. It also forms the flavor for mesquite ice cream. Start with a clarified Mesquite Broth (p. 76) for a beautiful, golden-colored syrup.

In a saucepan stir pectin into broth and bring to a boil over high heat. While stirring constantly, add sugar and lemon juice and return to boil. Boil mixture for 1 minute. Pour into hot, sterilized jars. Cover at once with lids. Allow jars to cool for several hours then store syrup in refrigerator.

NOTE: To make jelly use the whole packet of powdered pectin.

MAKES ABOUT 3 PINTS.

Ⓡ ⓖⒻ Ⓥ

OLIVE-MESQUITE TAPENADE

Contributed by Jill Lorenzini

Mesquite meal is the sweet balance to the savory essence of this rich, hearty spread. This is a special desert treat when made with home-cured black olives. The spread works well on any of the mesquite crackers in this cookbook, or you can just eat it straight from the jar. You can personalize this recipe to your own taste by adding your favorite herbs and greens.

Combine all ingredients. Use a food processor for a smooth paste, or chop by hand for a rustic, chunky version. Let flavors marry overnight, then re-taste and re-season, if needed. Serve with additional olive oil and crusty bread, crackers, veggie sticks, or chips. Also try on sandwiches, with pita and fixings, on pizza, and in lasagna, polenta, casseroles, dressings, or sauces.

MAKES ABOUT 2 CUPS.

2 cups olives, pitted

Juice and zest from one small lemon

3 to 4 cloves of garlic, or for a milder taste 3 to 4 green onions

1 cup peppery greens, such as arugula or garden or curly cress

2 teaspoons balsamic vinegar

1/4 cup fresh mixed herbs

1/3 cup mesquite flour

Up to 1/4 cup olive oil

(GF) (S) (V)

MESQUITE CHOCOLATE CHILE SAUCE

Contributed by Barbara Rose, Bean Tree Farm

1 quart strained mesquite reduction (reduced from 3 gallons Mesquite Atole, p. 107)

1/2 cup cocoa powder

1 tablespoon hot chile powder, or to taste (I like using chiltepin or chipotle)

Spices, your choice: cinnamon, vanilla, cloves, cardamom, etc.

Sweetener, your choice, if desired

Tequila, if desired

Rich, nuanced flavors infuse this thick, dark, decadent sauce, versatile in a variety of serving options. I often make this with just the first 3 ingredients. If the mesquite is tasty, the cocoa is high quality, and the chiles are fresh and powerful, nothing else is really needed.

In a medium saucepan, combine mesquite broth, cocoa, and chile powder over medium heat. Let simmer to blend flavors, taking care not to scorch. A solar oven is great for this! Add small amounts of remaining ingredients, to taste. Finish with a splash of good tequila! Serve hot or cold over ice cream, on chèvre, or on fresh fruit.

MAKES 1 QUART.

MESQUITE:
SWEETS

Mammoth Mesquite Chocolate Swirl Cookies

Photo: Christian Timmerman

GF

MESQUITE ICE CREAM

Contributed by Lori Adkison

6 large egg yolks

1 cup Mesquite Syrup (p. 80)

2 teaspoons all-purpose flour

1/2 teaspoon salt

1 1/2 cups milk

1 cup heavy cream

1/2 teaspoon vanilla extract

1 tablespoon mesquite flour
(for garnish)

Lori's ice creams are legendary. This original recipe steals the show at mesquite tasting parties!

In a medium mixing bowl, beat the eggs yolks, mesquite syrup, flour, and salt. In a saucepan bring the milk to a simmer over medium heat. With the mixer running, slowly pour hot milk into the egg mixture. Return mixture back to the saucepan. Cook on low heat stirring constantly until the custard thickens slightly. It is important to not let the mixture boil or the eggs will scramble. Pour the custard through a strainer into a large bowl. After mixture cools slightly, add the heavy cream and vanilla extract. Refrigerate overnight and then freeze in an ice cream machine according to the manufacturer's instructions. Serve with a sprinkling of sweet mesquite flour on top.

VARIATIONS: Make this ice cream extra special by adding Mesquite Toffee (p. 88) at the final stages of freezing. Use prickly pear syrup in place of the mesquite syrup to change the flavor of this dessert and make it a beautiful color.

MAKES ABOUT 5 CUPS.

GF V

REFRESHING MESQUITE SORBET

Contributed by Daniel Moss

Inspired by the delicious, hearty flavor of a good mesquite broth, I wanted to see if I could also enjoy it cold, and so the sorbet was born. The result is a delicious and refreshingly light summer treat.

Dissolve sugar into mesquite broth, and mix in cardamom. Let mixture cool in refrigerator. Freeze mixture in ice cream maker according to manufacturer's instructions. Sprinkle some mesquite flour over a dish of sorbet for color and extra flavor!

MAKES ABOUT 5 CUPS.

1/2 cup sugar

3 cups non-clarified Mesquite Broth (p. 76)

1 teaspoon fresh-ground cardamom

MESQUITE RUGELACH

Contributed by Sara Jones

DOUGH:

1 cup butter (2 sticks), cold, cut into chunks

2 cups all-purpose flour

2 tablespoons sugar

Pinch of salt

8 ounces (1 package) cream cheese

FILLING:

About 1 cup finely chopped semisweet chocolate

3/4 cup mesquite flour

1 teaspoon cinnamon

Powdered sugar for dusting (optional)

These cookies are like mini cinnamon buns, but made crunchier with mesquite and grated chocolate filling. The mesquite is used as a filling, rather than in the dough itself, keeping the cookies light and flaky.

Preheat oven to 350° F. In a food processor, pulse together butter, flour, sugar, and salt until butter is broken down into at least nickel-size pieces. Add the cream cheese and pulse a few times to integrate. Process until dough comes together. Shape dough into 3 equal-size disks. Wrap in plastic wrap and refrigerate for at least 30 minutes. Meanwhile, in a small bowl toss chocolate, mesquite flour, and cinnamon together and set aside until ready to use.

On a floured surface, roll each disk into a round about 12 inches in diameter and 1/8 inch thick. Cover each disk with 1/3 of the mesquite mixture. Press filling gently into dough. Cut each round like a pizza, into 8 slices. Roll each slice from wider, outer edge toward the center, forming a crescent shape. Place crescents 1 inch apart onto an ungreased baking sheet. Bake for 20 minutes, until lightly golden brown. Cool and dust with powdered sugar, if desired.

NOTE: You can also use this filling to make crescents with excess pie dough. Follow the directions above for placing the filling, cutting the dough, shaping, and baking.

MAKES 24 COOKIES.

ROSE'S MESQUITE HERMITS

Contributed by Rose Marie Licher

This recipe was developed from recipes in four old cookbooks (including my great-grandmother's from the 1890s) and modified to include mesquite flour and provide a more healthful snack. You can freeze part of the dough in rolls, wrapped in plastic .wrap, to slice and bake later.

Preheat the oven to 375° F. Simmer the dried fruit, raisins, and water until softened and water is absorbed. Let cool slightly. In a medium bowl, cream the butter and Sucanat. Blend in the maple syrup and beat in the eggs, one at a time. Sift the flours, spices, and salt into the creamed mixture. Add the fruits and nuts, blending just until mixed. Drop by spoonfuls (a small ice cream scoop works well) onto a greased cookie sheet, flatten slightly, and bake 15 minutes.

MAKES ABOUT 3 DOZEN COOKIES.

3/4 cup mixed dried fruits, cut in small pieces (apricots, figs, blueberries, etc)

1/2 cup currants or raisins, or dried hackberries or wolfberries

1/2 cup water, more or less, as needed to soften fruits

3/4 cup butter or coconut oil

1/2 cup Sucanat* or brown sugar

1/2 cup maple syrup or blackstrap molasses

3 medium eggs (or 2 large)

1 cup mesquite flour

1 1/2 cups whole grain flour

1 teaspoon cinnamon

1/4 teaspoon cloves

1/4 teaspoon nutmeg

1/4 teaspoon sea salt

1 cup chopped nuts

*SUCANAT is pure evaporated sugarcane juice (the word comes from "Sucre de canne naturel"). It contains the natural nutrients left in molasses unlike refined white sugar.

MESQUITE TOFFEE

Contributed by Lori Adkison

1/2 cup coarsely chopped toasted almonds or pecans (or a mixture of both)

1 cup butter

1 cup sugar

1 tablespoon Mesquite Syrup (p. 80)

3 tablespoons water

3/4 cup semisweet or bittersweet chocolate pieces

1/2 cup finely chopped nuts (dust-like)

This toffee combines decadently with Lori's Mesquite Ice Cream (p. 84). It also holds its own on any dessert table. Mesquite married to toffee is a dreamy combination.

Line a baking sheet with foil. Sprinkle the coarsely chopped nuts on the sheet. In a heavy 2-quart saucepan, melt butter. Add sugar, mesquite syrup, and water. Cook and stir over medium-high heat.

Clip candy thermometer to pan. Stirring, cook over medium heat until thermometer reaches 290° F (about 15 minutes) for soft-crack stage. Remove pan from heat and pour mixture over nuts in prepared pan. Sprinkle the chocolate pieces over the hot toffee. Let stand for 1 to 2 minutes. Spread softened chocolate over mixture. While chocolate is still soft, dust with finely chopped nuts. Chill until firm. Break candy into pieces and store remainder (if there is any!) in an airtight container.

GF R V

MESQUITE MACAROONS

Contributed by Aaron Wright

This easy, 10-minute recipe is a unique twist on a traditional Jewish delicacy, fusing mesquite, coconut, and maple syrup into nutritious, savory sweet treats.

In a large bowl, combine all ingredients. Mix with your hands until a crumbly dough forms. Squeeze small amounts of dough in your palms and then roll into balls of desired size. Refrigerate in an airtight container.

VARIATION: Garnish by rolling balls in flavorful dusting of cacao powder, mesquite flour, coconut crumbs, or something else.

MAKES 18 to 20 MACAROONS.

1 cup shredded unsweetened coconut

1 cup mesquite flour

1/4 cup maple syrup or raw honey

3 tablespoons coconut oil

1 teaspoon vanilla (or almond) extract

1/2 teaspoon sea salt

PUMPKIN CHEESECAKE BARS

Contributed by Carlos Nagel

16 ounces pound cake mix

4 tablespoons mesquite flour, divided

1/4 cup melted butter

3 eggs, divided

8 ounces (1 package) soft cream cheese

4 to 6 teaspoons pumpkin pie spice, divided

1 cup (8-ounce can) sweetened condensed milk

2 cups (16 ounces) pumpkin

1/2 teaspoon salt

1 cup chopped nuts (walnuts or pecans)

These bars were a favorite among our testers. The autumn flavors of pumpkin and mesquite are unbeatable.

Preheat oven to 350° F. In a large bowl combine cake mix, melted butter, 1 egg, 2 to 3 teaspoons pumpkin pie spice, and 2 tablespoons mesquite flour and mix until crumbly. Press into the bottom of a 10- x 15-inch jelly roll pan and set aside.

In a large bowl, beat the cream cheese until fluffy. Gradually beat in sweetened condensed milk, the remaining 2 eggs, pumpkin, the remaining 2 tablespoons mesquite flour, salt, and 2 to 3 teaspoons pumpkin pie spice. Scrape down the sides and beat again. When well mixed, pour over crust. Sprinkle nuts on top. Bake for 30 to 35 minutes until set. Cool, cut into bars, and refrigerate.

MAKES 24 BARS.

DESERT WILD FOODS	**Mesquite**
HARVEST SEASON	Dry Summer
CULINARY ROOTS	Southwest

MAMMOTH MESQUITE CHOCOLATE SWIRL COOKIES

Contributed by Jeau Allen of The Mesquitery

These big, chewy, and gooey cookies are named for the 3,000-acre mesquite bosque (forest) along the San Pedro River in Mammoth, Arizona, one of the largest remaining bosques of its kind in the Southwest. Fresh pecans add extra southwestern flavor and crunch! The trick to these cookies is to follow the directions precisely. If you work quickly, the chocolate bits will melt slightly and swirl in the warm batter prior to baking.

1 large egg yolk

1 large egg

1/2 teaspoon vanilla extract

1/3 cup granulated sugar

3/4 cup light brown sugar, packed

1 1/3 cups all-purpose flour

1/2 cup velvet mesquite flour

1/2 teaspoon salt (or 1 teaspoon if using unsalted butter)

1/2 teaspoon baking soda

1/2 cup American native pecan pieces

1 cup (2 sticks) butter

1 cup chocolate bits (6 ounces)

Move oven rack to the upper-middle position. Preheat the oven to 375º F. Line two cookie sheets with parchment paper and set aside. Separate the first egg and put the egg yolk in a small bowl (you won't need the egg white). Add the second egg (both yolk and white) and vanilla. In a large heat-proof bowl, combine sugars. In a medium bowl, combine flours, salt, and baking soda and mix thoroughly. Toast pecans over medium heat in dry stainless steel skillet by stirring continually to avoid scorching, about 3 to 4 minutes, until fragrant. Transfer to a small bowl and let cool. In a large stainless steel skillet, melt the butter over medium-high heat and brown by continually swirling the skillet for another 2 to 3 minutes. When the butter is a deep earthy brown, add it to the sugar mixture, scraping it thoroughly out of the skillet with a flexible heat-proof spatula. Quickly mix the butter and sugars together. (If doubling the recipe, you will have better results if you brown each stick of butter separately.) Stir the egg and vanilla mixture into the sugar and butter mixture until the sugars have dissolved and the mixture doesn't feel grainy. Fold in the flour mixture until all the flour is incorporated. Work gently but quickly. Do not overmix. Fold in the pecans and chocolate chips. The goal is to have chocolate swirls, not chocolate batter, so be careful not to overmix.

While the dough is still warm and soft, measure level 1/3-cup portions onto parchment-lined cookie sheets, about 5 cookies per sheet. Bake one sheet at a time, about 12 minutes. Cookies are done when the edges are firm and the centers are round and puffy. They should look slightly underdone, as they will continue to cook after removal from the oven. Remove the cookie sheet from the oven gently so that the cookies don't collapse. Place the cookie sheet on a wire rack to allow air circulation beneath the sheet, allowing the cookies to cool. Do not remove the cookies from the parchment paper and cookie sheet until they are cool enough to maintain their shape. Repeat this step with the second cookie sheet.

MAKES 10 REALLY BIG COOKIES

MESQUITE CHILTEPIN MILANO COOKIES

Contributed by Mikaela Jones

1 1/2 cups all-purpose flour

1 cup mesquite flour

1 teaspoon kosher salt

1 cup unsalted butter (2 sticks), softened

1 1/3 cups sugar

2 whole eggs

1 egg white

2 teaspoons vanilla extract

8 ounces dark chocolate, chopped

4 to 6 dried chiltepines, ground

This is a spicy, Sonoran version of the Milano cookies you find in the grocery store. They are easy and fun to make and they look great, so take them to any potluck or party.

Preheat oven to 325° F. Line two baking sheets with parchment or silicone mats. In a large bowl, combine flours and salt and set aside. In another large bowl, cream together butter and sugar. Beat in whole eggs and egg white, then vanilla, and continue to beat on high until light and fluffy. Lower speed and gradually beat in flour mixture until just incorporated.

Transfer batter to a plastic freezer bag with a 1/2-inch hole snipped in one corner. Pipe batter into 2-inch long strips. Bake for 13 to 15 minutes, or until the edges of the cookies just begin to brown. Remove from oven and let cool on the baking sheet for 5 minutes, then transfer to cooling racks. Allow cookies to cool completely. Arrange cookie halves in pairs of similar shape and size.

Melt chocolate and ground chiltepin in a double boiler until smooth, then remove from heat and let cool for 10 minutes. Spoon the chocolate onto one cookie half. Gently press the other half on top until the chocolate just reaches the edges. Repeat with the remaining cookies and let the sandwiches sit until the chocolate has set. Any extra cookies will keep well in an airtight container in the freezer.

MAKES 3 DOZEN COOKIES.

GF

SECRET MESQUITE CHOCOLATE CHIP COOKIES

Contributed by Gail Ryser

In addition to mesquite, these cookies have a secret ingredient that adds vitamin C and natural sweetness.

Preheat oven to 375° F. In a large mixing bowl, cream butter and sugar until blended. Add egg and mix until blended. Add sweet potato, yogurt, and vanilla and blend. Add baking soda, salt, xanthan gum, oats, and mesquite flour and mix until all ingredients are well blended. Add chocolate chips and mix until incorporated. Let sit for 30 minutes. Spoon dough onto a clay baking stone or cookie sheet. Bake for 12 to 15 minutes or until lightly browned.

VARIATION: Add dried cranberries or fruits as desired.

MAKES 1 DOZEN COOKIES.

2 tablespoons butter

1/4 cup brown sugar

1 egg

1/4 cup cooked sweet potato, peeled and mashed

1 tablespoon plain yogurt

1/2 teaspoon vanilla

1/2 teaspoon baking soda

1/4 teaspoon salt

1/2 teaspoon xanthan gum

2/3 cup rolled oats

1/3 cup mesquite flour

1/4 cup chocolate chips

PEANUT BUTTER MESQUITE COOKIES

Reprinted with permission from *Mesquite Meal Recipes*
(San Pedro Mesquite Company)

1 cup butter

1 cup natural peanut butter

3/4 cup granulated sugar

3/4 cup brown sugar

1 teaspoon vanilla

2 eggs

1 cup whole wheat flour

1 cup all-purpose flour

1 cup mesquite flour

1 1/4 teaspoons baking soda

1 1/2 cups chocolate chips
(optional)

Preheat oven to 350° F. In a large bowl, beat butter, peanut butter, sugars, and vanilla until fluffy. Mix in eggs. Add flours and baking soda, mixing well. Stir in chocolate chips, if using. Cover dough with a damp cloth and refrigerate for 1 hour. Scoop dough with a tablespoon and roll into balls. Place on a greased baking sheet and flatten by hand. Bake for 12 to 14 minutes until golden brown.

VARIATIONS: Add any additional items you have on hand such as chia seeds, barrel cactus seeds, dried saguaro fruit, or any other dried berries. Fold into mixture last after everything has been mixed, when you would add the chocolate chips.

MAKES 3 1/2 DOZEN COOKIES.

Ⓢ

KUKUKADOO SOLAR COOKIES

Contributed by Garth and Suzanne Mackzum

These are fun, creative cookies you can make with the sun!

In a large bowl, cream butter, sugar and vanilla. In a separate bowl, mix dry ingredients, using only 1 cup of the oats. Combine the two mixes and then add water. Add as much of the remaining oats as necessary to reach desired consistency (it should be dry enough to form into cookies). Mix in nuts. Add optional additional ingredients, if using.

Drop 1-inch spoonfuls of batter onto cookie sheet. Make sure your cookie sheet fits into your solar oven—normal-sized cookie sheets are usually too large. Bake in a solar oven for between 20 minutes and 1 1/2 hours or more, depending on the size of the cookies and the temperature of oven, which depends on how hot the day is!

VARIATIONS: These cookies are even better with dried fruits and seeds added to the batter. Consider using chia seeds, barrel cactus seeds, dried saguaro fruit, raisins, dried cranberries, sesame seeds, toasted pumpkin seeds, carob chips, chocolate chips, or whatever you have in the pantry.

MAKES ABOUT 20 COOKIES.

1/3 cup (about 5 tablespoons) butter, softened

1/4 cup Sucanat or sugar

1 teaspoon of vanilla

3/4 cup whole wheat flour

3/4 cup mesquite flour

1/2 teaspoon baking soda

Salt to taste

1 1/2 cups rolled oats, divided

1/2 cup water

1/2 cup chopped nuts

GF

AMY'S APPLE CRISP

Contributed by Amy Valdés Schwemm, Mano y Metate

FILLING:

2 pounds apples, local organic heirlooms if possible

2 tablespoons orange or apple juice

TOPPING:

1 cup mesquite flour

1 cup rolled oats

1/4 cup amaranth seeds

1/4 cup brown sugar

1/4 cup chopped pecans (optional)

1/4 teaspoon cinnamon, ground

1/4 teaspoon cardamom, ground

1/2 cup (1 stick) butter

2 tablespoons milk
(or kefir, rice/soy milk)

This dish holds well in the oven, while you're eating dinner. It isn't overly sweet so serve it warm with ice cream or eat it for breakfast with yogurt or kefir.

Preheat oven to 375° F. Core and thinly slice the apples (no need to peel them). Place sliced apples in an 8- x 8-inch greased baking dish and sprinkle with juice. Bake for 15 minutes.

Meanwhile combine (by pulsing) all topping ingredients in a food processor until mixed and slightly moist. Add more liquid if necessary. Remove the apples from the oven, spread the topping over the apples, and return to the oven. Bake for 30 minutes or until the apples are tender and the topping is browned.

MAKES 6 to 9 SERVINGS.

Ⓥ

CHOCOLATE CRAZY CAKE

Contributed by Deb Hilbert

Rumor has it that this cake was developed during the Depression by enterprising bakers who were hampered by a lack of culinary staples, like eggs, milk, and butter. This simple yet delicious cake is not only vegan—you don't even need a bowl for mixing!

Preheat oven to 350° F. Mix together all dry ingredients in a greased, 8 x 8-inch square pan. Make 3 depressions in the mixture, 2 small and 1 larger. Pour vinegar in one small depression and vanilla into the other. Pour oil in the larger depression. Pour water over all and mix well until smooth. Bake on middle rack for 35 minutes or until toothpick comes out clean. Serve with a dusting of powdered sugar or with whipped coconut or other non-dairy cream.

MAKES 12 SERVINGS.

1 cup all-purpose flour

1/3 cup mesquite flour

1/3 cup whole wheat flour

3 tablespoons baking cocoa powder

2/3 cup granulated sugar

1 teaspoon baking soda

1/2 teaspoon salt

1 1/2 teaspoons white vinegar

1 1/2 teaspoons vanilla

5 1/2 tablespoons vegetable oil

1 cup water

Powdered sugar or whipped coconut or other non-dairy cream

ALMOND MESQUITE CAKE

Contributed by Jim Byrd

CAKE BATTER:

2 1/4 cups flour

3/4 cup mesquite flour

1/2 teaspoon salt

2 1/2 teaspoons baking powder

3/4 cup butter, softened

1 1/3 cups sugar

2 eggs, large

2 teaspoons almond extract

1 1/3 cups milk

2 cups slivered almonds, divided

ALMOND BUTTER FROSTING:

1 cup butter

2/3 cup almond butter

2 teaspoons vanilla extract

2 teaspoons molasses

2 1/2 cups powdered sugar

Mesquite flour has a natural nutty flavor that complements well with almonds in this beautiful layer cake.

Preheat oven to 350º F. In a large bowl, sift together flours, salt, and baking powder. In a separate bowl, beat butter, sugar, eggs, and almond extract until well incorporated. Mix the contents of the two bowls together slowly, adding milk. Beat until smooth. Add 1 cup of slivered almonds to batter and mix briefly until incorporated. Pour batter into two oiled and floured 9-inch round cake pans. Bake 35 to 40 minutes or until a toothpick comes out clean. Remove from oven and allow to cool completely.

While cake is cooling, whip butter until fluffy. Add almond butter and continue whipping. Add vanilla extract and molasses. Slowly add powdered sugar and whip until blended and fluffy. Remove cakes from pans. Place first cake onto plate and frost all around. Stack second layer on top and do the same. Press slivered almonds into the side of the cakes.

VARIATION: To make cupcakes instead of a layer cake, simply divide the batter into lined cupcake tins and bake for 20 to 25 minutes. Remove from oven, allow to cool completely, then frost and serve.

MAKES 8 SERVINGS OF CAKE OR ABOUT 16 CUPCAKES.

VALENCIAN EASTER CAKE OR "LA MONA DE PASQUA"

Contributed by Maite Guardiola

Originating from 15th-century Spain, this small round or doughnut-shaped cake topped with hard-boiled eggs is traditionally given as a gift to a godchild from his or her godparents at Easter time. The name, La Mona de Pasqua, comes from the Moroccan word "mona" meaning "gift." Traditionally, the cake was shaped like a donut or figure eight, with hard-boiled eggs in the holes. The number of eggs depended on the age of the child. Modern cakes are quite fancy. They are glazed with chocolate and can be topped with chocolate eggs, almonds, and colorful feathers.

1/4 cup mesquite flour

3/4 cup whole wheat or white flour

5 eggs at room temperature, separated

1 cup white sugar

Zest from 1/2 orange

1/2 teaspoon vanilla

Pinch of salt

1/2 cup orange marmalade (traditional) or prickly pear jelly

Juice from 1/2 orange

1/2 cup white sugar

Powdered sugar or chocolate glaze

Preheat oven to 350° F. Grease and flour a 12-inch round cake pan and set aside. In a small bowl, sift mesquite and wheat flour together and set aside.

In a large bowl, beat the egg yolks, 1 cup sugar, and orange zest with an electric mixer set on high for 2 to 3 minutes, until thick and cream colored, and set aside.

In a large bowl, beat egg whites on high, to soft peak stage (until very fluffy and beginning to hold a shape when the beaters are removed). Gently fold egg yolk mixture, vanilla, and salt into beaten whites using a large spoon or silicon spatula. Sprinkle flour, a few tablespoons at a time, over egg mixture, folding gently to incorporate each time. When batter is smooth, pour into prepared cake pan and place in middle rack in oven. Bake 25 to 30 minutes or until a toothpick comes out clean.

Cool cake then remove from pan. Cut in half, through the middle, so that you have two circular halves. Make orange syrup by combining the orange juice and 1/2 cup sugar in a saucepan over medium heat and stirring until sugar is completely dissolved. Pour the syrup over the cut surface of both halves of the cake. Spread the marmalade or jelly over bottom half of cake and top with second half. Dust cake with powdered sugar or drizzle with a chocolate glaze.

MAKES 6 SERVINGS.

Ⓥ

MESQUITE PIE CRUST

Contributed by Ian Fritz and Turtle Southern

1 cup unbleached white flour

1 cup whole wheat pastry flour

1/3 cup mesquite flour, sifted

1/2 teaspoon salt

2/3 cup plus a fat tablespoon vegan margarine*

2/3 cup ice water

*SPECIAL NOTE ON MARGARINE: Many butter substitutes contain unhealthy hydrogenated oils. We use Earth Balance non-hydrogenated margarine, which is a tasty blend of oils without trans fat or genetically engineered ingredients. A vegan staple. Yum!

This pie crust comes to us from the founders of the Tucson Pie Party. We take pie seriously around these parts, and this crust recipe proves it.

Mix flours and salt in a bowl. Add (but do not mix) margarine. Put the bowl in the freezer to chill. When it is "good n' cold" (at least 30 minutes), pull it out of the freezer and use a pastry blender or two table knives to cut the margarine into the flour until you have pea-sized chunks. Add water (a sprinkle at a time) to the flour, stirring with a fork and lifting from the bottom of the bowl to incorporate any dry flour. Add just enough water to barely hold the flour together. Knead briefly, then divide the dough in half and roll it out on a floured surface. If you are not ready to roll out and use the dough immediately, wrap it in a sealed plastic bag or in plastic and put it back in the freezer to stay chilled until you are ready.

If you are blind baking the crust for a chilled pie, bake at 425º F for 15 minutes and then reduce to 375º F for 10 minutes.

NOTE: The more diligent you are about keeping everything cold (the ingredients, the mixing bowl, the rolling pin, the counter), the better your pie crust will turn out. Flaky crust happens when pockets of "fat" melt quickly, leaving only air behind. If your margarine is allowed to soften into the flour before the crust goes in the oven, the two will join together prematurely and cause a dense crust. Always remember that pie takes practice, and the more pies you make, the better your crust will become.

MAKES TWO 9-INCH PIE CRUSTS.

SOUTHERN ARIZONA PECAN DATE PIE WITH MESQUITE CRUST

Contributed by Emily Rockey. Inspired by Judy Rockey, Bodie Robins, and the Sonoran Desert

This award-winning pie features wild and local ingredients: local mesquite, local honey, Colorado River Medjool dates, Amado pecans, unsmoked Whiskey Del Bac, and local eggs. It was inspired by Emily's mother's traditional pecan pie, and local baker Bodie Robins's mesquite crust. The pie won 2nd place in the "Other" category at the 2015 Tucson Pie Party along with the best "Home Slice/Closest to Home" Award for incorporating local ingredients.

Preheat oven to 350° F. Make sure oven racks are in middle of oven.

MESQUITE CRUSTS:

Mix the flours and salt in a large mixing bowl. Add about one-third of the butter, cutting it in using a fork or pastry blender until the butter is combined. Add in the remaining butter and mix to form coarse crumbs. Add the vinegar, incorporating while adding 1/3 cup ice water. Test a little of the dough by forming a small ball and squeeze: it should just hold its shape. If it's still crumbly, add in a bit more ice water by the tablespoonful. (Do not overwork the dough.) Turn the dough out onto a large piece of plastic wrap or plastic bag. Wrap the dough, then press and flatten into a round. Refrigerate 1/2 to 1 hour.

Roll out the dough into about a 12-inch round, about 1/8 inch thick, on a lightly floured surface. Center over a 9-inch pie dish. Trim edge and design as desired. Refrigerate 30 minutes before using. Before adding filling, make a foil cover in a ring shape just to cover the crust's edges to prevent burning during baking. (This is easier to do before the filling is in the crusts.)

FILLING:

In mixing bowl, combine brown sugar and flour. Mix together eggs, honey, and brown rice syrup and add to flour and brown sugar mixture. Stir well. Add butter, vanilla, vinegar, salt, and whiskey and mix until combined. Set aside. Place pecans in the pie crust shells as a solid layer. Distribute dates evenly on top of the pecans. Slowly pour filling over pecans and dates. Place pre-made foil protector over edges of crusts. Gently place in preheated oven. Bake 40 minutes, or until filling is set and is only slightly jiggly in the center. Allow to cool before serving.

MAKES 2 9-INCH PIES.

MESQUITE CRUST (2 SHELLS):

1 cup all-purpose flour, plus more for dusting work surface

3/4 cup mesquite flour

1/2 teaspoon salt

12 tablespoons (1 1/2 sticks) unsalted butter, diced and chilled

4 teaspoons apple cider vinegar or white vinegar

1/3 cup ice water

FILLING:

Approx. 2 cups halved pecans

10 to 12 chopped and pitted Medjool dates (1/4-inch cubes)

1 cup + 2 tablespoons brown sugar

A little less than 1/2 cup all-purpose flour

9 eggs (small)

1 cup local honey

1/2 cup brown rice syrup

1 cup unsalted butter

2/3 tablespoon vanilla

1 teaspoon vinegar

1 teaspoon salt

2 tablespoons Whiskey Del Bac, unsmoked

GF V

DESERT GRANOLA BARS

Contributed by Mikaela Jones

3 cups rolled oats

1/2 cup each slivered almonds, pecans, sunflower seeds, peanuts

24 or more Medjool dates, pitted

3 tablespoons coconut oil

1/2 cup peanut butter

1/4 cup agave syrup or honey

1/4 cup chia or barrel cactus seeds

1 cup mesquite flour

I really like having granola bars with me on hikes or at work when I only have time for a quick snack, but I don't like all the mysterious ingredients in store-bought bars. These granola bars are easy to make and use recognizable and completely natural ingredients. They are the perfect snack to take with you wherever you go and store well in the fridge or freezer. I cut mine up and wrap them in cling wrap. The best thing about making your own granola bars is you can make them to suit your taste. Use this recipe as a guide, but feel free to add anything!

Preheat oven to 350° F. Place oats and nuts on a cookie sheet and toast for 25 minutes. Remove from oven and let cool. Blend pitted dates in a food processor until a date "dough" ball forms.

Heat coconut oil on stove and add peanut butter and agave syrup.

Place toasted oats and nuts, chia seeds, and mesquite flour into a large mixing bowl. Pour coconut oil mixture onto oats. Stir thoroughly. Add date dough ball and mix together with hands, fully incorporating dates and granola. You want the mixture to be sticky all the way through; if there are dry parts in the bowl, your bars won't hold together.

Place mixture into a 9- x 13-inch baking pan. Press mixture firmly into pan and put into preheated oven for 10 minutes. Remove from oven and allow to cool. Cut into desired sizes and wrap in plastic wrap. Keeps in fridge for 1 month.

MAKES 10 to 20 BARS.

BRAD'S NEIGHBORHOOD MESQUITE HOLIDAY BARS

Contributed by Brad Lancaster. Adapted from Carolyn Niethammer's
The Tumbleweed Gourmet: Cooking with Wild Southwestern Plants (University of Arizona Press, 1987)

These are made with mesquite flour ground from pods harvested from native mesquite trees planted along our neighborhood streets during our annual tree plantings. Our bees visited the same trees and made the honey. We like to celebrate the desert's bounty by giving these holiday bars to our neighbors (especially those that helped us plant the trees).

Preheat oven to 350° F. Lightly grease two 8- x 8-inch pans.

In a large saucepan, slowly heat honey, water, and butter until melted. Mix flours, baking powder, and spices in a medium bowl. Add to honey mixture and stir until well combined. Stir in nuts and raisins. Divide batter between pans and spread evenly.

Bake for 20 to 25 minutes for crunchy bars, or less for a softer bite. Cool in pans and slice into bars.

VARIATIONS: Substitute dried desert hackberries or wolfberries for raisins.

For drop cookies, spoon 2 or 3 tablespoons of batter onto baking sheet, and bake for 8 minutes.

MAKES ABOUT 16 BARS.

1/2 cup organic honey

1/3 cup water

3 tablespoons organic butter

1 1/2 cups organic whole wheat flour

1 1/2 cups mesquite flour

1 tablespoon baking powder

1 to 2 teaspoons cinnamon

1/8 teaspoon nutmeg

1/2 cup organic nuts

1/2 cup organic raisins

MESQUITE:
DRINKS
Dirty Mesquite Chai with Mesquite Syrup and rim salt

MESQUITE MILKSHAKE

Contributed by Laurie Melrood

2 cups low-fat milk

2 cups low-fat plain yogurt

2 cups Mesquite Broth (p. 76)

Dash cinnamon and nutmeg

Ice cubes

2 tablespoons honey (optional)

Laurie ends her mesquite demos with this simple and delicious milkshake. If participants are new to mesquite and just beginning to learn all the diverse variety of recipes for which mesquite is used, she says, "The milkshakes will hook them forever!"

Put liquid ingredients and spices in a blender and whip until frothy. Add ice cubes and continue blending. Pour into glasses and enjoy.

VARIATION: For a special sweeter treat, substitute vanilla ice cream for yogurt.

MAKES 5 MILKSHAKES.

GF S V

MESQUITE ATOLE

Contributed by Barbara Rose, Bean Tree Farm

This is a desert version of the nutritious and energizing drink from Mesoamerica, traditionally made from corn and sometimes chocolate.

In a large pot, soak pods overnight, then simmer in solar oven or on stove until fibers soften and pods are falling apart. Cool to handling temperature and squeeze, mash, and stir to release as much non-fibrous pulp as you can—that's where the flavor is. Strain out long tough fibers and seeds (good for mulch!). Add pinch of salt and cinnamon if desired, and serve hot or cold. The atole can also be reduced to a sauce, butter, or syrup. Great job for free sun-power from your solar oven!

MAKES ABOUT 2 QUARTS.

1 gallon dry, delicious mesquite pods

Water to cover

Pinch of salt

Cinnamon if desired

(GF) (V)

MESQCAFÉ OLÉ

Contributed by Barbara Rose, Bean Tree Farm

2 cups mesquite chaff (from milling pods)

2 cups ripe mesquite pods

2 cups dark-roasted mesquite pods (try roasting in a solar oven) for a coffee-like flavor

8 to 10 cups water, or to cover

Chiltepin or other spicy chile pepper, ground and added to taste

Dried cinnamon, nutmeg, ginger, other spices, to taste

Dash of salt

2 to 3 cups coconut milk, milk, or cream

I always save mesquite pods before grinding them all into flour, for the purpose of making mesquite broth for beverages, soups, and sauces. This recipe uses mesquite pods to make an atole/champurrado-like Sonoran eggless nog!

Place first four ingredients in a large pot, and simmer on low-heat for several hours or days until pods fall apart, and liquid is reduced by about half. Cool and strain out fibers (great for compost or chickens). To strained liquid add chiles, spices, and milk of your choice. Reheat and adjust flavors as needed. Serve hot or cold.

MAKES ABOUT 8 CUPS.

GF V

DIRTY MESQUITE CHAI

Contributed by Barbara Rose, Bean Tree Farm

This rich, delicious beverage is perfect on cold winter days, when the summer mesquite harvest is a distant memory, but flavors linger on. Not only is this beverage deeply satisfying, it is also warming and nourishing.

In a saucepan, heat Mesquite Broth, chai, milk, and seasonings until steaming. Dip mug rims in chocolate, carob, or mesquite molasses. Pour chai into warmed mugs and dust with salt, pepper, and chile. Sweeten if desired.

VARIATIONS: Add a shot of strong coffee or espresso if you're still missing that buzz. Also good with a spot of Saguaro Cordial (p. 127) or tequila!

MAKES ABOUT 6 CUPS.

2 cups Mesquite Broth, p. 76

2 cups chai tea

1 to 2 cups milk, cream, or milk substitute of your choice

Your choice of seasonings: cocoa, cinnamon, nutmeg, allspice, ginger, chile powders

Chocolate, carob, or mesquite molasses

Pinch of salt, pepper, and chile to taste in each mug

(V)

MESQUITE BEER

Contributed by Jack Strasburg and Sky Jacobs of Cabeza Cerveza

12 to 15 gallons filtered rainwater

20 to 22 pounds 2-Row Barley

1 pound 40L Crystal Barley

1 pound 20L Crystal Barley

1/2 pound 10L Crystal Barley

About 2 1/2 gallons (volume) mesquite chaff (from milling pods)

2 ounces Cascade Pellet Hops

2 ounces Saaz Domestic Hops

2 packages Nottingham Ale Yeast

This beer recipe requires some prior know-how and special equipment. But for brewers, adding mesquite to your brews is a special way to connect to place. Go for it!

Heat around 8 gallons of water to somewhere around 180° F. Add enough water to the grain and mesquite chaff in your "mash tun" (look up if needed) until proper consistency (think overly wet oatmeal) and temperature is reached (ideally about 153° F to 155° F). Add more hot or cold water to get proper temperature. Stir vigorously off and on for 10 to 15 minutes. After this do not disturb the grain bed until after the sparge—your grain bed becomes your filter!

You are aiming to keep your steeping temp between at least between 150° F and 160° F through 1 hour of steeping. This is the best temperature range for getting sugars that will ferment into alcohol. The lower the temp in this range the higher the alcohol; the opposite is higher body.

The next step is to "sparge." That is draining off the steeped tea (wort) into the boiling pot. You do this by heating another 5 gallons of water to about 170° F and adding it very slowly to the top of the mash tun (without disturbing the grain bed) while draining it out the wort from the bottom. Try to keep 1 to 2 inches of water above the grain bed while doing this to keep the surface of the grain from caramelizing and impeding the even flow of water through the grain. Sparge slowly, especially at first, to make sure you are extracting all the sugars from the grain.

You now bring your 11 to 12 gallons of wort to a boil. About 5 minutes into the boil we added 1 ounce of the Cascade hops. After 10 more minutes we added the other ounce of Cascade. These are the bittering hops. After about 45 minutes into the boil we added 1 ounce of Saaz. This is the flavoring hops. After another 10 minutes we added the last ounce of Saaz for aroma. At 1 hour we turned off the heat. You then need to cool the wort to around 70° F to 85° F. Remember at this point you need to prevent any contamination by biotic organisms—sanitize everything that comes into contact with your wort. Drain the wort into your fermenting container(s). At this point it is a good idea to agitate your wort somehow to oxygenate it. Add your yeast and seal your container(s) with airlocks.

After half a day or less your airlocks should be bubbling as the yeast do their magic. Ideally after a few days to a week you will transfer your proto-beer into a "secondary" fermenter to leave behind the dead yeast accumulating at the bottom. Let your beer ferment for at least 2 to 3 weeks before bottling/kegging.

There are many details to brewing beer, so consult online resources for further details.

MAKES ABOUT 10 GALLONS.

(V)

NUTTY LU DESERT BROWN ALE

Contributed by John Adkisson, Iron John Brewery

This recipe evolved from a hazelnut brown ale to reflect the local ingredients of our home in Tucson. It has become a satisfying way to evoke a sense of place that is unique about the area. We think of it as English nut brown ale with a Baja Arizona spin. Toasted mesquite pods, pecans, and bellotas (acorns) give this beer a unique nutty character with spice notes similar to cinnamon, hazelnut, and nutmeg. Nicely balanced malt character provides a slightly sweet base and hops lend woody and floral elements. Easy drinking and a wonderful complement to lighter fare.

Mill and mash the grains at 150° F, then sparge to collect wort and boil for 90 minutes, adding hops at 75 minutes and 20 minutes time remaining. Cool to under 70° F, pitch yeast, and ferment for 1 week. Transfer, cold crash to clarify, then bottle or keg for consumption.

NOTE: This is a beer recipe that requires familiarity with brewing processes. Please consult your local home brew shop or home brewing friend for assistance.

MAKES 5 GALLONS.

8 pounds Maris Otter Malt

1 1/2 pounds Biscuit Malt

1 1/2 pounds Victory Malt

1/2 pound Wheat Malt

1/3 pound Brown Malt

1/4 pound Torrified Wheat

2 ounces toasted ground pecans

2 ounces toasted ground mesquite pods

1 ounce toasted ground acorns

1/2 ounce Northern Brewer hops

1/2 ounce Challenger Hops

1 packet British Dry Ale Yeast

ABV: 6.6% IBU: 25 SRM: 20

LURING BREWERIES AND BEER DRINKERS TO THE FANTASTIC FLAVORS OF LOCAL WILD FOODS

The year-long Baja Brews Project in Tucson inspired many local craft brewers to utilize local wild food ingredients in their brews to create new flavors and beers truly unique to this place, which were then shared with an enthusiastic beer-drinking public. The project's calendar of bi-monthly beer tastings highlighted the local ingredients harvestable/available throughout the year's seasons and was created in collaboration with *Edible Baja Arizona* magazine, the Baja Arizona region's local craft breweries, and non-profit organizations (including Desert Harvesters) that are focused on growing and sourcing local foods. Proceeds went to the non-profits. Many of the delicious brews featured in the project, such as Nutty Lu Desert Brown Ale, continue to be seasonally brewed and enjoyed at the breweries of their creation.

- Brad Lancaster

MEET
SAGUARO

Carnegiea gigantea

O'ODHAM *has:añ, bahidaj* (fruit), *juñ* (dried fruit)

SPANISH *saguaro*

One of the largest columnar cacti in the world, the saguaro cactus grows

wild nowhere else but the Sonoran Desert. These amazing plants produce gorgeous white flowers and enormous quantities of delectable fruits that feed people and animals alike. They stand as sentinels to the passage of time and seasons, and are an iconic symbol of this one-of-a-kind Southwest desert we call home. For the Tohono O'odham, saguaros are people.

Saguaro fruit ripens and is gathered during the hottest and driest time of the year in the Sonoran Desert, sometimes called Dry Summer, usually in late May and through June, right before the summer monsoon and rainy season begins. Like many cactus foods, this highly nutritious fruit has a cooling, moistening nature, along with natural antioxidant and anti-inflammatory qualities. It has a delicious sweetness both fresh and dried. Saguaro seeds are high in protein and fat, and add a nutty-crunchy undertone to the sweet flavor of the fruit. The dark magenta-red pulp and shiny black seeds make saguaro one of the most beautiful and delicious fruits in the world. From the desert, no less!

Saguaro fruit is a prized food source for many native peoples of the Sonoran Desert. The O'odham people gather and process the fruits in an event that is seasonal, migratory, social, and spiritual. Fruit gatherers sing songs for a good harvest and extract and drink the precious fruit juice. Tradition says to place emptied fruit husks at the base of the giant saguaro from which it came, turned skyward to bring the rain. Seeds that fall from the husks to touch soil can then take advantage of those rains, having a better chance at germinating, growing, and providing food for future generations.

Juicy fruit is cooked in a pot over a fire, where it breaks down into a thick liquid. Debris or gravel from harvesting is skimmed off or strained out. Jams and syrups are often made from this juice concentrate and stored to preserve and extend the season of use for saguaro fruit. Seeds are separated from pulp and juice, dried, and often ground into flour and formed into cakes for storing and later use. Ceremonial wine is also prepared from the juice.

Photo: Steven Meckler

Tanisha Tucker and niece Ryanna Butler harvesting saguaro fruit with a kui'pud

A favored snack that requires no processing is called juñ, saguaro fruit that dries atop the saguaro or when it falls into tree branches or on the ground below. It has a chewy-crispy consistency, with concentrated sweetness.

Many desert animals also count on this rich summer food source at a time when few other foods are available. Birds, bats, and insects pollinate saguaro's huge, white flowers. Birds adore the plentiful fruit, and are lucky to reach it more easily than most other creatures! All other critters, from ants to rabbits, javelina to coyotes, and foxes to desert tortoises, indulge and gorge themselves on ripe fruits that eventually fall to the ground for the taking.

Saguaros often grow taller than the native legume trees that "nursed" them (protected them from cold and heat when young). Fruits mostly grow at the tip of the saguaro's arms and central trunk, making them a challenge to reach and harvest. One of the traditional methods for harvesting fresh ripe saguaro fruit is by constructing and using a reaching tool called a "ku'ipad" (pronounced kwee-pahd), made of saguaro ribs lashed together for length, with a "t" made of creosote bush or jojoba at the end used for loosening fruits from saguaro arms and trunks. Dislodged fruits are caught in a bucket or basket below, or gathered off the ground or in nearby trees they fall into, fresh or dried. Small stones and sand may get embedded in fruits that fall to the ground, so it's good practice to inspect and clean fruit before eating and using. Again, you can strain these stones later if making syrup or jam. Avoid fruits with signs of spoilage or damage.

-Jill Lorenzini

SAGUARO BASICS

FLOWER BUD & BLOOM SEASON	LATE SPRING | DRY SUMMER – April, May.
FRUIT/SEED SEASON	DRY SUMMER – June, early July.
PARTS USED	Ripe fruit, seeds.
HARVESTING TIPS	Cool mornings and evenings are most comfortable harvest times. Use a "ku' ipad" (long stick) to gently dislodge ripe fruits from top of saguaro or pick up dried fruit from the ground.
BEST HARVESTING PRACTICES	Saguaro is a protected species, and may not be harvested except by permission on private land. Allow animals and birds to harvest freely at season outset, then harvest using best practices and harvest ethics. Leave skin from first fruit open and skyward to invite summer rains. Anoint heart and forehead with saguaro juice from first fruit in reverence.
CAUTION	Sharp thorns, and rattlesnake season during harvest time.
NUTRITION	Protein, potassium, calcium, fat, dietary fiber, vitamin C, vitamin B-12, hydrating, gluten-free.
PLANTING TIPS	With summer rains with a light, protective covering in the top zone of a rain garden, under a nurse plant, on the warm south side of the tree. Seed scarification: Age seeds a year or two before planting, then leach/soak seed in water just before planting. Note: If growing cacti in nursery pots, let soil dry out between each watering. Small pots and seed trays drain better than large pots.
OTHER USES	Saguaro ribs are used for harvesting fruits high up on saguaro arms and trunks. Woody strong ribs were also used traditionally to create structures and ceilings. Saguaros make wonderful living totems—gift a young 6- to 12-inch-tall saguaro to family, friends, and neighbors to mark a birth, wedding, graduation, home purchase, etc. Plant it together and remember as it grows with you and outlives us all. Medicinal.

THE SAGUARO FRUIT HARVEST: LEARNING FROM STELLA TUCKER

as told to Kimi Eisele

Tohono O'odham elder Stella Tucker, 70, has taught countless desert dwellers both the practical and spiritual practice of saguaro fruit harvesting. She offers workshops and classes through Saguaro National Park and other local organizations. Stella's daughter Tanisha Tucker, 35, is carrying on the family tradition, helping her mother harvest fruit, make syrup, and educate the public about the saguaro harvest. This interview was conducted by Kimi Eisele as part of a yearlong performance project in Saguaro National Park called Standing with Saguaros.

Stella and Tanisha Tucker

Photo: Kathleen Dreier

STELLA: When I was very young, like maybe four or five years old, my grandfather used to take us camping to their saguaro harvest camp between Topawa, Arizona, and Sells. We used to go there by wagon wheel, horse, carry all our bedding, our water, our food. I'll always remember those days. After I got older I went to visit my grandmother's camp at the Saguaro National Monument. I just fell in love out there. So that's how I started harvesting. I was working at the time and I'd take the summers off and during my vacation I'd go out to the camp and help my grandmother pick. I always loved my grandmother's place. We slept outside and did [things] the old way, a whole different way of living.

My grandmother camped out there before Saguaro National Monument came in. She was kind of pushed away from the area where she wanted to be. A lot of her friends from the Arizona-Sonora Desert Museum wrote a letter for my grandmother to Washington, D.C., and gave them the story about what she did out there and why she lived out there during the harvest. Washington came back and said, "Give her an area there so she can stay there and do her harvest." And that's how

we got this little area. It's about two acres of land where we can camp and do our harvest.

[Harvesting] was a part of what we lived on, the desert. This is our way of living. We are still around because of all the good nutritional value that the desert gives us. In our stories that we tell we look at the saguaros as people. I have my favorite saguaros that I go and talk to and see how they're doing, see what kind of damage they've [had]. I've been out there almost 30 years picking the fruit and a lot of these saguaros are no longer there. They just died and [fell] to the ground. They gave me so much fruit, you know? I always thank them for that.

Everybody asks me, how do you know when to harvest? We don't know. We just come when the fruit's ready, when we see it opening. We used to go out at the beginning of May, and the fruit would be ready. Now it's backing up to June. We only pick the ones that are red and ripe. Later in June they start to dry out and fall down by themselves to the ground. Those are the best ones to pick, 'cause they're clean and you can take them home with you and have fruit anytime you want during the year.

TANISHA: Of course all the animals know it's time. The birds are the first ones to get the fruit way up on

Breaking up fruit and soaking in water

Photo: Kathleen Dreier

top. The animals are buzzing around the whole desert because it's time for the harvest. There's also the Big Dipper. When the handle turns on the Big Dipper that's when it's ready and you can see it in the stars. Oh, it's time to pick.

When you pick your first fruit you open it, take a little piece, and you bless your heart or your third eye with either a heart, a cross, or a star, whichever symbol you'd like. That's also to bless you for protection out there when you're picking. It symbolizes the start of the harvest, that you're ready to pick and to say thank you to the saguaro. When you take the fruit out of the pod you leave the pod face up to the sun, to the sky, to say thank you and to welcome rain for the next season.

STELLA: After we've picked the fruit we bring it back to the camp and that's when we start our hard work. We soak the fruit in water. I've done it so

many times I can't tell you in measurements, I just see it. When you've been doing something for so long you know what you're doing and you know it's the right thing.

It soaks in water and then you put it over a wood fire of mesquite wood and let it come to a boil. After it boils then that's when all the grass or the ants that you picked up with the fruit come to the top. You skim that off—well, you can't get everything off, but you do your best. Then you take it off the fire and it is strained through a wire screen, into another pot. That separates the fiber and the seed from the juice. The fiber and the seed will go out and lay in the sun. The liquid will go into another strainer, through cheesecloth, and into another pot. That last straining will be the juice that will make the syrup or jam.

That juice will cook for about two to three hours, depending on how much fruit you're cooking. After it's cooled down then we put it in jars and you look

Photo: Kimi Eisele

Boiling fruit and water to skim off grass and ants

Photo: Kathleen Dreier

Pouring cooked fruit and water through a screen to separate fiber and seed from juice

at your product and you say, "Well this is what I've done for the day." It's a lot of work.

TANISHA: When it's starting to form into the syrup it's got that yummy smell and you see it forming into that nice thick rich syrup. It makes you feel like, "Yes, this is my accomplishment and I worked hard today and this is my prize." It's beautiful, a liquid gold.

STELLA: Tanisha grew up out there. She was just a little girl when I took her out there. She didn't know a thing about picking the fruit. I'm glad Tanisha will take over. They will come to her and ask her, How do you make the syrup? I guess you have to have it in your heart to do it. And that's something I taught Tanisha.

It's a dying culture. One day nobody will know how to do it. I want them to learn. It's really important to me that they learn and keep this culture going.

Photo: Kimi Eisele

Saguaro syrup

SAGUARO FRUIT

Chocolate-Dipped Juń

GF V

SWEET SMOKY SAGUARO SEED BLEND

Contributed by Jill Lorenzini

EQUAL PARTS:

Dried saguaro seed
and some dry, crumbly pulp

Canyon hackberry,
dried or toasted

Wolfberry, dried or toasted

Barrel cactus seeds, toasted

Chipotle flakes to taste

Local seed/spice blends can be used as a condiment on almost any food and are an easy way to bring a little bit of the desert into every meal! This one is simultaneously sweet, smoky, and spicy.

In a spice grinder or mill set to coarse grind, grind seeds to desired coarseness. Sprinkle over hot cereal, yogurt, salads. Store in jar in refrigerator.

DESERT WILD FOODS	Saguaro, Cholla
HARVEST SEASON	Dry Summer
CULINARY ROOTS	Tohono O'odham

(GF) (V)

KAIJ ATOL / SAGUARO SEED PORRIDGE

Reproduced with permission from *From I'itoi's Garden: Tohono O'odham Food Traditions*
by Tohono O'odham Community Action with Mary Paganelli Votto and Frances Manuel

This nutritious porridge can be eaten any time, not just for breakfast.

Bring water to a boil and add salt and ground cholla buds. Cover and boil for 30 minutes. Add ground saguaro seeds and whole wheat flour mixture. Don't worry if it's a bit lumpy. Stir briskly and constantly over high heat until porridge thickens into the consistency of thin gravy.

MAKES ABOUT 4 CUPS.

4 cups water

2 teaspoons salt

1 tablespoon coarsely ground sun-dried cholla buds

1 cup finely ground toasted saguaro seeds

1 cup whole wheat flour combined with 1 cup water

GF V

SAGUARO SEED NUT BUTTER

Reproduced with permission from *From I'itoi's Garden: Tohono O'Odham Food Traditions* by Tohono O'odham Community Action with Mary Paganelli Votto and Frances Manuel

Toasted saguaro seeds

The delicious jet-black butter made from saguaro seeds can be eaten plain or used in place of any nut butter. It has a slightly sweet taste, and the consistency of thick peanut butter, but with less oil. Frances Manuel called it "Indian chocolate."

Grind toasted saguaro seeds by the handful in an old-fashioned, hand-cranked meat grinder, poppy seed grinder, spice grinder, blender, or food processor set fine so that the seeds are ground into the consistency of paste. Roll into balls and eat or store for later. Saguaro seed nut butter does not need to be refrigerated—it will keep for several months in tightly sealed jars or plastic bags.

SAGUARO FRUIT GLAZE

Reprinted with permission from Barbara Rose and Jill Lorenzini's
Wild Recipes: Seasonal Samplings (2008)

In a saucepan, combine fruit and alcohol and simmer on low heat until most alcohol evaporates, while mashing fruit into a purée without crushing seeds. Remove from heat, let sit 5 minutes. Add sweetener if using and cornstarch or chia seeds to thicken if needed. Add creosote drops, if desired. Cool completely. Spread over cheesecake or other desserts and garnish with flower blossoms and mint leaves.

MAKES 2 CUPS.

2 cups fresh, sweet, ripe saguaro fruit

1/2 cup tequila or liqueur of your choice

Dash of sweetener, if desired: stevia, honey, sugar, agave, or maple syrup

A little cornstarch to thicken, if needed, or 1 tablespoon chia seeds

A couple drops creosote (*Larrea tridentata*) tincture, or tea, for that desert smell/taste (optional)

GF V

SAGUARO CASHEW ICE CREAM

Contributed by Lori Adkison

2 1/2 cups raw cashews, unsalted

1/2 cup agave syrup

1/2 cup maple syrup

2 1/2 cups fresh saguaro fruit

Here's a vegan ice cream perfect for those lactose-intolerant folks! Now you don't have to miss out on cold creamy deliciousness and you get the special taste of saguaro.

Blend cashews with sweeteners until smooth. Vitamix blenders do the best job, as others can leave the cashews gritty. Add saguaro fruit (reserving some as chunks) and blend briefly until incorporated, but not long enough to break up too many of the seeds. If the mixture has gotten warm from blending, refrigerate until cool. Put mixture into an ice cream maker and follow instructions. Add chunks of saguaro fruit once mixture has begun to thicken but before completely frozen.

MAKES 4 to 6 SERVINGS.

Ⓥ

SONORAN PIE

Contributed by Carlos Nagel

This pie marries three quintessential place-based flavors: saguaro fruit, prickly pear fruit, and mesquite. You won't eat this anywhere but in the Sonoran Desert.

In large bowl, combine all filling ingredients. Pour into prepared pie crust. Chill for 3 to 4 hours and serve.

VARIATIONS: Substitute dried figs, cranberries, raisins, hackberry, or any other dried fruit for saguaro fruit.

MAKES 10 to 12 SERVINGS.

CRUST:
Follow recipe for Mesquite Pie Crust (p. 100) or use other baked pie crust of your choice

FILLING:
1 1/2 cups coconut milk

1 1/2 cups Mesquite Broth (p. 76)

1/2 cup prickly pear juice

1 1/2 cups chia seeds

1 cup dried saguaro fruit, broken into small crumbles

2 teaspoons lemon rind, grated

1 teaspoon vanilla

Dash of salt

3 tablespoons agave syrup or to taste

SONORAN DESERT CHOCOLATE

Contributed by Jill Lorenzini

10-ounce bag (1 1/4 cups) organic semisweet chocolate chips

Coconut oil

OPTIONAL ADD-INS:

Up to 6 ounces (3/4 cup) of:

- Dried fruits: saguaro, wolfberry, goji berries, golden raisins, dates, currants, mango, coconut, etc.

- Nuts and seeds: peanuts, cashews, walnuts, almonds, pine nuts, Arizona pecans, Brazil nuts, macadamia nuts, hemp seeds, sesame seeds, barrel cactus seeds, chia seeds, etc.

- Spices: grated ginger, cayenne, sea salt, desert lavender, dried palo verde or ironwood flowers, etc.

Sea salt, to taste

This delectable decadence is full of sweet desert treasures and other tasty goodies, trapped in melted semisweet or bittersweet chocolate. Heaven! Custom-make distinctive chocolate for every season. Summer: saguaro fruit. Spring: desert lavender, chia seeds. Fall: wolfberries, aloysia. Winter: barrel cactus seeds, mesquite flour. The possibilities are endless.

In a glass bowl, melt chocolate chips in a solar oven. This may only take minutes, so be careful not to burn it! Mix chosen add-ins into melted chocolate. Grease a shallow glass dish with coconut oil. Pour chocolate mixture into dish. Sprinkle additional add-ins and sea salt to taste over top of chocolate. Refrigerate until solid. Remove from fridge and let sit 10 minutes. Use butter knife at edge of chocolate to lift out of dish. Break into pieces and store in bags or jars. Keep refrigerated.

MAKES EIGHT 2-OUNCE PIECES.

SAGUARO CORDIAL

Contributed by Barbara Rose, Bean Tree Farm

Nothing rivals the unique sweetness of saguaro fruit, except maybe the piquant earthy flavor of tequila. Combine the two and you might just capture desert heaven in a bottle.

Dried saguaro fruit (juñ)

OR

Saguaro syrup

Tequila

OPTION 1:

Steep a jar full of juñ (dried saguaro fruit) in tequila to cover until all seeds and fiber have sunk to the bottom. Strain (use seeds and fiber in baking) and bottle.

OPTION 2:

Mix saguaro syrup with equal or greater volume of tequila, depending on how strong you like it.

Add a chile pepper or other herbs/spices of your choice. Flavor will improve with age.

(GF) (S) (V)

CHOCOLATE-DIPPED JUÑ

Contributed by Jill Lorenzini

8 ounces semisweet, dairy-free chocolate chips

3 dozen large juñ pieces

1 ounce each: barrel cactus seeds, chia seeds, hemp seeds

When saguaro fruit ripens in the height of summer, it falls from the tops of saguaro arms and trunks into branches of nurse trees below, where it naturally dries in the sun. The Tohono O'odham call the fruit at this stage "juñ." It's hard to imagine improving on the exquisite taste of this dried saguaro fruit, but perhaps chocolate is the only way!

In shallow baking dish, melt chocolate chips in a solar oven. Watch carefully so chocolate doesn't scorch or burn. Remove from oven. Hold juñ at narrow end and dip up to an inch into the melted chocolate. Then dip chocolate-covered end in hemp, chia, or barrel cactus seeds. Set on a plate and refrigerate until chocolate sets. Loosen from plate to serve or store.

MAKES 3 DOZEN.

MEET
IRONWOOD

Olneya tesota

O'ODHAM *ho'idkam*

SPANISH *palo fierro, tésota, uña de gato*

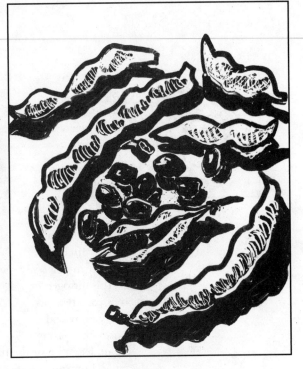

A staple food source for many animals and native desert people, desert ironwood offers abundance during hot pre-monsoon summer months, much like the other main food-producing legumes of the Sonoran Desert, mesquite and palo verde. Ironwood offers both flowers and protein-rich seeds, which taste great and connect us to the sultry summer season in which they thrive.

Seeds may be collected and eaten fresh when green and soft, shelled from the pod like peas, and with a similar flavor. Fresh green seeds can be added to salads, salsas, and savory dishes. They are great this way in salads and salsas, especially. At this stage, ironwood seeds can be blanched in the pod then put in containers to be frozen for later use. Thawed pods can then be steamed or boiled and, after seeds are removed from pods, eaten as edamame or added to other savory foods. These seeds may also be dried fully for storage; ground into a nutritious flour for baked goods, sauces, soups; or used as a sprinkle or garnish.

In later summer months mature ironwood seeds turn brown and hard in the dried seedpod, and can also be harvested at this stage. Seeds removed from dried pods store well, extending ironwood's culinary season. Mature ironwood seeds can also be soaked and sprouted, like popular alfalfa and mung beans, and put in salads and on sandwiches.

Simply soak seeds as you would other sprouting seeds, rinsing daily. Once seeds rehydrate, swell, and split their seed coats open, they can then be squeezed out of compostable seed coats and used in salads, stir-fries, salsas, and as a beautiful, buttery-tasting garnish. If you plan to eat a lot of ironwood seeds, lightly steam or stir-fry them. As the seeds are high in phytates, it's best not to consume high quantities of them raw.

Often referred to as a Sonoran Desert keystone species, desert ironwood provides enriched and protected micro-environments under and near its canopy. Many desert plants, like the mighty saguaro, germinate and grow to maturity under this canopy. Without desert ironwood "nurse

plants," the array of desert flora and associated animals we recognize here would be very different.

In association with soil bacteria and mycorrhizal fungi, desert ironwood fixes nitrogen in the soil, a nutrient often in low supply in desert soils. This nitrogen in its root zone benefits not only ironwood but also other plants

Desert ironwood seeds, pods, and leaves

Photo: Brad Lancaster

living under and near the tree. All plants require nitrogen for growth, and like other desert legumes, ironwood provides and shares it.

Like many other desert trees and shrubs, ironwood sheds its leaves before flowering, in times of drought, and when temperatures dip below freezing. But mostly it remains evergreen, creating crucial, cool oases of shade underneath, where other plants survive extreme heat (and cold), and animals take refuge. Animal droppings and the seeds within, nesting materials, fur, antlers, and even bones decompose and add even more nutrients and carbon to desert soils, which typically lack organic matter.

Ironwood is one of the desert's tallest trees, growing up to 35 feet tall. In its natural growth pattern (unpruned), ironwood trunks and branches grow up, out, and then toward the ground again at the edge of the tree's canopy, forming a small, enclosed area around the tree. Ironwood's preferred habitat is in frost-protected areas, lowlands, and in and along the edges of washes. When rains cause seasonal flooding in summer and winter, organic debris flows with water down once-dry washes, where ironwood branches touching the ground trap it, again enhancing the soil in their environment.

What an apt name, ironwood. This wood is so dense and solid it sinks, rather than floats, in water! It is also nearly indestructible, with chemicals in the heartwood that resist decay and decomposition. Dense wood burns hot, so ironwood was heavily harvested for firewood and charcoal production in earlier times. Dense stands of ironwood were also cleared for agricultural use of the land and the development of built environments that took their place.

Desert ironwood is long-lived, growing to 500 years and often much longer. Trees also provide long-term habitat for other life even when dead. Ancient ironwood stumps, impossible to budge from their strong, deep root systems, erode very gradually and elegantly from the sculpting forces of wind, water, lichen, and time.

- Jill Lorenzini

IRONWOOD BASICS

LEAF DROP	Leaves yellow and drop in late March and April in preparation for new leaf growth and flowering.
FLOWERS BUD/ BLOOM	SPRING – April, May.
GREEN SEED HARVEST	DRY SUMMER – May, June.
RIPE DRY SEED HARVEST	DRY SUMMER ǀ WET SUMMER – June, July, August.
PARTS USED	Flowers, green and dried seeds.
HARVESTING TIPS	Harvest green or dried pods into a basket or a cloth bag. Use a sturdy ladder or a harvest hoe to reach pods on higher branches.
BEST HARVESTING PRACTICES	Pick off trees, not the ground. Pick only what you can process, store, and use.
CAUTION	Watch for curved sharp thorns on branches while harvesting pods, and for foraging bees and other pollinators while harvesting flowers.
PROCESSING TIPS	Blanch green seeds in pod, remove seeds from pod, then eat, use in a recipe, or freeze for later use. Blanched green seeds may also be completely dried and ground into flour. Soak and sprout dry ripe seeds or use in recipes, store for later use, or dry and grind into flour.
NUTRITION	Protein, vitamins, gluten-free.
PLANTING TIPS	With summer rains, in frost-free microclimates below 3,500 feet and with ample moisture, in terrace or top zone of a rain garden. No seed scarification needed.
OTHER USES	Excellent rot-resistant wood for building and utilitarian uses and also carving. Ironwood also makes a great hot-burning firewood. Nitrogen-fixing bacteria in its roots and nitrogen in its leaf drop enhance soil fertility. Wonderful shade tree. Keystone species supporting myriad wildlife and understory vegetation. Produces fodder for honeybees/pollinators, desert tortoise, chickens, and goats. Seeds used for tanning hides. Citrus can often be grown where ironwood grows as they both have a similar intolerance to hard freezing temperatures. Medicinal.

Desert ironwood seedpods on tree in foreground, ripe saguaro fruit above

IRONWOOD

Sprouted Ironwood Stir-Fry

Photo: Barbara Rose

Ironwood 133

GF V S

IRONWOOD FLOUR

Contributed by Jill Lorenzini

12 ounces of ironwood beans, harvested green, blanched, then dried in solar oven, low oven, or air-dried

Salt and seasonings

Water

Oil

This light green delicious and nutritious powder can be used as a flour, blended into a dressing or sauce, or sprinkled as a garnish on many foods. It's a great way to use surplus ironwood seeds that were harvested green and then blanched, dried, and stored.

Pulverize dried beans into a fine powder in Vitamix blender or electric food mill. Use flour in baked goods, sauces, soups, salsas, casseroles, pestos, etc. Add salt and seasonings for use as a sprinkle or garnish on all kinds of savory dishes like popcorn, rice, garlic bread, etc. Mix powder with oil, water, or broth and seasonings for a beautiful sauce for pasta, tamales, potatoes, etc.

VARIATION: This recipe can also be made with blanched and dried green palo verde beans.

MAKES ABOUT 8 OUNCES.

(GF) (V)

IRONWOOD EDAMAME

Contributed by Barbara Rose, Bean Tree Farm

This delicious snack offers a Sonoran Desert twist on the Japanese edamame, showing off the nutty flavor of ironwood seeds eaten straight out of the pod.

Harvest tightly filled ironwood pods. The outer pods will feel somewhat sticky and they'll look like over-ripe garden peas. In a pot, simmer whole pods in water for 15 to 30 minutes, or until they begin to split open. Drain, sprinkle with a little salt, lime juice, and chile and eat!

Ironwood seeds, plump green in pods

Salt

Lime juice

Chile

GF V

PALO FIERRO TEMPEH

Contributed by Paula Verde

3 cups blanched green desert ironwood seeds/beans, patted dry

2 teaspoons white or apple cider vinegar

1 teaspoon tempeh starter culture*

2 quart-size Ziploc bags, poked with holes at 2-inch intervals, from bottom up and across (Use a skewer or toothpick to poke holes.)

*NOTE: Tempeh starter cultures are available at health food stores and elsewhere. One brand, of many, is Cultures for Health. You can also make your own.

Palo fierro is Spanish for ironwood. Once you have success making this tempeh at home, you'll never want to buy it from the store again! Tempeh is a nutty, hearty, healthful food that can be marinated, grilled, stir-fried, or steamed and added to stews, casseroles, tacos, nori rolls, sandwiches, chili, and any number of savory dishes.

Toss ironwood seeds/beans in a large bowl with vinegar to coat. Add tempeh starter culture and mix thoroughly. Spoon one-half tempeh mixture into each prepared bag. Flatten mixture evenly in bag and zip bag closed. Put on a rack in a consistently warm place (85º F to 90º F required) for 24 to 48 hours. This will incubate the starter and grow the mycelium that binds the seeds/beans together into a firm white cake. One option for incubating with temperature control is to put in the oven with the light on and the door cracked open. Another option is to use a heating pad beneath a rack in a non-drafty spot. When a white covering forms over the tempeh, it is done. Cool and transfer to bags or containers and refrigerate for later use. Steam tempeh cakes for 15 minutes before freezing for later use.

MAKES 2 TEMPEH CAKES.

GF S V

THREE SISTERS AND FRIEND SNACK MIX

Contributed by Barbara Rose, Bean Tree Farm

A crunchy, crispy, delicious and nutritious snack mix.

To prepare seeds, soak overnight in water with a little vinegar to make seeds more digestible. Rinse and drain seeds. Mix in seasonings, adding a little oil if desired. Spread thinly on cookie sheets. Slow-roast in oven set at 250º F or dry in solar oven until crunchy. Check often to prevent burning. Vary ingredient volumes to suit your preferences. Remove from oven. Add popcorn and more seasoning and toss to mix. Add oil if desired.

MAKES ABOUT 5 CUPS.

1/2 to 1 cup pre-soaked mature ironwood seeds

1 cup pre-soaked pumpkin or squash seeds

1 cup pre-soaked sunflower seeds

Seasonings to taste: salt, herbs, chiltepin or other chile powder, minced garlic, oil, etc.

2+ cups freshly popped or parched corn

GF V

SPROUTED IRONWOOD STIR-FRY

Reprinted with permission from Barbara Rose and
Jill Lorenzini's *Wild Recipes: Seasonal Samplings* (2008)

1 cup sprouted ironwood seeds

4 medium potatoes, diced

1 medium onion, chopped

Small bunch l'itoi onion, chopped

Oil of your choice

Garlic, chile, curry, salt to taste

1 to 4 cups wild or cultivated seasonal greens (e.g., lamb's quarter, amaranth, chard, kale, etc.)

A savory and hearty desert meal from ironwood tree seeds and seasonal greens.

Sprout ironwood seeds by soaking in water overnight or until seeds swell and seed coat opens. Drain, remove seed coats, and rinse. Steam or stir-fry potatoes and onions in fat. When half done, add spices and sprouted seeds. When browned and nearly done, toss in greens, cook briefly, and serve. Non-vegans can top each serving with grated cheese or an egg.

MAKES AROUND 6 CUPS.

Sprouting ironwood seeds

Photo: Barbara Rose

MEET
ACORN

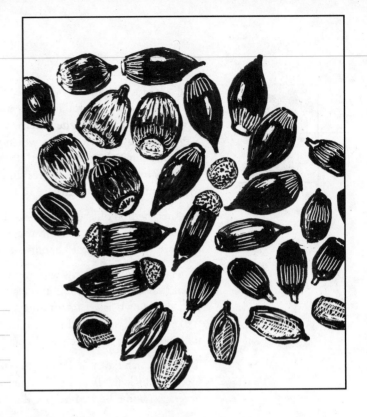

Quercus spp.

O'ODHAM	*wiyi:di*
APACHE	*chichn'il*
SPANISH	*bellota, encino*

"Mighty oaks from tiny acorns grow," wrote Chaucer.

And for thousands of years, those tiny acorns have provided a highly valued staple food for indigenous cultures. This food tradition continues today. Of the 600 species of oak trees that flourish all over the world, around 20 species occur in higher elevations of the Sky Islands adjacent to the Sonoran Desert. Some of the most common to Arizona are Emory (*Quercus emoryi*), Arizona white (*Q. arizonica*), shrub live (*Q. turbinella*), and scrub (*Q. dumosa*) oaks. Others include canyon live (*Q. chrysolepsis*), net leaf (*Q. rugosa*), Mexican blue (*Q. oblongifolia*), Engelmann (*Q. palmeri*), silverleaf (*Q. hypoleucoides*), and Gambel (*Q. gambelii*) oaks. The low-tannin Emory oak acorns are the most commonly harvested, and can also be found in the transitional zones where the Sonoran Desert meets higher-elevation microclimates.

In the Sonoran Desert and its interspersed Sky Island biomes, various oaks grow wild on hilly desert grassland environments up to higher pine-oak forest communities. Oaks may also be found in the lowest valley floor where they are used in landscaping. Desert oaks differ from other oaks in that most are not seasonally deciduous and only drop some leaves in response to new growth cycles in spring and summer or to drought. Desert oaks also tend toward smaller-than-average leaf size—a trait common to many other desert trees.

Many desert animals, from small and large mammals to birds, eat acorns. No doubt people took a cue from these fellow foragers and sampled acorns, but perhaps had aversion to the taste of acorn's bitter tannins. Since acorns supplied ample protein, fat, and other essential nutrients in large quantities every year, multiple methods were developed to leach out the acorn's bitter and astringent flavor components. Soaking whole shelled acorns in baskets along streams and burying acorns in the sand along flowing washes are some of the strategies. In other regions, acorns were buried in riverbank mud and allowed to ferment for several months before use. Gatherers also collected from and returned to favorite trees that produced the least bitter acorns.

To leach bitter tannins, food forager John Slattery suggests gently simmering acorns in water enough to cover them for about 30 minutes before soaking them overnight. Pour off the water in the morning and test the bitterness and astringency. If needed, repeat. You can also dry acorns in an oven on low heat, which further diminishes tannins while also drying the acorns and imparting a delicious toasted flavor. Shell the nut meat, discard the shells, grind what you are ready to use, and store the rest in the freezer or place in an airtight jar. (Note: Acorns tend to mold in hot, damp weather.)

Another method of leaching tannins is to grind acorns into a meal or flour to increase surface area, and then soak the meal in water, several times if necessary. Thoroughly strained acorn meal can then be used as is, or be fully dried and stored for later use.

Some oaks produce acorns with minimal amounts of tannins, which taste agreeable and may be eaten fresh from the shell, in moderate amounts. In the Sonoran Desert, the productive Emory oak, also known as *bellota*, produces a low-tannin nut. Along with mild flavor, the *bellota* shell is easy to crack, making this acorn highly desirable and accessible. Roasting whole *bellotas* or toasting coarse meal (leached) deepens the flavor.

The nutty, rich flavor of acorn flour enriches both savory and sweet baked goods. It can also be used as a thickener in sauces, beverages, stews, and soups, and makes a great addition to coffee beverages, home-brewed beer, and baked goods.

- Jill Lorenzini

Emory oak acorns aka bellotas

Photo: Jill Lorenzini

Ground Emory oak acorns

Photo: Jill Lorenzini

ACORN BASICS

FLOWER BUD & BLOOM SEASON	SPRING | WET SUMMER – April, May and July, August.
NUT HARVEST SEASON	WET SUMMER | FALL. Some oaks such as Emory oak ripen in July and can be harvested through September. Others such as Mexican blue oak ripen October through December.
PARTS USED	Fruit/nut.
HARVESTING TIPS	Check trees early in the season to harvest as soon as acorns ripen. This ensures you get some before the animals do. Waiting longer can also mean moldy acorns.
BEST HARVESTING PRACTICES	Harvest before rains to avoid mold and spoilage.
PROCESSING TIPS	Find good tips for leaching tannins out of acorns on p. 139. You can also put shelled acorns in a net, cheesecloth, or jellybag within your clean toilet tank (not the dirty bowl). Play it extra safe by scrubbing, draining, then refilling your tank. Each flush changes the water, removing tannins. This tecnhique mimics the traditional method of leaching the shelled acorns in a flowing stream. And since most flush toilets in the U.S. currently flush with potable-grade (drinking) water, it may even be cleaner! Depending upon how often you flush, leaching may be complete in about 48 hours. Taste to test. They're done when no longer bitter.
CAUTION	Most acorns require leaching to remove bitter tannins. See "Processing Tips" above.
NUTRITION	Protein, fat, carbohydrates.
PLANTING TIPS	Plant with summer rains in terrace or bottom zone of rain garden at appropriate elevations. Acorns benefit from mycorrhizal fungi in the soil, which you can introduce with a little leaf litter/soil duff taken from under wild oaks of same species, taking care not to leave patches of bare soil when you harvest that duff. Fresh seed is important. Collect seed and put in fridge to keep it fresh. Have patience, as oaks set down their taproot before their aboveground growth shoot. Mexican blue oak (*Quercus oblongifolia*) acorns, which ripen and drop in November, germinate with the winter rains, but wait till spring before they send up their aboveground growth shoot.
OTHER USES	Oak wood is hard and desirable for many utilitarian purposes such as bows, digging sticks, and firewood. Bark used for tanning hides. Acorn caps, oak galls, and bark used for dye. Medicinal.

SKY ISLANDS FULL OF FOOD

The desert Southwest is known for its magnificent, expansive vistas and views and intriguing plant life, especially the iconic saguaro. The region is also celebrated for its many "Sky Islands," isolated mountain ranges interspersed in a vast sea of different lowland desert environments. These high elevations are also habitat islands: Separated from other mountain ranges, they support some of the most biodiverse ecosystems in the world.

A layer cake of life zones represented by distinct elevation ranges and changes is one reason such biodiversity exists in Sky Islands. A trip from valley floor to the top of Sky Islands presents adventurers with no fewer than eight life zones to observe and explore, along with interesting geological and historical information. Edges are rich places too. Where Sky Islands and deserts meet, at the bottom of mountain watershed drainages, there are often canyons and riparian areas, oases replete with even more life and beauty featuring the element that threads through all desert landscapes: water.

Fruit- and nut-bearing trees form forests with an understory full of additional fruit- and seed-bearing plants; plenty of edible and nutritious herbs, greens, roots, and berries; mushrooms and game; and myriad medicinals for self and community care. Various species of oak trees produce acorns, a cherished staple food that indigenous cultures have harvested and used for thousands of years. Arizona walnut may be found in riparian areas, along with naturalized pecan trees and moisture-loving elderberry. Mulberry trees prefer protected canyons and moist shady microclimates. Piñon pine trees periodically produce bumper crops of nuts in the pine-conifer forest zone.

Fruit trees like apple and plum, which require cold temperatures to set fruit, are found at higher-elevation zones. Currant and berry bushes, wild grapes, greens, herbs, and medicinal plants round out a vast Sky Island food palette.

Many desert dwellers escape to the cooler temperatures, elevated perspective, and fresh forested mountains of the Sky Islands during summertime, when temperatures can reach over 100° F on the valley floor. Many trails lead to or flank riparian areas, a welcome, refreshing reprieve from hot, dry summer blues. In the winter, the Sky Islands are sometimes blanketed with snow, a special treat for desert dwellers.

Santa Rita Mountains of Southern Arizona

Photo: Ben Johnson

ACORN

Acorn Saguaro Seed Bread, wild and garden greens salad, palo verde and chuparosa blossom garnishes

Photo: Christian Timmerman

(GF) (R) (V)

EMORY OAK ACORN FLOUR

Contributed by Patty West as told by Elizabeth Rocha, an Apache elder and teacher
whose passion is maintaining traditions and language

Acorns

Acorn flour adds a nutty flavor to stews and can be used similarly to mesquite flour in cupcakes or bread. As Elizabeth Rocha says, "I like it in stew, or even just dipping it in coffee. Or on your fried potatoes you can just sprinkle it on there to get the flavor."

Pick acorns in the late summer or early fall. You can gather them from the ground before it rains. After the rain, you can still collect, but you must crack the shells open so they dry without discoloring. Crack acorns with a mortar and pestle and pull yellow flesh out of shell. Good acorn will be bright yellow. Sometimes yellow acorn grubs live inside even if there is not an obvious hole there. Discard any grub-eaten and darkened acorns. (These discards are great for your chickens!) Remove from good acorns the thin layer between the flesh and the shell, unless it is well adhered to the flesh, in which case leave it on. Allow the flesh to dry and grind into flour using a grain grinder or *mano y metate*. Store flour in jars or bags in the refrigerator or freezer. Before people had refrigeration, the acorns were not cracked open until needed.

Ⓥ

ACORNTILLAS

Contributed by Paula Verde

This innovative version of a corn tortilla, made with acorn instead of maize, is a great way to celebrate the nut's unique flavor.

In a large bowl, mix dry ingredients together. Make a well in the center and add oil and most of the water. Stir carefully until just mixed: use rest of the water if needed. Turn dough out onto floured surface and knead for 5 to 7 minutes. Form dough into a ball, lightly coat with oil, cover, and let sit for an hour or more in a warm area until dough rises. Heat a griddle or cast iron skillet to medium heat. Divide dough into 6 to 8 parts. Roll each part into a ball, then flatten thin with a rolling pin or your hands. Oil griddle with remaining oil and lightly cook each side until browned and bubbly. Serve hot or cool with your favorite desert salads, soups, casseroles, beans, dips, spreads, and more.

MAKES 6 to 8 ACORNTILLAS.

2 1/4 cups whole spelt or wheat flour

3/4 cup acorn flour

1 1/2 teaspoons salt

3 tablespoons olive oil

1 cup water

GF

ACORN BREAD

Contributed by David "Farmer" Valenciano

1 3/4 cups wheat or spelt flour

1 cup acorn flour

2 teaspoons baking powder

1/2 teaspoon baking soda

1/2 teaspoon salt

2 eggs

1 3/4 cups milk

2 tablespoons oil

1 to 2 tablespoons agave nectar

Acorn's nutty flavor and fragrance make this quick bread a treat to bake and eat! Wonderful moist, crumbly, cake-like bread that's great with butter and jam.

Preheat oven to 425° F. Grease a 9- x 13-inch baking pan or an 8-inch cast iron skillet. In a large bowl, mix together flours, baking powder, baking soda, and salt. In a separate bowl, mix together eggs, milk, oil, and agave nectar. Slowly stir the wet ingredients into the dry ingredients. Do not overstir. Pour the batter into the prepared pan or skillet and bake until firm, 20 to 30 minutes.

MAKES ABOUT 12 SERVINGS.

GF V

ACORN SAGUARO SEED BREAD

Contributed by John Slattery

This bread can be served with soup or stew and also makes a delicious dessert served with prickly pear jelly or organ pipe cactus marmalade.

Preheat oven to 350º F. In a large bowl, mix all dry ingredients. Bring the coconut oil to a liquid temperature and combine with all wet ingredients. Combine wet and dry ingredients, blending well and quickly. Transfer batter into a 9- x 9-inch greased baking pan. It may take some molding with your hands to get the batter evenly placed throughout the pan. Bake for 25 to 30 minutes or until a toothpick comes out clean. Serve hot with non-dairy butter. Toast leftover bread in cast iron pan with butter before serving. Enjoy!

VARIATIONS: Use quinoa flour as a substitute for all-purpose flour for a nuttier flavor. Use full fat coconut milk (canned) in place of coconut milk beverage. Add some honey and cinnamon for a sweet bread.

MAKES 6 to 8 SERVINGS.

1 cup acorn flour, leached

1/2 cup saguaro seed meal or barrel cactus seed meal

1 1/2 cups gluten-free all-purpose flour

1 tablespoon baking powder

1/4 teaspoon sea salt

2 large eggs

1/2 cup coconut oil or extra virgin olive oil

1 1/4 cups coconut, almond, or hazelnut milk

Non-dairy butter

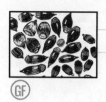

GF

ACORN BURGERS WITH
MOUNTAIN SPICE AND CHILTEPIN

Contributed by John Slattery

1/2 cup acorn flour, leached

3 tablespoons pecan meal

1 large egg

1 to 2 tablespoons broth, gravy, water, or milk

1 tablespoon coconut oil

2 medium I'Itoi onions, chopped

1 teaspoon Mountain Spice Blend* (from Desert Tortoise Botanicals)

2 chiltepines, crushed

Pinch of sea salt

Bacon fat, or other oil for frying

*MOUNTAIN SPICE BLEND
Contains wild oregano, false tarragon, Mexican oregano, oreganillo, black sage, yerba santa, and desert lavender.

These "veggie" burgers are a great way to savor the sweetness of local acorns. Serve them as a main dish over a bed of greens, on a bun, as a side dish, or like falafel in a pita.

In a large bowl, combine all ingredients except fat or oil and mix by hand. Set aside in the refrigerator, covered, for at least 4 hours, or overnight. When ready to make, heat oil in a large skillet on medium heat. Mold mixture into burgers with your hands to desired size. Cook burgers over medium-low heat until they begin to brown. Flip and brown the other side. Remove from heat and place on paper towels to absorb oil. Serve on an acorn biscuit or atop a bed of fresh or sautéed greens. I like to top with London rocket (wild arugula) pesto or elderberry ketchup. (Also try Sky Island Pesto, p. 289.)

VARIATIONS: Add to burger mix chopped tart apple and yellow or sweet onions. You can also add saguaro seed meal, barrel cactus seed meal, mesquite flour, prickly pear syrup, and/or saguaro syrup. Top with organ pipe cactus (pitaya) marmalade.

MAKES ABOUT 4 BURGERS.

ACORN COOKIES

Contributed by Paula Verde. Adapted from *Gourmet Magazine*

Cookies that look and taste like acorns! These festive treats have an irresistible nutty-buttery flavor, accented by chocolate and the crunch of chia and barrel cactus seeds. Yum!

Preheat oven to 375º F. In a large bowl, sift together flours, baking powder, and salt. In a separate bowl, blend butter, sugar, and vanilla with a mixer or by hand until fluffy. Slowly add flour mix into butter mixture until well combined. Form oval-shaped cookies from about 2 teaspoons of dough and arrange on ungreased baking sheet. Bake about 10 minutes, until edges are browned lightly. Remove and cool on racks. To create acorn "caps," dip one end of cookie into melted chocolate and the barrel cactus and chia seeds. Arrange cookies on parchment or wax paper to let chocolate harden. Eat right away or store in a sealed container in refrigerator or freezer.

MAKES ABOUT 4 DOZEN.

ACORN DOUGH:

2 1/4 cups flour

3/4 cup acorn flour

1/2 teaspoon baking powder

1/4 teaspoon salt

1 cup butter, melted and cooled

3/4 cup packed brown sugar

1 teaspoon vanilla

ACORN CAPS:

8 ounces semisweet chocolate bits, melted

1/3 cup barrel cactus and chia seeds

MEET
PRICKLY PEAR FRUIT
AKA TUNAS

Opuntia spp.

O'ODHAM *i'ipai (fruit)*

SPANISH *tuna*

Isn't it surprising that in the very hot, dry, rain-limited Sonoran Desert, one of the most widespread species are succulent, water-storing cacti? What is less surprising is how these qualities make prickly pear one of the Sonoran Desert's most place-appropriate foods. Juicy, hydrating, and nutritious like a super food, prickly pear is also heat and drought tolerant, dependably productive, and easily cultivated and harvested. It offers not one, but two edible parts: the tender newly grown pads and the magenta-colored fruit.

Prickly pear cactus is native to the Americas and has a long and interesting history of use. About 18 species are present in the Sonoran Desert, some of which have formed hybrids. Early cultures that depended on the cactus and developed harvesting and culinary traditions likely recognized even more varieties. The most common prickly pear used was Engelmann's (*Opuntia engelmannii*), but other species like beaver tail, pancake, and wild ficus-indica were also harvested, relished, cultivated, and even traded.

Cacti are of course known—sometimes painfully so—for their sharp spines. In addition to spines, only the *Opuntia* species grow glochids, tiny clumps of bristly hairs that hide amidst larger spine clusters and easily lodge into skin. They are thin and plentiful and as they tend to break off once embedded in the skin, they are difficult to find and remove. But prickly pear food is worth the temporary discomfort, and true desert rats always carry tweezers! Some even consider the inevitable pain of glochids and spines an initiation into desert living and to desert foods gathering. Free acupuncture!

Opuntia species are also different from other cacti in that they have segmented stems. In prickly pear, these stems present as roundish segments known as pads, which sprout each spring, funded by winter rains and encouraged by longer, warmer days. The tender new pads, known as nopales, are edible at this young, green stage—but not for long, because soon a tough inner "skeleton" of fibrous tissue forms inside, along with increasing amounts of oxalic acid, which requires processing to improve edibility. But the fresh pads are tender and edible and delicious!

Prickly pear flower buds emerge in spring and are also edible. They can be harvested, processed, and used in the same way as cholla buds. Fresh flower petals are a great occasional snack on a hike, and later in the season, whole dried flowers are easy to pull from the tops of green, developing fruits, for use in teas. Flowers feed many pollinators who fumble around in the plant's thigmotactic anthers—central anthers that curl when touched—assuring an abundant fruit harvest in late summer after seasonal rains have plumped pads and ripening fruits. New pads may emerge in this season too, triggered by summer rains.

Both ripe fruits and pads have glochids, so tongs are required for harvesting. Ripe fruit should come off pads easily, and can be collected into buckets for later processing. Fruits may be juiced fresh (in a blender, food processor, or juicer for ease) and carefully strained (using a fine strainer or a pillowcase) or frozen then thawed, pressed, and meticulously strained, to prevent any glochids from getting into the juice.

Prickly pear fruits ripen in the hot and humid months of July and August—a perfect time to take advantage of their sweet, cooling qualities by mixing up a colorful pitcher of prickly pear lemonade!

- Jill Lorenzini

Harvesting prickly pear fruit

Photo: Brad Lancaster

PRICKLY PEAR BASICS

FLOWER BUD & BLOOM SEASON	SPRING | DRY SUMMER – April, May, June.
FRUIT HARVEST SEASON	WET SUMMER | FALL – Late July, August, September, October.
PARTS USED	Tender young pads; ripe fruit; fresh flower bud, flower petals, dried flowers.
HARVESTING TIPS	Watch for spines and glochids!
BEST HARVESTING PRACTICES	Harvest undamaged ripe fruit with tongs. An easy way to get juice is to freeze the fruit, thaw, press juice, and then filter through a very fine strainer or fine cloth to remove spiny glochids.
CAUTION	Fruit juice has a cooling effect; drink small amounts at a time, especially in winter.
NUTRITION	Omega-3 and omega-6 fatty acids, vitamin C, calcium, magnesium, dietary fiber, potassium, vitamin A, phosphorus.
PLANTING TIPS	Plant single pads and larger cuttings in enough dirt that at least some areoles are buried and can take root. Plant with summer rains, when plant is plump from moisture, in top or terrace zone of rain garden. If growing cacti in nursery pots, let soil dry out between each watering. Small pots and seed trays drain better than large pots.
OTHER USES	Source of pigment/dye. Living fence. Fodder for desert tortoise. Medicinal.

A GATEWAY TASTE:
JEAU ALLEN'S PRICKLY PEAR POPS

by Kimi Eisele

The first prickly pear fruit Jeau Allen ever harvested was on High Jinks Ranch (once owned by Buffalo Bill Cody), in Oracle, Arizona, where she lived for a time.

"There was a huge prickly pear 30 feet from my door," she said.

One morning she went out to pick and ended up filling a five-gallon bucket. Once she processed the fruit, she had more juice than she knew what to do with. She ended up selling bottles of the syrup at the Cascabel Christmas fair. "I needed something to go with the syrup, so I made blue corn pancakes from a mix," she said.

When Jeau's husband got a job with the Nature Conservancy, they moved from the ranch to the edge of the wilderness in Aravaipa Canyon, where she began wandering the desert looking for foods. Jeau had gathered wild edible and medicinal plants growing up in New England, but was new to the practice in the desert. She began wandering and picking, learning mostly from Wendy Hodgson's *Food Plants of the Sonoran Desert* (University of Arizona Press, 2001).

Jeau said prickly pear was her "gateway drug" to desert foods, followed by mesquite, hackberry, and saguaro.

"I love coming back all sweaty and bloody and exhausted," she said of harvesting. "I love how it feels like you did something ambitious."

Jeau turned her wanderings into products and prickly pear syrups and jellies and mesquite flour mixes and named her business "The Mesquitery."

One of the places she sold her products was Santa Cruz River Farmers' Market, which for a time was

Jeau Allen

Photo: George L. Bradley

held on a hot and shadeless parking lot just west of Interstate 10. One summer, the Market held a Prickly Pear Festival, and the director asked Jeau if she might offer any additional treats.

Jeau considered renting a snowcone machine, but the location didn't have electricity. "There was nothing else at that market that was cold and wet, not even water fountains," she said.

So she bought plastic molds and made 100 popsicles with prickly pear juice. She sold them for $1 each. "They were gone within 20 minutes," she said. "I realized this might be a thing."

It was.

After that, she made mesquite pops for one of the Desert Harvesters' annual milling fiestas, using mesquite syrup flavored with mesquite honey. She now reserves mesquite pops for special occasions since they're more labor intensive. But she has added other

Mashing frozen, then thawed prickly pear fruit through a screen

Photo: Brad Lancaster

flavors to her fleet, including watermelon, cucumber, and other locally grown, heirloom crops, along with barrel cactus and Meyer lemon.

"I like to have texture in the pops so I include seeds," she says. "They're a little atypical from what we grew up with."

They're also healthier. The original prickly pop has only 8 grams of sugar "compared to 20 to 30 grams you find in your everyday Dryer's fruit popsicles." For people who don't eat sugar, she has a prickly pear pop sweetened with stevia.

Jeau makes the pops by hand in a commercial kitchen and they now sell for $3. She's working on a paleta cart (*paleta* is a Mexican term for popsicle),

so she can make the business portable and become a more consistent part of local culinary events, kids' events, and community events.

She is also using her pops in support of political causes she supports. In the spring of 2017, she made protest pops for a number of planned protests—for political policies discounting science and climate change, in particular. "They'll be by donation. I'll put a jar on top of the cart. It will be hot. People will want them," she said.

Since her pops are truly "desert-to-market" treats, part of what makes the work so satisfying for her is talking about the harvesting process with customers.

"I'm not that good at keeping trade secrets. It's always

Fine straining of juice before canning, freezing, or use

Photo: Barbara Rose

a neat opportunity for education and tiny tutorials," she says. Once she shared her harvesting technique with a family who'd been burning off the spines of prickly pear fruit. "I told them it doesn't have to be that hard!"

Jeau says she loves introducing people to the flavors of the desert. She says there's nothing like "that feeling you have when you've opened up the world to somebody, a world that is all around them but that they've never tasted before, and you open that door for them."

Read more about Jeau Allen and order her products at MesquiteFlour.com.

PRICKLY PEAR FRUIT

Prickly Pear Lemonade

(GF) (R) (V)

SEASONAL SALSA OR SUMMER SOPA

Contributed by Barbara Rose, Bean Tree Farm

1 pint chopped tomatoes with juice (or canned)

OR

1 pint citrus chunks and juice (grapefruit, orange, tangelo, or combination)

OR

1 pint prickly pear concentrate

1/4 cup chia seeds

2 cups onion, chopped small

Minced garlic and chiltepin to taste

1/4 cup cilantro/herbs

Your choice of seasonings

1 cup desert food options: cholla buds, nopalitos, green palo verde or ironwood seeds, wolfberries, hackberries, saguaro fruit, pincushion cactus fruit, pickled devil's claw pods, pickled verdolagas (purslane), etc.

Almost monsoon? Hot and humid? Sweaty and hungry? Here's a cooling salsa or soup/ sopa. One becomes the other, depending on how you vary quantities and ingredients.

Combine 1 pint fruit and juice of your choice with chia seeds. Let sit 15 minutes. Add onion, garlic, chiles, herbs, and seasonings. Add in desert food options. Taste and adjust seasonings as needed. Chill for 1/2 hour before serving. Add more or less juice for thinner soup or thicker salsa, or vice versa-tile! Garnish with avocado, oil, seasonal flowers, and serve with warm tortillas, chips, or bread.

MAKES ABOUT 3 CUPS.

PRICKLY PEAR BORSCHT

Contributed by Barbara Rose, Bean Tree Farm

I come from Belarus and Ukraine people. My grandma Evie, born in 1900, always had fermenting crocks of garlicky green tomatoes and cucumbers, and pots of simmering chicken soup "with the feet" (her way of saying the whole chicken) in her kitchen. She fed us dense black sourdough pumpernickel smeared with onion-infused chicken fat, and a sweet-sour broth-based cold borscht, always served with a hot boiled potato and dollop of sour cream. Evie left us at 103, with all her "marbles" intact into her last days, having shared with me a treasure of food and family stories.

Beets have been pickled and soured by lactic acid fermentation for ages. So why not a fermented prickly pear borscht? I love beets, but my garden lives on my rainwater budget, and I'm not so good at growing beets. Prickly pears thrive without my attention (beyond some subtle rainwater harvesting earthworks nearby), are delicious, nutritious, and a gorgeous color. It was a no-brainer: A red desert fruit that sours nicely and has a sweet earthy flavor. Carrying a family food tradition from far away into a desert food forest is very satisfying to me. I hope you enjoy the recipe, expand on it, and make it your own.

1 quart fermented, sweet-sour prickly pear fruit juice*

1 quart broth, strained and chilled (chicken, vegetable, bone, mesquite, or combo, flavored with herbs, alliums, chiles, etc.)

1 hot boiled potato per serving

Sour cream, yogurt, or kefir for garnish

Combine prickly pear mixture and broth. Serve cold or heat on stovetop for a hot soup. Season to taste with salt, chile, pepper, etc. To each bowl of borscht add potato, garnish with sour cream, and serve with sides of hard-boiled eggs, green onion, sliced cucumbers, etc.

MAKES 2 QUARTS.

*TO FERMENT PRICKLY PEAR JUICE:

Add 1/2 cup of kombucha or whey (liquid strained from yogurt or cheese-making) to 1 quart of prickly pear juice a day or so ahead. Cover with cloth and taste on occasion. It will develop a sweet-sour flavor as it ferments. When it has that "tang" but still retains some sweetness, it's ready to use. Sometimes I combine citrus juice with the prickly pear and ferment both. This juice will store in fridge for some time, becoming more sour from fermentation.

DESERT WILD FOODS   Prickly Pear

HARVEST SEASON   Wet Summer

CULINARY ROOTS   Southwest

GF

PRICKLY PEAR MUSTARD

Contributed by Chef Greg Smith

1/4 cup prickly pear jelly, melted

1 tablespoon yellow, Dijon, or other mustard

This Sonoran Desert-inspired condiment is great on baked ham and hot dogs or simmered with meatballs for a tangy twist. When quadrupled, it is also the base for Asian/Sonoran Sweet and Sour Sauce (p. 161). The recipe came about as a way to get creative with all the prickly pear juice and jelly we harvested and processed. There are only so many peanut butter and prickly pear jelly sandwiches one can eat!

Heat the prickly pear jelly until it is liquid. Add the prepared mustard and whisk until smooth.

MAKES ABOUT 1/4 CUP.

GF

ASIAN/SONORAN SWEET AND SOUR SAUCE

Contributed by Chef Greg Smith

East meets West in this sweet and sour sauce/glaze made with prickly pear jelly.

Combine first five ingredients in a small saucepan over low heat, whisking constantly until well incorporated. Remove from heat. Toss with rice noodles and garnish with sesame seeds, brush onto chicken for grilling or baking, or use as a dip for fried wontons.

MAKES ABOUT 1 1/2 CUPS.

1 cup Prickly Pear Mustard (p. 160; quadruple recipe)

3/4 teaspoon sesame oil

2 teaspoons rice vinegar

1/2 teaspoon prepared wasabi (or to taste)

3 tablespoons peanut oil

Cooked rice noodles

Sesame seeds to garnish

PRICKLY PEAR UPSIDE-DOWN CAKE

Contributed by Amy Valdés Schwemm, Mano y Metate

TOPPING:

3 tablespoons butter

1/3 cup brown sugar

3 or more prickly pear fruits, de-spined, peeled, seeded, and sliced

CAKE:

3/4 cup whole wheat flour

3/4 cup unbleached all-purpose flour

3/4 cup sugar

1 teaspoon baking powder

1/4 teaspoon salt

3/4 cup prickly pear juice

1/2 cup melted butter

1 teaspoon vanilla

This desert version of the original upside-down cake replaces pineapple with prickly pear fruit. The dark pink color makes for a dramatic and beautiful dessert. If you don't want to go upside-down, you can decorate the top of the unbaked cake batter with the colorful fruit.

Preheat oven to 325° F. Place a springform pan on a cookie sheet. Place butter in springform and melt in oven. Remove from oven. Sprinkle brown sugar and arrange prickly pear in the pan. Set aside.

In a large bowl, sift dry ingredients together. In a separate bowl, whisk together wet ingredients. Combine the two mixtures and pour into cake pan. Bake for 30 minutes or until toothpick inserted comes out clean. Cool, flip onto a platter, and serve.

MAKES 6 to 8 SERVINGS.

PRICKLY PEAR THUMBPRINT COOKIES

Contributed by Mikaela Jones

This is a desert twist on a traditional cookie. I think of them as tea cookies—good, afternoon cookies. They are buttery and sweet, but very small so not overwhelming. They make a great last-minute gift, because they are simple and so pretty.

Follow the Pomona's directions for making jam from fruit juice using the listed ingredients. In a large bowl, cream together butter and sugar. Beat in extract. In a separate bowl, sift together flours. Slowly incorporate flours into butter mixture. Cover and refrigerate dough for half an hour. Preheat oven to 350° F. Roll dough into 1-inch balls and place 1 inch apart on an ungreased cookie sheet. With the end of a wooden spoon, make an indent in each cookie and fill with jam. Bake for 14 to 18 minutes.

VARIATION: If you do not have prickly pear juice on hand, you can use store-bought prickly pear jelly as well.

MAKES 2 to 3 DOZEN COOKIES.

PRICKLY PEAR JAM:

4 cups prickly pear juice

1/4 cup lemon or lime juice

4 teaspoons Pomona's calcium water

2 cups sugar, or sugar substitute

4 teaspoons Pomona's pectin powder

SHORTBREAD COOKIE:

3/4 cup butter, melted

2/3 cup sugar, or substitute

1/2 teaspoon vanilla or almond extract

1 cup all-purpose flour

1 cup mesquite flour

GF R

PRICKLY PEAR LEMONADE

Contributed by Amy Valdés Schwemm, Mano y Metate

3 to 5 tablespoons honey or agave syrup

1 1/2 quarts cold water

5 lemon juice ice cubes

2 to 5 prickly pear ice cubes

Fresh mint, lemon, or basil balm (optional)

This gloriously colored refreshing drink is a Sonoran Desert delicacy that will delight any party! Freezing prickly pear juice and lemon juice separately in ice cube trays is a great way to store it and have it ready to use.

Dissolve honey in a cup of hot, but not boiling, water. Cool to room temperature. Fill a 2-quart pitcher three-quarters full of cold water. Add 5 lemon cubes and 2 to 5 prickly pear cubes, depending on your preference. Add honey mixture or agave syrup to taste. Mix, sample, and adjust. Serve with ice and sprigs of fresh mint, lemon, or basil balm.

VARIATIONS: To reduce or eliminate sweeteners, use mesquite broth or syrup instead of honey or agave. Replace some of the lemon juice with sweet orange juice or use sour orange juice, utilizing some of the "ornamental" harvest that goes to waste! Replace some of the water with apple juice. No additional sweetening required.

For a refreshing and cooling summer dessert, turn this lemonade into a sorbet! Make a stronger prickly pear lemonade (using less water) in a shallow pan, stirring periodically as it solidifies. (Alternatively, freeze in an ice cream maker.)

NOTE: Prickly pear juice is very cooling. Do not consume high quantities of non-diluted raw juice as it is occasionally known to cause chills and body aches. Drinking a few glasses of lemonade is absolutely fine and will give you the cooling effect you're seeking in the heat of August.

(GF) (S) (V)

PRICKLY PEAR JAMAICA SUN TEA

Contributed by Anastasia Rabin

This is a refreshing, no-sugar-added version of the classic Mexican drink jamiaca, *or hibiscus in English. It can be easily altered to a variety of tastes. I juice my prickly pear fruits by freezing, thawing, slicing them open, and then straining and squeezing the juice through a cloth-lined colander. Afterwards, I sun-dry the seeds and skins, which can be stored indefinitely in a sealed jar or container. That is what I use for this recipe.*

Dried prickly pear skin

Jamaica (hibiscus flowers)

Use a ratio of approximately 2:1 prickly pear skins to dried jamaica. Fill a 1 gallon glass jar about 2 inches high (or more for higher concentrate) with the dried fruits skins and flowers. Fill the jar with water, and then set in the sun for a couple of hours. Chill and strain to serve.

MAKES 1 GALLON.

GF R V

PRICKLY PEAR WINE OR SOFT DRINK

Contributed by Dan Dorsey

1 quart prickly pear juice

2 quarts purified, non-chlorinated water

3 to 4 cups organic cane sugar (or honey)

Pinch of storebought bread yeast (optional)

Any other flavorings you want to add (optional)

This fermented juice from prickly pear fruit makes a tasty soft drink or alcoholic table wine. Many cultures let the foods they could gather or grow naturally ferment into beverages. My grandmother made these types of simple fermented wines and passed the idea down to me. I teach classes on fermentation through the Sonoran Permaculture Guild and enjoy reviving the tradition of indigenous peoples and early pioneer settlers of making homemade country wines using locally available ingredients for flavoring.

Pour the prickly pear juice into a clean, 1-gallon, food-grade plastic bucket, glass container, or food-grade ceramic crock. A container with a wide mouth works best. Add water and sugar, stirring until the sugar dissolves. Add pinch of yeast to speed up fermentation process if you like. Cover with a permeable cover, such as cheesecloth, to keep dust and insects out but allow air to circulate freely. Set the container on a counter or shelf inside the house at room temperature but not in direct sun for a few days to a week, stirring the liquid one to two times per day.

Within a week, the liquid should start to bubble. This is wild yeast from the fruit or the air that is starting to turn the sugar into carbon dioxide gas and ethyl (drinking) alcohol. After the liquid is bubbling vigorously, wait for another day or so.

FOR SOFT DRINKS:

Transfer the liquid with a funnel from the container to clean, food-grade plastic containers (water bottles with caps work well). Fill containers to within an inch or so from the top. Cap tightly. If you use glass bottles, be very careful, as they can shatter from the pressure of the carbon dioxide inside, causing injury and/or a big mess. Let the containers sit out at room temperature until they inflate with carbon dioxide and it is hard to push in the sides of the containers. Refrigerate bottles and enjoy! Best if consumed within a month or two.

FOR WINE:

Allow the bubbling to subside. Sample to taste alcohol. Don't worry if there is a white layer at the bottom of the container: This is the by-product of yeast converting the sugar to drinking alcohol. These are called the lees, drinkable and high in B vitamins. If you don't want the yeasty flavor from the lees, scoop or siphon the wine from just the top three fourths of the container. Enjoy the wine immediately or transfer it via funnel into clean, food-grade containers with a screw-on cap and place them in the refrigerator immediately. Drink within a few weeks before the wine starts turning into vinegar. It is beyond the scope of this recipe to discuss racking and bottling the wine with a cork for further aging.

MAKES 2 to 2 1/2 QUARTS.

GF R

PRICKLY LASSI

Contributed by Barbara Rose, Bean Tree Farm

This beverage blends the tangy yogurt flavor of Indian lassi drinks with sweet prickly pear to make a beautifully pink fruit-drink treat.

Blend all ingredients together in blender or by hand. Garnish with drizzle of yogurt.

MAKES ABOUT 20 OUNCES.

1 to 2 ounces prickly pear juice (use more depending on desired color and flavor)

1 tablespoon (or to taste) lemon or sour orange juice or kombucha

1 pint plain yogurt, kefir, or greek yogurt if thicker lassi is desired

Salt, pinch

Spice of your choice, pinch

Ginger, fresh, grated, to taste

Stevia or other sweetener as desired

10 to 12 ice cubes

GF V

PRICKLY PEAR SYRUP & JELLY

Contributed by Pearl Mast

4 cups prickly pear juice

1/4 cup lemon juice

2 teaspoons Pomona's calcium water (see box instructions)

2 cups sugar

2 teaspoons Pomona's pectin powder (tan powder in the box)

Prickly pear syrup is a delightful desert treat whose color alone is more than half the fun! Use not just over pancakes, but add to any mixed cocktail or beverage, or drizzle over ice cream to impress all of your friends. This is the traditional syrup of the Cascabel Milling and Pancake and Waffle Breakfast (see p. 34).

SYRUP

Use the recipe for grape jelly found inside the box of Pomona's pectin (PomonaPectin.com), but halve both the amount of pectin and calcium.

Sometimes the syrup will be very thin, especially if made with reduced sugar, honey, or part sugar and part honey. If too thick, bring to room temperature and shake well before serving.

JELLY

Follow the instructions for grape jelly included in Pomona's Universal Pectin. You may need to boil for a longer time period to achieve the desired consistency.

MEET
DEVIL'S CLAW

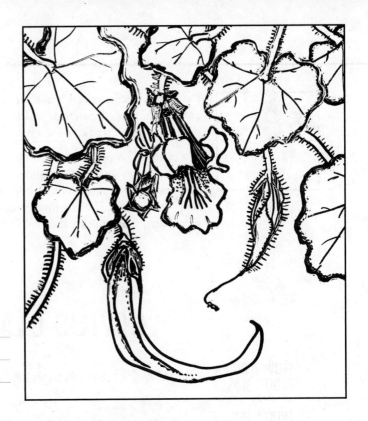

Proboscidea spp.

O'odham: *eehuk*

Spanish: *garra del diablo, cuernitos*

Native to the desert borderlands of the U.S. Southwest and

northwest Mexico, two species of devil's claw grow in the Sonoran Desert. One is a perennial (*Proboscidea altheaeifolia*), the other an annual (*Proboscidea parviflora*). Denizens of the desert, these plants love the heat and are triggered to germinate by high temperatures and summer rains. Sun-worshipping, shiny-green leaves are heliotropic and track the sun throughout the day. Droopy, resting leaves "wake up" in the morning and turn toward the light.

Perennial devil's claw blooms yellow, while the annual species blooms pinkish-purple. Flowers resemble those of snapdragon or desert willow. The curving stems and the immature fruit of devil's claw are sticky and covered with soft, dewy, whitish hairs that sparkle in the light.

But it's the fruit or seedpod of devil's claw that most delights. Flowers give way to fuzzy green fruits that resemble long thin peppers with curved tails at the end, like horns, which is how devil's claw gets its nickname: unicorn plant. At this stage the tender green seedpods are edible, and may be eaten raw, if peeled. They can also be blanched, pickled, or sautéed, and eaten plain or with seasoning or added to soups, salads, and other favorite savory foods.

Once the pod develops beyond the immature green stage, it is no longer edible. At full maturity the pod dries, browns, and develops intricate textures and tufts on the surface. The long tail splits open into two curved horns, or claws, with a delicate second set of hairs in between at the end of the comb-like tufts.

These twin sets of claws are sharp and can jab or rip skin or grab onto clothing and hold on diligently! Yet devil's claw pods are one of the most elegant seedpods in nature. Though bothersome, pods that cling carry seeds to new locations where they may germinate, successfully grow, and spread. Splitting in half is another seed-dispersal strategy, allowing the rough, black seeds to release from the pod.

Devil's claw seeds are edible and nutritious, packed with loads of protein and oil. Seeds may be eaten fresh, toasted, parched, or dried. To harvest, hold claws near seed chamber, open sides of pod, and tap out seeds, or use a nut pick or similar tool to retrieve seeds from inside pod.

The plant is also popular with Tohono O'odham basket weavers, who use its dark-colored fiber for design accents. Due to loss of wild devil's claw populations to cattle grazing and other factors, Tohono O'odham communities began cultivating *Proboscidea parviflora* var. *hohokamiana* and selecting for desired traits: long capsules and claws, white seeds that germinated more quickly than wild black ones, and pliable fibers for basketry.

-Jill Lorenzini

DEVIL'S CLAW BASICS

FLOWER BUD & BLOOM SEASON	SUMMER – May through July.
FRUIT HARVEST SEASON	WET SUMMER – July, August.
PARTS USED	Unripe green pod, seeds; dry pod.
HARVESTING TIPS/TOOLS	Wear gloves when gathering green pods to avoid sticky hairs, and when gathering dried pods to avoid sharp claws.
BEST HARVESTING PRACTICES	Carefully pick immature green pods from plant; peel or blanch to remove bitterness. Don't take all pods from one plant, no matter how beautiful they are.
CAUTION	Mature claws are sharp and easily catch on pant legs, etc. Summer is snake season, so use care when harvesting around plants close to the ground.
NUTRITION	Good protein and oil source.
PLANTING TIPS	Plant devil's claw with summer rains in terrace zone of rain garden. Seed scarification: Germination can be difficult. Let the pods age on a shelf with seed, and let the seed sit for at least a year. Germination rates increase more after the seed sits for two to three years, though plant nursery man Miles Anderson reported that others have had success with a Madagascar variety when they planted the seed within the first couple of weeks of the ripe fruit opening. Note that the annual variety of native devil's claw (*P. parviflora*) is very easy to grow with no scarification or long-term storage.
OTHER USES	Long, dark pod fibers are traditionally used in basketry. Medicinal.

DEVIL'S CLAW

Spicy Devil's Claw Pod Pickles

GF V

SPICY DEVIL'S CLAW POD PICKLES

Contributed by Patty West

4 cups rinsed young, green devil's claw pods

1 cup water

1/2 cup red wine or apple cider vinegar

1 1/2 to 2 cups white vinegar

1 6-ounce can tomato paste

3/4 cup sugar (or 1/4 teaspoon stevia)

1 onion, finely chopped

2 to 3 hot peppers of your choice

5 cloves garlic

1 teaspoon black peppercorns

2 teaspoons ground cinnamon

1/2 teaspoon dill seeds

Devil's claw is a wonderful plant that gifts humans with basketry fibers and beauty. Many people have never tasted the pods and are at first wary, but then relax into the new flavor. These spicy pickles are a great way to introduce the taste and texture of this beautiful plant. They make a tasty side dish, appetizer, or just a yummy snack.

Select only young pods that are between 1 1/2 to 3 inches and still have soft tips. (It is sometimes difficult to find this many small pods at one time, so pods can be parboiled and frozen or refrigerated until you get enough.) Rinse fresh pods in water and drain. Soak rinsed pods overnight in salt water (1/4 cup salt to 2 cups water). Discard or reuse salt water and rinse pods with fresh water.

In saucepan heat water and vinegars until warm but not boiling. In a separate bowl, add enough of water and vinegar mixture to tomato paste to make a liquid. Return liquid tomato paste to saucepan and add all other ingredients, including pods. Simmer for 15 to 25 minutes until pods are softened. Place pods in appropriate-sized jars, leaving 2 inches of space above the pods. Pour seasoned liquid into the jars to cover pods by at least 1 inch. Put lids on jars and refrigerate. Use within 1 month. To make a larger batch and can them, use safe/proper canning methods.

MAKES ABOUT 4 CUPS.

MEET
WOLFBERRY

Lycium spp.

O'ODHAM   *kuáwul*

SPANISH   *tomatillo, frutilla*

Deciduous, thorny wolfberry bushes that appear lifeless in winter turn bright green in spring, covered with copious new leaf growth, new branches, and flower buds. Blossoms appear soon after, in a variety of colors, depending on the species. *Lycium fremontii* blooms purple and produces large, teardrop-shaped red berries, favored by many desert foragers. Other Sonoran Desert wolfberries such as water jacket (*Lycium andersonii*) and narrow-leaf wolfberry (*Lycium berlanderii*) produce lavender-colored flowers and smaller, round red berries. Many desert wild foods enthusiasts prefer pale-leaf wolfberry (*Lycium pallida*) with its fragrant, light green flowers and big, oval-shaped, juicy red berries.

Wolfberry bushes are leafless in other seasons too, shedding foliage as a water conservation strategy during exceedingly hot and dry summer months. Sometimes plants go dormant until conditions improve. After plentiful summer rains, they revive to leaf out, flower, and fruit again, for early fall harvests. In years when rains aren't favorable or other conditions limit growth, wolfberry may not produce fruit at all. Every year, every season is different, as we know from our own lives.

Wolfberry bushes also tolerate alkaline and saline desert soils. They thrive under the protection of mesquite and ironwood trees, where they grow largest. Wolfberry occupies a wide variety of habitats, from mesquite to cactus forests, from valley floor to mountain elevations, and from wash margins to urban landscapes.

Thorny thickets of wolfberry branches are a favorite night roosting spot for many desert birds, like quail and curve-billed thrasher, because they are protected, hidden from night predators, and likely warmer than out in the open. These animals and many others feed on both berries and leaves. Pollinators love wolfberry flowers and bushes may be found abuzz and aflutter with them in spring!

Sometimes referred to as "desert goji," wolfberry provides health benefits similar to its highly marketed Asian counterpart, goji berries, including antioxidant qualities, high nutrition, and assistance with eye health, longevity, and weight-loss. The taste of fresh wolfberries is a blend of bitter and sweet. They can be astringent, so sampling in small quantities is advised. Wolfberries sweeten once dried and mix well in granola, trail mix, and cereals or cooked in soups, stews, stuffing, and jams.

-Jill Lorenzini

WOLFBERRY BASICS

FLOWER BUD & BLOOM SEASON	SPRING | SUMMER – February, March and July, August.
FRUIT/SEED HARVEST SEASON	SPRING | WET SUMMER – March, April and August, September.
PARTS USED	Fruit.
HARVESTING TIPS	Try to avoid thorn sets along branches, which are small but can scratch skin.
BEST HARVESTING PRACTICES	Pick by hand at peak ripeness. Try not to bruise fruits. Process soon after harvest to prevent spoilage.
CAUTION	Don't eat too many raw as they have a light astringency. Some berries are more bitter than sweet.
NUTRITION	Vitamins A, B2, and C; calcium; potassium; iron; zinc.
PLANTING TIPS	Plant with winter and summer rains in terrace, bottom, or top zone of rain garden. No seed scarification needed.
OTHER USES	Great plant for the chicken yard—the hens love its fruit, leaves, and shelter. Medicinal. Hummingbirds and other pollinators love the flowers. Birds favor roosting and nesting in the thick network of branches.

WOLFBERRY

Solar-Baked Wolfberry Bread

Photo: Jill Lorenzini

Ⓢ Ⓥ

SOLAR-BAKED WOLFBERRY BREAD

Contributed by Jill Lorenzini. Adapted from
John Robbins's *May All Be Fed: A Diet for a New World* (Harper Perennial, 1993)

1 cup whole spelt flour

1 cup mesquite flour

1 teaspoon salt

1 teaspoon baking soda

1/2 teaspoon baking powder

1/4 teaspoon cardamom

1/4 cup soy, coconut, almond, or other milk

1/8 cup olive oil

1/8 cup maple or agave syrup

2 1/4 cups mashed bananas

1-inch piece ginger, peeled and grated

1 1/2 cups fresh wolfberries

1/8 cup chia seeds

Summer rains in the desert promote the leafing out, flowering, and fruiting of both wolfberries and hackberries, which provide juicy tastes of autumn, as seasons shift. Bright red wolfberries add visual interest, nutrition, and heartiness to this tasty loaf. Perfect toasted or eat warm from the solar oven.

Preheat solar oven. (If using regular oven, preheat to 350º F.) Grease two 9-inch round cake pans. In a large bowl, combine dry ingredients. In a separate bowl, whisk together wet ingredients, including banana and ginger, until well mixed. Add dry ingredients to wet mixture and fold together lightly. Fold in wolfberries and chia seeds, saving a portion of each for topping. Divide batter evenly into cake pans. Smooth top and sprinkle on remaining wolfberries and chia seeds. Bake in solar oven until done, turning oven regularly to track the sun. Make sure bottom is baked completely. If using regular oven, bake for 30 to 35 minutes. Test with toothpick in center of loaf for doneness.

MAKES TWO 9-INCH ROUND LOAVES.

(GF) (R) (V)

AUTUMN CHUTNEY

Contributed by Jill Lorenzini

This gorgeous, colorful, and spicy condiment honors the desert autumn abundance with apples, pears, and wolfberries, with chutney seasonings.

In a medium bowl, combine all ingredients until well mixed. Store in a glass jar and use on any dish you like.

VARIATION: Use desert hackberry in place of wolfberry.

ABOUT 8 CUPS.

3 cups wolfberries

2 cups grated apples

2 cups grated pears or Asian pears or combo

1 onion, chopped

4 cloves minced garlic

4 tablespoons grated ginger

1 red or yellow pepper, chopped

1/2 cup golden raisins

3 cups apple cider vinegar

1 teaspoon salt or to taste

1 1/2 teaspoons cinnamon

1 teaspoon hot red pepper, or a dash of chiltepin to taste

1/2 teaspoon celery seed

1 teaspoon turmeric

GF V

FERMENTED FALL FRUITS

Contributed by Paula Verde

1 cup fermented fruit (starter)*

1/2 cup diced canned peaches

1/2 cup diced canned pears

1/2 cup pineapple tidbits

1/2 cup fresh, dried, toasted, or honey-marinated wolfberries (can mix with hackberries, golden raisins, goji, or currants)

1 1/4 cups raw organic sugar (or equivalent sweetener)

2 tablespoons grated fresh ginger

*NOTE:
GET STARTER FROM:

1. A friend in a gesture of welcome and solidarity, as with sourdough starter, kefir crystals, or kombucha, or yogurt starter.

2. Part of a batch you make and save.

3. Natural processes. Allowing the jar to sit in warm conditions with a loose cover also invites fermentation to begin in the fruit-sugar mixture, even without friendship starter, though it might take a lot longer.

From a recipe in my mother's file called Vintage Friendship Fruit Sauce, from friend Mary Pace. My mom made it and jarred it annually for our pantry, with peaches and pears we'd canned in the summer. We called it Fermented Fruit. By the time we got to the last jar, it had acquired quite a high alcohol content, and a zesty, effervescent tang. Delicious on ice cream, pound cake, cheesecake, and even on savory foods, as a fruit chutney.

Combine all fruit with sugar and ginger in a large glass jar with a loose or cloth cover. Set in a consistently warm place, on a partially sunny counter, on top of the refrigerator, etc. Stir well daily for a week, with a long wooden spoon handle. After 1 week, sauce should be thick, fermented, sweet, and ready to eat (taste it to see, and let sit a few days longer if you think it needs to). Eat some, save some, share some, and store some in jars for later use. No need to refrigerate, but store in a cool dark pantry.

Always save at least a third of the fermented fruit mixture in the jar, so you have starter for friends, but also so that, if you want to, every 2 weeks fruit and sugar may be added to the starter mixture to make more fermented fruit sauce. It's a recipe that keeps on giving!

MAKES 3 to 4 CUPS.

(GF) (V)

WOLFBERRY-APPLE MOLE WITH BARREL CACTUS SEEDS

Contributed by Barbara Rose, Bean Tree Farm

This rich sauce has a wealth of subtle flavor combinations to enhance any dish. Warming for cool-season fare, and slow-cooked for maximum tastiness!

In large pan, sauté onion, garlic, herbs, mole, and chiles in oil over medium heat until fragrant and beginning to brown. Add tomatoes (or reductions), apples, and barrel cactus seeds. Simmer slowly. When thickened, mash or blend into a smooth sauce. Add wolfberries and simmer a bit more. Seaons with salt, pepper, and vinegar to taste. Drizzle warm sauce over your favorite protein, tamales, eggs, pancakes or waffles, spuds, etc.

MAKES ABOUT 6 CUPS.

1 large onion, chopped

3 cloves garlic, minced

2 teaspoons aloysia or oregano

2 tablespoons mole powder*

2 chiles, minced

Oil for frying

2 cups chopped tomatoes (or substitute reduction Mesquite Broth, p. 76 or prickly pear juice)

2 cups apples, chopped

1 cup barrel cactus seeds, ground

1 cup wolfberries

Salt and pepper, vinegar to taste

*NOTE: A favorite mole powder is Mano y Metate Mole. These freshly ground blends of whole spices, nuts, seeds, and chiles are an easy way to make the celebrated Mexican sauces. Found locally in Tucson and Southern Arizona or online at ManoYMetate.com.

(GF) (R) (V)

WOLFBERRY VINEGAR

Contributed by Paula Verde

1 cup fresh wolfberries

1 quart organic raw apple cider vinegar

Adding wolfberries to vinegar infuses the vinegar with the healthful attributes of these desert berries in a versatile form for use in the kitchen. You can also use the pickled fruits in chutney, soup, salsa, and salad dressing.

Make sure berries are clean, dry, and free of debris and insects. Toast lightly on low heat in a dry cast iron skillet, shaking often so berries roll around and toast evenly. Remove from heat. Allow to cool completely.

Open vinegar and pour off 1 cup; set aside. Using a funnel, slowly pour toasted wolfberries into vinegar until vinegar nears top of jar. Add reserved vinegar to fill the jar if needed. Let vinegar steep for a few weeks in a cool dark place. Then strain, re-bottle vinegar, and label for later use, saving strained wolfberries to use elsewhere.

MAKES 1 1/4 QUARTS.

(V)

WOLFBERRY COOKIES

Contributed by Paula Verde

These chewy, spicy, sweet, nutty cookies also have a unique taste of the desert inside and are full of nutrition and flavor. Eat the season!

Preheat oven to 350° F. Grease cookie sheets. In a large bowl, combine all dry ingredients. In a separate bowl, combine syrup, oil, vanilla, and ginger. Add wet ingredients to dry ingredients. Fold carrots, berries, and nuts into dough. Drop by heaping tablespoonful onto a greased baking sheet. Bake for 14 to 18 minutes, until edges brown. Cool, then remove from sheets. Store in a lidded cookie jar or tin. Great snack at tea or coffee break!

VARIATION: Use desert hackberry in place of wolfberry.

MAKES ABOUT 3 DOZEN.

1 1/3 cups spelt or wheat flour

1/2 cup mesquite flour

2 teaspoons baking powder

1 teaspoon baking soda

1 teaspoon salt

2 cups rolled oats

1 1/4 cups maple syrup or 1 cup agave syrup

1/2 cup mild olive oil

1 teaspoon vanilla

2 tablespoons fresh-grated ginger

1 cup grated carrots

1 cup dried or toasted wolfberries

1/2 cup chopped Arizona pecans or walnuts

MEET
HACKBERRY

DESERT (BUSH)	*Celtis pallida*
CANYON (TREE)	*Celtis reticulata*
O'ODHAM	*ko:m, kuwavul*
SPANISH	*granjeno, garambullo, garabato, capul*

There are two kinds of hackberry in the Sonoran Desert: desert hackberry, a bush, and canyon hackberry, a tree. They both offer delicious berries for harvest. The recipes in this book feature desert hackberry.

In late June, July, and August, summer rains recharge watersheds and trigger flowering and fruiting of the desert hackberry bush. Tiny white stigmas visited by pollinators turn to roundish green fruits that later swell and ripen to a bright orange color, in late September, October, and November. Sometimes hackberry blooms in spring as well, inspired by winter rains and other beneficial conditions.

Inside the fleshy fruit is a rather large seed that adds a crunchy-nutty contrast to the melon-apricot flavor of the sweet juicy fruit. Desert hackberries are best eaten fresh. Because they are soft and full of sugars, they can damage and spoil easily, even in the fridge. To best store hackberries, air-dry or toast them, or freeze them fresh. They can also be cooked into sauces, jams, and chutneys and canned; or baked into breads, cookies, or muffins and frozen. They may be added to agave syrup, honey, or alcohol as a way to preserve as well.

Desert hackberry has its share of thorns, like so many native desert food plants, so harvesting requires careful reaches in and out to get individual berries. Thorn pairs hide behind leaves and can scratch fingers and forearms intent on reaching handfuls of sweetness. Do spiny-thorny desert plants remind us that every pleasure exacts its pain?

Hackberry drops its leaves in times of extreme cold or heat/drought, which adds organic matter to desert soils right beneath it. Canyon hackberry trees often act as nurse or structure trees for desert hackberry bushes, and other understory plants. Both hackberry trees and bushes provide significant food and shelter for native and migratory birds and other wildlife, whose droppings

add even more nutrients to soils under and around hackberry canopies.

Canyon hackberry, sometimes called sugar berry, also ripens in the fall. Harvesting from a tall tree might require more equipment or physical skills than gathering from a bush, but the sweet harvest might well be worth it! Even when canyon hackberry fruit have dried on the tree, they are still sweet to eat and can be ground seed and all into a sweet sugar substitute. Use caution, in any case, since the seed inside can be very hard, and hard on the teeth. Crunch carefully!

- Jill Lorenzini

Desert hackberry harvest

Photo: Jill Lorenzini

DESERT HACKBERRY BASICS

FLOWER BUD & BLOOM SEASON	WET SUMMER – July, August.
FRUIT/SEED HARVEST SEASON	FALL – September, October, November.
PARTS USED	Fruit.
HARVESTING TIPS	Fruit are delicate. Handle carefully or just eat fresh.
BEST HARVESTING PRACTICES	Carefully pick ripe berries from bushes; they should come off easily. Leave plenty of fruit for birds and other animals.
CAUTION	Avoid hidden thorns on branches.
NUTRITION	Niacin, magnesium, calcium, protein, phosphorus.
PLANTING TIPS	Plant desert hackberry with summer rains in terrace or top zones of rain garden. Plant canyon hackberry with summer rains in terrace or bottom zone of rain garden. No seed scarification needed if seed is fresh, otherwise soak in lemon juice or citric acid for 24 hours.
OTHER USES	Fodder for honeybees/pollinators, chickens, and cattle. Wood for bows. Medicinal.

DESERT HACKBERRY

Fresh desert hackberries, Drunken Hackberries, Autumn Chutney with hackberry

Photo: Jill Lorenzini

GF V

HACKBERRY FLOUR

Contributed by Paula Verde

2 cups fresh-picked desert hackberries, clean and free of stems, debris, and insects.

Berries must be dried or toasted before grinding into flour.

Hackberry flour adds beautiful color and a sweet and nutty flavor to any recipe, plus added nutrition and a sense of connection to place.

TO AIR-DRY:

Put berries in a basket or wooden bowl and cover securely with a cloth. Put outside in a shady spot with good air flow. Shake or toss lightly every day so berries dry evenly. In Tucson's dry, warm, fall climate, this may be only a couple of days; in other places, it might take longer, or require the use of an oven on low heat to prevent spoilage. Once dry, store in jars in a cool, dry, dark place.

TO TOAST:

Cover the bottom of a dry skillet with berries, and toast on low heat until berries shrivel and toast on all sides. Shake skillet (versus stirring berries) to evenly toast on all sides. Alternatively, toast on a baking tray in a low-temp oven with door open, shaking to toast berries evenly. Cool and air-dry as per above directions. Store in jars in a cool, dry, dark place.

TO GRIND:

Grind dried or toasted berries in an electric grinder or with a hand-mill. Sift flour if necessary before adding to your favorite baked goods recipes, smoothies, sauces, salsas, soups, and beverages.

VARIATION: Substitute dried wolfberries for hackberries.

MAKES ABOUT 1 CUP.

(GF) (R) (V)

HACKBERRY MILK

Contributed by Jill Lorenzini

The eye eats first! This light-orange milk has a beautiful hue and is a sweet treat in the early fall, when bodies crave more than just water as days shorten and temperatures finally start to cool.

In small bowl, combine milk and berries. Add salt. Mash berries with potato or bean masher until milk turns berry-colored. Alternatively, pulse berries and milk in a blender or food processor. Strain milk through fine sieve into drinking mug. Add sweetener to taste and top with a dusting of freshly ground nutmeg to perfect the experience!

MAKES 1 CUP.

1 cup soy, coconut, almond, or other milk

1/2 cup fresh desert hackberries

Pinch of salt

Sweetener, to taste

Nutmeg, for garnish

(GF) (V)

ASPEN'S HACKBERRY MARMALADE

Contributed by Aspen Samuelson

2 cups desert hackberries

1/4 cup coconut sugar or brown sugar

Juice and zest from 1 lemon

1 teaspoon balsamic, prickly pear, or apple cider vinegar

1 teaspoon fresh ginger, minced

Hackberry's beautiful orange color makes this marmalade stand out, as do the sweet, spicy flavors. A perfect desert recipe for transitioning into autumn.

In a medium saucepan, combine all ingredients and simmer on low for 30 minutes. Adjust sweetness and spices to taste. Serve with chèvre and crackers, or on toasted bread with butter.

MAKES ABOUT 2 CUPS.

HACKBERRY EI KEUCHEN

Contributed by Jill Lorenzini

Adapted from my mother's recipe file, ei keuchen is a super-simple but delectably delicate egg-cake, more like a crepe than a pancake. A favorite from her German-Dutch immigrant heritage, this recipe somehow elevates the most basic of ingredients into the finest of treats.

Preheat a griddle or cast iron skillet to medium heat. In a small bowl, whisk eggs and milk together. In a separate bowl, combine dry ingredients plus hackberries. Add wet ingredients to dry ingredients and mix well, but loosely, with a fork. Add oil to skillet and bring to high heat (but not smoking!). Pour 1/2 cup of batter at a time into skillet. Cakes should slip around and curl up and brown around the edges. Flip with a spatula, or in the air if you're good at it! Serve with syrup, fresh fruit, or Fermented Fall Fruits (p. 178). Yum!

MAKES ABOUT 8 SERVINGS.

4 eggs, beaten

1 1/2 cups milk

4 tablespoons flour (2 tablespoons mesquite pastry flour + 2 tablespoons spelt flour)

2 teaspoons sugar or other sweetener

Salt to taste

Cinnamon to taste

1/2 cup fresh, dried, or toasted desert hackberries

Coconut or olive oil for cooking

(GF) (R) (V)

DRUNKEN HACKBERRIES

Contributed by Jill Lorenzini

2 cups clean fresh desert hackberries (or wolfberries or a combination of the two)

32 ounces tequila of your choice

2 sprigs Mexican oregano OR 1/2 teaspoon creosote flowers

Hackberries and wolfberries have a small window of harvest time and they produce in profusion. But they also spoil very quickly once picked. So this recipe came from thinking up all the ways to preserve surplus berries. It's an easy way to make these colorful berries intoxicatingly tasty for use as a garnish for desserts, salads, and beverages.

Put berries into a large jar. Add tequila and herbs or flowers. Steep for at least a month in a cool dark place. Check weekly, shake lightly, loosen lid to release any pressure. Pour mixture through a strainer to separate berries, and remove creosote flowers or oregano sprigs. Re-jar tequila for use in margaritas or other mixed drinks. Serve drunken hackberries over ice cream, on pancakes or french toast with syrup, as a garnish on pumpkin pie with whipped cream, in salads, as a garnish on savory or sweet dishes, and in beverages.

MAKES 32 OUNCES OF TEQUILA and 2 CUPS OF BERRIES.

MEET
CHILTEPIN

Capsicum annuum var. *glabriusculum*

O'odham: *a'al kokoli*

Spanish: *chiltepín, chiltipiquín, piquín, tepin*

Hot stuff!
Tiny, tasty, and terrifically hot are apt ways to describe this little pepper, a native of the U.S. Southwest and northwest Mexico. Chiltepin is known as "the mother of all peppers," the original wild chile from which all other chiles evolved.

Wild chiltepin bushes typically grow up to 4 feet high. They thrive in the mountains of the borderlands, in partly shaded canyon sites, or under the canopy of desert legume trees, which protect them from hot and cold extremes. Under such legume canopies they can often grow to double their typical size! These indigenous perennials may live up to 35 to 50 years in ideal growing conditions and areas without hard frost in winter.

The spicy fruits are round to oval in shape, colored dark green and sometimes purplish-black when immature, ripening fully to a bright red or red-orange hue. They are also known as bird's eye, turkey, or bird pepper, since many birds delightedly consume the peppers and help spread the seeds far and wide. Birds are insensitive to the intense heat but value the chiltepin's nutrition and abundance, consuming large quantities from colorful, fruit-filled bushes.

But for humans, the heat from a chiltepin is hot to handle. Use caution to avoid contact with bare skin, eyes, and mucous membranes, as the peppers contain capsaicin, an oily chemical that causes a painful burning sensation on skin if you handle peppers without protection, such as gloves or a mask. The dry powder of ground peppers may also irritate skin and the respiratory system.

A great solution to avoid handling hot peppers is to use a wooden chiltepin grinder. Seri and other native crafters carve desert ironwood into beautiful, decorative mortar and pestle sets for grinding dried chiltepin peppers.

Eating chiltepin peppers—raw, dried, pickled, green, or ripe—can cause a pungent, burning sensation in the mouth, throat, and stomach that is intense but fairly short-lived. It even has a distinctive smoky bite to go with the burn. Because where there's smoke, there's often fire! Coughing, blowing the nose, and shedding tears are not unheard of. Connoisseurs of this fiery

experience claim they feel a pain-induced "high" from the heat. Interestingly enough, ingesting capsaicin triggers a pain-stimulated release of endorphins, the body's natural painkillers, causing mild euphoric sensations. Those chile lovers aren't crazy! Consuming hot chiltepin peppers also causes the body to sweat, which is a great evaporative cooling strategy. Almost all cuisines from hot climates include some sort of hot pepper and/or spice for this and other body benefits.

Chiltepin is the only wild chile native to the United States. As such, it is protected in several national and state parks, including Organ Pipe National Park. In 1999, Native Seeds/SEARCH and the U.S. Forest Service established the Wild Chile Botanical Area in the Coronado National Forest near Tumacacori, Arizona. This preserve protects a large wild chiltepin population for study, and to conserve this valuable genetic resource.

Like the saguaro harvest in summer, the wild chiltepin harvest is a seasonal ritual in many native borderlands communities, where families make harvesting camps in the mountains during the lingering heat of September and early October to harvest and process the peppers. Ripe fruits are harvested by hand and then dried whole in the sun to be stored for later use.

Dried peppers may be ground fresh in a grinder and sprinkled onto many foods for the spicy taste and to add vitamin C to the diet. Fresh fruit may also be fermented into sauces or pickled with wild oregano, garlic, and salt as a traditional tabletop condiment. The green or dried red fruit are often mixed with wild greens and onions as a typical Sonoran dish.

The chiltepin pepper can also be used medicinally. In native traditions it has been used internally for head and stomach pain, and in a liniment formula for sore muscles. Curiously enough, red-hot capsaicin, when used topically in analgesic formulas for muscle soreness and achy joints, actually helps relieve pain and inflammation! Hot stuff!

- Jill Lorenzini

CHILTEPIN BASICS

FLOWER BUD & BLOOM SEASON	WET SUMMER I FALL – July, August, September, October.
FRUIT SEASON	FALL – September, October. But if cultivated and watered, chiltepin might continue to fruit or fruit out of season.
PARTS USED	Fruit.
HARVESTING TIPS	Avoid skin and eye contact with spicy-hot oils of fruits.
BEST HARVESTING PRACTICES	Harvest early or around dusk.
CAUTION	One of the hottest peppers in the world!
NUTRITION	Vitamins A and C, riboflavin.
PLANTING TIPS	Plant chiltepin with summer rains in top or terrace zone of rain garden. No seed scarification needed. Frost sensitive.

SWEET AND SPICY: EXO COFFEE
AND THE DESERT COLD BREWS

by Kimi Eisele

When Amy and Doug Smith were planning the coffee menu for their downtown Tucson café, EXO Roast Co., they wanted to include flavors of the region. Both had strong ties to the Sonoran Desert and an affinity for place-based endeavors. Doug was trained as an anthropologist and wrote a dissertation on coffee production in central Mexico, and Amy had spent nearly a decade teaching social studies at City High School, known for its placed-based curricula.

But now they were in the coffee business. How could they make place-based coffee in a habitat where coffee beans do not grow?

They had sampled Blue Bottle Coffee's New Orleans-inspired cold brew made with sugar, milk, and roasted chicory, a root traditionally used in French Louisiana as a coffee substitute and additive.

"I wondered what the Tucson version of that would be," Amy said. "We couldn't really add grapefruit!"

Like chicory, mesquite was sometimes used as a coffee substitute, and it offered a quintessential Sonoran Desert flavor. So one of EXO's employees at the time, Cate Maxon, contacted Desert Harvesters, and soon Cate and Amy were attending harvesting workshops, learning to taste the pods before picking to get the sweetest ones.

Amy began experimenting with using the pods, drawing lessons from the cookbook *From I'toi's Garden: Tohono O'odham Food Traditions*, and soaking the pods in a crockpot to extract the flavor.

Eventually EXO created their signature Mesquite Toddy, a "parfait" of cold brew coffee, mesquite extract, and cream over ice.

Amy, Alma, and Doug Smith

Photo: Liora K courtesy of
Edible Baja Magazine

"They became so popular that we had to harvest a lot of mesquite," Amy said. "We actually had to train someone to harvest for us and instructed him to pick only from native velvet mesquite and at the right time of year," she said. Honey mesquite pods did not produce as sweet of an extract due to the weaker sugars, she said, adding that they had all pods tested for aflatoxins.

Eventually they started selling the mesquite extract to other businesses in town, like the Good Oak Bar, for use in its Mesquite Old Fashioned cocktail.

But they didn't stop at mesquite. Amy and Doug were also familiar with the Mexican tradition of chocolate and chiles, so they started experimenting with chiltepines in a cold brew coffee.

Chiletpines

Photo: Jill Lorenzini

"It was way too hot at first," Amy said. But then they added a house-made chocolate truffle and organic cream, both of which tempered the heat, she said.

Their Chiltepin Cold Brew (see p. 200) is now one of their most popular items. "We're able to offer it all year round, using dried peppers from a friend's 'mother bush' he grows in his backyard," Amy said.

In 2016 EXO added to their menu of pour-overs and cold brews a series of lectures and programming related to regional practices, research, and activism. They expanded into the back room of the café and called it the Southern Arizona Workspace, or SAWS. They also built a small kitchen and started serving breakfast, with some of the offerings made with wild, desert foods (see Meals of the Moment, p. 275).

Amy said the expansion was simply an expression of her own affinity for the Sonoran Desert, as well as her staff's.

Indeed, the EXO staff is not your average set of baristas. "Everyone who works here is so invested in Tucson," said Lia Griesser, EXO's kitchen manager. "When you come in they're going to tell you emphatically about chiltepin. They have an investment in the desert."

Using desert flavors "fits our personality," Amy said. "We wanted to stand out and offer something original, culling from regional flavors. We wanted to pay homage to traditions, bringing attention to native and wild foods to inspire others."

Learn more about EXO's desert offerings at ExoCoffee.com and SouthernArizonaWorkspace.com.

CHILTEPIN

Chiltepin Flan with wolfberry garnish

Photo: Christian Timmerman

GF V

CHILTEPIN SALSA

Contributed by Janos Wilder, Downtown Kitchen+Cocktails

4 plum tomatoes, halved and seeded, or 1/2 14.5-ounce can fire-roasted diced tomatoes

3 to 6 chiltepines (depending on desired level of heat!)

1/2 white onion, roughly chopped

1 tablespoon dried oregano

3 tablespoons distilled white wine vinegar

2 tablespoons tomato paste

Salt to taste

Chiltepines make a fiery salsa so only a few of the small chiles are needed to make a small batch. The flavors are unique to this region and if you can find Mexican oregano, all the better.

Preheat oven to 400° F. If using fresh tomatoes, roast them for 30 minutes. Allow to cool completely. Puree with other ingredients in a blender until completely smooth.

VARIATION: Add 2 to 4 roasted poblano or hatch chiles for a different flavor profile.

MAKES 2+ CUPS.

GF V

SPICY TEPARY BEAN SPREAD

Contributed by Janos Wilder, Downtown Kitchen+Cocktails

This flavorful spread uses one of the oldest, drought-resistant beans found in the region. These wonderful flavors come together to create a spread that is served cold as a dip, spread on tortillas as a base for quesadillas, or used as a spread on sandwiches. Once you've made this the first time you will look for ways to use it every day.

In a food processor puree jalapeños or chiltepines, chipotle, and smoked poblano chiles. Add tomato paste, tepary beans, and crushed garlic to the paste. With the motor running, slowly add the olive oil and red wine vinegar. Adjust the seasoning with salt and pepper.

MAKES 2 QUARTS.

1 1/2 jalapeños OR 1 (or more) chiltepines

1 chipotle

1 1/2 smoked poblano chiles

1/2 cup tomato paste

1 1/2 quarts cooked tepary beans at room temperature

2 1/2 tablespoons crushed garlic

3/4 cup olive oil

1/2 cup red wine vinegar

Salt and pepper to taste

GF V

CHILTEPIN BEET HUMMUS

Contributed by Mikaela Jones

1 small roasted beet

Olive oil

Salt and black pepper

1 15-ounce can (1 3/4 cups) cooked chickpeas, mostly drained

1/4 cup palo verde beans

Zest of large lemon

Juice of half a large lemon

2 large cloves garlic, minced

2 heaping tablespoons tahini

8 dried chiltepines (or less/more depending on desired spiciness)

This hummus is spicy and colorful fun. The roasted beets make it a beautiful fuchsia color that children are guaranteed to love. You can make it as spicy or as mellow as you like.

Preheat oven to 350º F. Slice beets thinly. Place on cookie sheet, drizzle with olive oil, and sprinkle with salt and black pepper. Bake for 15 to 20 minutes or until tender. Place the remaining ingredients (except chiltepines) into a food processor, blender, or bowl if you have a hand blender. Add beets and blend until smooth. You can adjust the proportions until you have the consistency you like your hummus. If you like a tangy hummus add more lemon juice. If you like thick hummus, completely drain the can of beans before placing them in the food processor. Add the dried chiltepines just a few chiles at a time. Remember you can always add more, but you can never take them away. Chiltepines are very spicy, so start small and add more to taste. Blend completely into the hummus and enjoy.

MAKES ABOUT 2 CUPS.

CHILTEPIN FLAN

Contributed by the Hotel y Restaurante La Posada del Rio Sonora
and adapted by Lori Adkison

This dessert marries the creamy sweetness of flan with the heat of chiltepin for an exciting and delicious dessert. La Posada's head cocinera, Ana Patricia Galvez, makes the recipe in a round tin (the kind cookies come in), but you can use whatever dish you like. On most dining tables in homes and restaurants in Sonora, you find beautiful chiltepin grinders made from ironwood and carved into various animal shapes. So if you want to add more spice after the flan is served, you just grind some up and sprinkle it on carefully!

1 cup sugar

1 1/4 cups cream

1 14-ounce can sweetened condensed milk

1 12-ounce can evaporated milk

3 large eggs

1 tablespoon vanilla

12 chiltepines (or more, depending on taste)

TO PREPARE CARAMELIZED SUGAR:

In saucepan, heat sugar over low heat, stirring continuously until deep amber. Pour quickly into a 1 1/2-quart flan mold or round cookie tin, tilting mold so that sugar coats all surfaces. Set aside and allow mold to cool until sugar hardens. Be careful when working with caramelized sugar. If touched it can cause serious burns!

TO PREPARE FLAN:

Preheat oven to 425º F. Blend all remaining ingredients in blender. Pour mixture into mold and cover with foil. Place a rectangular baking dish in the oven with enough boiling water to reach halfway up the flan mold. Place the mold into the baking dish taking care not to get a steam burn from the water. Add boiling water as necessary to maintain water level halfway up the mold. Cooking times will vary depending on the depth and width of your mold. Start testing after an hour and a half. Flan is done when toothpick inserted in center comes out clean. Deeper molds will require longer cooking times. Remove mold from water pan and allow to thoroughly cool. Once cool, remove cover. Place plate on top and quickly turn over so that flan falls onto plate. Slice into serving pieces.

MAKES 8 to 12 SERVINGS.

GF V

CHILTEPIN COLD BREW

Contributed by Amy and Doug Smith of EXO Coffee

1 pound coarse-ground coffee

1 to 2 teaspoons dried, crushed chiltepin pepper

12 cups filtered or purified water

This is a slightly spicy, rich coffee drink with Sonoran roots! We like this recipe because it marries the chiltepin, a pepper native to the Southwest and Mexico, and the coffee we import from farther south in the Americas.

In a container that can be made airtight, mix 1 pound of coarse-ground coffee with the crushed chiltepines. Every chiltepin, depending on how old it was when picked, will be different! But they are always HOT so err on the side of less!

Thoroughly saturate grounds of coffee and crushed pepper with 12 cups of cold, filtered water. Cover and put in a room temperature environment for 24 hours. Strain coffee with a mesh colander with either cheesecloth or a coffee filter placed in colander basket. Serve with a splash of milk or coconut milk. Add your favorite chocolate sauce or simple syrup to sweeten.

MAKES ABOUT 5 CUPS.

MEET
BARREL CACTUS

Ferocactus spp.

O'odham: *chiávul*

Spanish: *biznaga (de agua)*

Roll out the barrel! We'll have a barrel of fun! The barrel cactus is one of a few desert perennial food plants that fruit during the fall-winter season when other wild foods are less plentiful. After late-June and July monsoon storms, barrel cacti swell up with rain and in August produce fat, teardrop-shaped flower buds that grow in a spiral out of the center of the cactus top. Barrels then bloom bright yellow, red, or orange, depending on the species.

Green fruits gradually develop from pollinated flowers, and by late October and November, fruits begin turning yellow, toward full ripeness. November through February are prime harvest months. Sometimes ripe yellow fruits persist on barrel into spring, or even into the next flowering season!

The fishhook or candy barrel (*Ferocactus wislizeni*) is the most common and the largest barrel cactus in Southern Arizona. It has sharply hooked, flattened central spines, light pink to red in color. The compass or California barrel (*Ferocactus cylindraceus*) is also found in Southern Arizona and is similar to fishhook except that the central spines curve downward, with no hook. Also, as the compass barrel grows the whole cactus leans south or southwestward, thus its name. Nothing like a cactus to keep you well oriented!

Like saguaro and organ pipe cacti, barrels are pleated columnar cacti that grow upward and can swell or shrink, depending on the availability of seasonal rains or supplemental water. Barrel cacti grow very slowly so are often under 4 feet tall, though older special specimens can reach up to 8 feet in height!

Bright yellow ripe fruits are smooth, and unlike other cactus fruits, have no spines or glochids, making harvest simpler. Still use caution with its sharp spines, which can rip both fruit and hands. Oblong fruits are topped by tufts of the tough dried flower, which serve as a great handle for pulling fruits from cactus areoles. These tufts also make the fruit resemble a small pineapple.

The yellow fruit is juicy, tart, lemony, and refreshing. Inside the fruit cavity is a network of fine white pulp, in which hundreds of shiny black and sometimes reddish seeds are clustered. The seeds are mildly nutty in flavor and packed with protein and oil. Seeds visually enliven any recipe, and add a wonderful crunch too!

Seeds and pulp are easily scooped out of fruits with thumb or spoon, and may be sorted by putting into a bowl of water, where viable seeds sink and lightweight pulp and non-viable seeds float. (The water from this processing is slippery and emollient and benefits the skin and hair!) Dry seeds thoroughly before storing. Seeds keep best frozen or toasted and stored in jars in a cool dry place.

Fruits may be sliced and used fresh in beverages, cooked into chutneys, main dishes, and preserves, or frozen for later use. Fruits may also be halved or sliced, then air-, solar-, or oven-dried and stored. Dried fruits may be reconstituted by soaking or may be ground into a tart spicy powder for adding to favorite foods and beverages.

- Jill Lorenzini

BARREL CACTUS BASICS

FLOWER BUD & BLOOM SEASON	WET SUMMER I EARLY FALL – July through September.
FRUIT/SEED HARVEST SEASON	WINTER I SPRING – November through April
PARTS USED	Fruit, seeds, flower buds.
HARVESTING TIPS	Use tongs to harvest flower buds. Use stiff tuft of spent flower as a handle for pulling fruit from cactus.
BEST HARVESTING PRACTICES	Ripe, undamaged fruit should pull easily from cactus. Leave enough flower buds and/or fruit for pollinators, animals, and birds to forage.
CAUTION	Use great caution around curved spines.
NUTRITION	Protein- and oil-rich seeds, fruit contains vitamins C and A, hydrating.
PLANTING TIPS	Plant with summer rains in the top or terrace zone of rain garden. Seed scarification: Plant last year's crop. Other than that, no scarification needed. Note: If growing cacti in nursery pots, let soil dry out between each watering. Small pots and seed trays drain better than large pots.
OTHER USES	Medicinal. Pigment/dye. Cut fruit (minus the seed) soaked in water for 20 minutes creates a mucilaginous hair conditioner.

HARVESTING AS HEALING:
ISKASHITAA REFUGEE NETWORK

by Kimi Eisele

When geologist-turned-gleaner Barbara Eiswerth suggested to Faeza Hillian, an Iraqi refugee in Tucson, that she incorporate prickly pear fruit into her baklava, Faeza made a funny face.

But Faeza was willing to try it. And her experiment, Eiswerth recounted, turned into "the most beautiful baklava you've ever seen—a pan of rosy, flaky sweetness and gorgeous local food."

That's the kind of innovative spirit that permeates Iskashitaa Refugee Network, a grassroots organization Barbara founded in 2003 that assists United Nations refugees and asylum seekers in creating a sense of home through food-based programs such as gleaning, harvesting, and production.

The Network grew out of a youth food mapping project Barbara initiated in one Tucson neighborhood. "The idea was to create awareness of food going to waste by creating a geographic information system (GIS) of those backyard resources," she said.

The first participants were Somali Bantu youth who had recently arrived in Tucson. "They'd come from agricultural backgrounds and had huge barriers to city life, our complex systems, community integration, and self-sufficiency," Barbara said. The project was a way to get them involved in indoor and outdoor activities, and also to help prevent thousands of citrus fruits that would fall on sidewalks and backyards from going to waste.

"Iskashitaa" is a Somali word for "working cooperatively together," and the project eventually expanded to other neighborhoods and brought in refugees from other countries to participate, putting to use their food preservation traditions.

Barbara Eiswerth

Photo: Bae Meckler

The Network's initial efforts involved gleaning excess citrus in Tucson neighborhoods. Now the refugees harvest both cultivated and wild foods, including 82 different fruits, vegetables, flowers, leaves, pods, and weeds.

From the resources they harvest, the Network produces date syrup, date vinegar, prickly pear syrup, pickled garlic (in prickly pear brine), and candied barrel cactus and citrus rind, which they sell in local markets. The group is currently exploring possible harvests of the California fan palm (*Washingtonia filifera*), native to the U.S. Southwest.

Iskashitaa also harvests cultivated foods. The Bhutanese are "avid gardeners," Barbara said. "Many of them grew up never buying food from a grocery store. They grew all their own food."

Using the bounty from the Iskashitaa garden in midtown Tucson, the Bhutanese began sharing their techniques for pickling, fermenting, and souring vegetables, such as pomegranates, pumpkin seeds, and radishes.

The Bhutanese use lime juice instead of vinegar to pickle. Others use fermented greens or fermented radishes to help sour foods, such as the broth used to cook lentils. "It's similar to how Mexican cuisine often uses lime juice in soups to bring the other flavors out," Barbara said.

While the refugees are inventive and skilled in the kitchen, recipe capture is a challenge. "It's often volunteers running around with tablespoons and cups to catch before it goes into the bowl. Nothing is measured and often, nothing is written down," Barbara said.

The Network also introduces refugees to orchards, farms, vineyards, and aquaponic endeavors in the region. These excursions help give the refugees a sense of purpose, Barbara said, but also often allow them to reconnect with an aspect of home.

Barbara recalled one trip to harvest saguaro fruit with the Tohono O'odham, when some of the folks exclaimed, "This is just like Bhutan!" upon seeing the Tucson Mountains towering over the desert.

Other groups help to harvest 5,000 pounds of garlic from Forever Yong farm in Amado, Arizona, each year. One man said, "I've been away from home for 20 years—18 years in a refugee camp and two years in Tucson. This is the first time my hands connected me to the healing soil of the earth."

Such outings also help refugees discover new resources. While harvesting the garlic, the refugees noticed lamb's quarter growing in between the rows. "We were done with the garlic and I saw them carrying over armfuls of the greens," Barbara said.

Iraqi and Syrian refugees also harvest purslane (verdolagas), which grows wild in urban environments.

"We stumbled upon this knowledge," Barbara said. "Someone would point to wild mustard growing after the monsoon and say, 'That's medicine. We use this for malaria.'"

During a funeral for a child of one of the Turkish families, the refugees discovered amaranth growing near a water treatment plant. "Nobody was paying attention to the funeral because everyone was collecting amaranth," Barbara said.

Afterwards members of the Network cooked a dinner, and one refugee commented, "Barbara, you transported me back to Nepal. I had a taste of home in my mouth."

In addition to extra income and knowledge, the Refugee Network has helped give newcomers to the region a sense of purpose, Barbara said. The Network donates 40 percent of the annual harvest to several of the community food banks and shares plentifully with new refugees.

Giving back to Tucson, a safe haven and a place that represents a second chance at life, is important to many refugee families, Barbara said.

"Food is a beautiful unifying thing. We say harvesting is healing. And we're creating a new fabric for them."

Speaking of fabric, Iskashitaa members have even created a special harvest bag for outings, which they sell along with their other products.

Barbara "gleaned" the bag several years ago when she went to pick up mesquite flour from a milling. Inside her mesquite pod bucket was an over-the-shoulder mesquite harvesting bag someone had misplaced there. Before returning it, she had a friend make a pattern from it and then gave the pattern to some of the refugees who re-created it using recycled sewing machines and recycled fabrics. "They doubled the bottom so it's stronger and put jeans pockets on the inside," Barbara said. "It's really a perfect thing to have in your car for spontaneous harvesting."

Learn more about Iskashitaa Refugee Network and their practices and products at Iskashitaa.org.

BARREL CACTUS

Barrel cactus fruit

GF S V

BARREL CACTUS SEED GOMASIO

Contributed by Barbara Rose, Bean Tree Farm

1 cup barrel cactus seeds

1/2 cup dulse, nori, or seaweed of your choice, flaked or chopped finely

1 teaspoon salt (or more, to taste)

Chiltepin to taste

Dried herbs (saltbush or Mexican oregano) to taste

Gomasio is a Japanese dry condiment usually made from unhulled sesame seeds and salt and used as a topping for many rice dishes. This version features seeds from a Sonoran Desert cactus in an easy and tasty blend.

Lightly roast barrel cactus seeds in a solar oven or stovetop skillet until they become fragrant. Add seaweed and salt and toast a bit more. Remove from heat, cool, and store in airtight container. Add chiltepin and dried herbs to gomasio and grind onto food before eating.

MAKES ABOUT 1 1/2 CUPS.

GF R V

SOOTHING BARREL CACTUS SEED BLEND

Contributed by Jill Lorenzini

Local seed/spice blends can be used as a condiment on almost any food and are an easy way to bring a little bit of the desert into every meal! This one is both soothing and nutritious.

In a spice grinder or mill, grind seeds into a powder to your desired coarseness. Sprinkle over salads or vegetable roasts or use as a rub. Store in jar in refrigerator.

EQUAL PARTS:

Amaranth seeds

Barrel cactus seeds

Chia seeds

Saguaro seeds

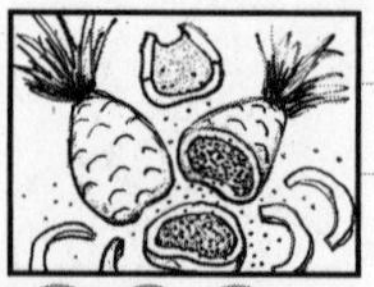

GF R V

DESERT WILD FOODS Barrel Cactus, Desert Herbs

HARVEST SEASON Fall | Winter

BARREL CACTUS SEASONING/RIM SALTS

Contributed by Barbara Rose, Bean Tree Farm

3 cups ripe fresh barrel cactus fruit, with or without seeds (dries to about 1 1/2 cups)

Salt to taste

Desert herbs such aloysia, lavender, or any chile powder, to your taste

Barrel cactus fruits, like other cacti, are hydrophilic, meaning they attract moisture. They taste very lemony and blend well with other flavors. This seasoning can be used on any dish or as coating on the rim of a glass holding your favorite cocktail!

Cut dried flower tops off barrel cactus fruits, far enough down to remove woody ends. Leave or remove seeds. Air-dry on a screen or in a basket covered with fabric until brittle. Grind to powder in a coffee grinder or similar processor. Add salt, herbs, and spices to taste and blend well. Store in airtight jar.

(GF) (S) (V)

BARREL CACTUS CHUTNEY

Contributed by Barbara Rose, Bean Tree Farm

This scrumptious condiment makes use of abundant, lemony-tart barrel cactus fruit and seeds, which are mingled with warming chutney spices. It makes a great side for curries, chèvre, or ice cream!

In a solar oven or stovetop pan, heat fruits and ginger in enough water to just cover, and simmer slowly for 1 hour or more until flavors and textures meld. Mixture should be thick and syrupy. Add chiles, seeds, spices, vinegar, sweetener, and salt to taste, and simmer again to blend flavors and thicken further. Put into sterilized jars. Let cool, then keep refrigerated.

MAKES ABOUT 8 CUPS.

8 cups cleaned barrel cactus fruit slices

1 1/2 cups raisins or chopped jujubes (a species of *Ziziphus* in the buckthorn family also called red dates or Chinese, Korean, or Indian dates)

1/2 cup fresh ginger, peeled and chopped fine

10 very hot chiles, chopped, or to taste

1/4 cup toasted barrel cactus seeds

1/4 cup ground spice mix: your choice cinnamon, cloves, allspice, mace, cardamom, black pepper, star anise, etc.

1/4 cup prickly pear vinegar or other vinegar

1 teaspoon stevia or other sweetener to taste

Salt to taste

GF V

GRAPEFRUIT BARREL CACTUS SEED DRESSING

Contributed by Iskashitaa Refugee Network

1 1/2 tablespoons dried desert barrel cactus seeds

1 cup gleaned grapefruit juice

1 cup olive oil (or an olive oil blend)

1 1/2 tablespoons local lemon juice

1 1/2 tablespoons Sonoran honey

Salt/pepper to taste

This tangy vinaigrette features the delicious tartness of local citrus with the desert crunch of barrel cactus seeds. An added bonus is that it stays emulsified once it is shaken and does not separate quickly into oil and water parts.

In a toaster oven, roast barrel cactus seeds at 400° F or toast in cast iron pan on stovetop over medium-high heat until fragrant. Combine seeds with all other ingredients in blender (or immersion blender). Adjust honey, lemon, or seed quantities to taste.

MAKES 2 CUPS.

GF V

BUTTERNUT-BARREL CACTUS RICE

Contributed by Jill Lorenzini

This rich winter dish will warm you up inside! Sweet winter squash is complemented by lemony-tart barrel fruit, and barrel seeds add a crunchy beautiful touch.

In a large cast iron skillet, sauté squash, barrel cactus fruit, onion, garlic, salt and pepper, and spices in olive oil until tender and caramelized. Remove 1 cup of the sautéed veggies and purée with 1/2 cup water in blender. Add this mixture and rest of water to rice and amaranth seeds. Cook until done. Combine rice and remainder of cooked squash mixture for risotto. Garnish with barrel cactus seeds. Serve with a salad and bread.

MAKES ABOUT 10 to 12 SERVINGS.

1 large butternut squash, peeled and cut into 1-inch cubes—approximately 3 to 4 cups (can substitute other winter squash like Magdalena Big Cheese, delicata, acorn, or red kuri)

20 barrel cactus fruit, seeded and sliced (reserve seeds)

1 large red onion, chopped

4 cloves garlic, minced

Salt and pepper to taste

1 teaspoon turmeric powder

1 teaspoon smoked paprika

1 teaspoon ginger powder

2 teaspoons dried desert lavender

4 tablespoons olive oil

3 1/2 cups water, divided

2 cups dry jasmine or basmati rice

2 tablespoons amaranth seeds

CANDIED BARREL CACTUS FRUIT SLICES

Contributed by Jill Lorenzini

20 ripe yellow barrel cactus fruits

1 cup organic raw cane sugar, more or less as needed

chiltepin, cayenne, or ginger powder to taste (optional)

Barrel cactus is one of my favorite wild foods because it brightens the winter season with its yellow, tart, tasty goodness. Barrel cactus fruit is also one of the easiest desert foods to harvest and use. These sweet-tart, crunchy-chewy slices are a decadent desert dessert and a perfect winter treat.

Preheat solar oven to 275º F. Rinse and dry ripe barrel cactus fruits. Slice off top of fruit below tough flower attachment, until seeds are visible. Remove white covering from bottom opening if still attached, using tweezers or small knife. Slice barrel fruit width-wise into 1/4-inch slices/rings. Try to keep seeds inside slices as much as possible. Sprinkle sugar evenly onto bottom of shallow glass baking dish. Arrange barrel slices flat and close together onto sugar in dish. Sprinkle remaining sugar on top of barrel slices. Add optional seasonings if desired. Bake until sugar dissolves, bubbles, and candies fruit, approximately 1 hour in winter sun. Check often and be careful not to overcook or burn. It may be helpful to slightly crack oven door open, to let moisture escape and to keep temperature moderate. Remove from oven and use a wooden or metal spatula to lift up individual barrel slices. Arrange in sealed containers and store in a cool place or in the fridge. Keeps well, if you don't eat them all at once!

NOTE: If using a conventional oven, put covered glass dish of sugared barrel fruit in oven and turn oven on to 300º F. Bake for 20 to 25 minutes, until fruit and sugar are bubbling.

MAKES ABOUT 3 CUPS.

MEET
NOPAL
AKA PRICKLY PEAR PAD

Opuntia spp.

O'odham: *I:ibhai naw*

Spanish: *nopal*

One of many signs of spring in the desert is when prickly pear cacti begin to sprout new pads, funded by winter rains and encouraged by longer, warmer days. "Nopales" in Spanish, these tender new pads emerge mostly from areoles on the top edges of existing prickly pear pads. New pads are shiny, bright green, and covered in succulent leafy appendages at each new areole. As the pad grows and matures, these appendages shrivel and fall off, and spines and glochids develop in their place.

Pads are edible when tender and young, before a tough inner network of fibrous tissue forms inside. Different species of prickly pear have varying numbers of spines and glochids. To reduce labor, choose species like Indian fig (*Opuntia ficus-indica*) that have the fewest or no spines and glochids. These species are the ones commonly found in southwestern grocery stores and are readily available at plant nurseries.

Harvest nopales with tongs, holding young pad at base and twisting or tipping to the side where it connects to mature pad below. Remove areoles with spines and glochids with a knife or vegetable peeler or carefully burn off over a flame then scrape clean. Don't forget the edges of the pad. Rinse, dry, and cut prepared pads into small pieces, known as nopalitos, for convenient storage or immediate use in recipes.

Nopales are excellent grilled, sautéed, or breaded and fried. They can also be pickled, dried, or marinated and slow-cooked into a jerky-like texture. They contain vitamin C and other nutritious and tonic components, and are valued as a prolific and accessible green vegetable in spring, before summer when heavy hitters like bean trees and saguaros offer their abundant harvests.

Like other cactus foods, nopales have a slimy, mucilaginous nature, which can be reduced by cooking. The sugars and other components that create this slimy characteristic are also what help regulate blood sugar and supply prolonged hydration in hot dry times.

- Jill Lorenzini

PRICKLY PEAR PAD/NOPAL BASICS

FLOWER BUD & BLOOM SEASON	SPRING	DRY SUMMER – April, May, June.
NOPAL HARVEST SEASON	SPRING – April, May
HARVESTING TIPS	Harvest tender green pads with tongs, then remove spines and glochid clusters before rinsing and preparing for use.
CAUTION	Prickly pear cactus contains oxalic acid, which requires processing or cooking to improve edibility, but the acid occurs in the least amounts in new pads.
NUTRITION	Vitamins A and C, calcium, fiber, magnesium, phosphorus.
PLANTING TIPS	Plant single pads and larger cuttings in dirt enough that at least some areoles are buried and can take root. Plant with summer rains, when plant is plump from moisture, in top or terrace zone of rain garden. If growing cacti in nursery pots, let soil dry out between each watering. Small pots and seed trays drain better than large pots. Prickly pear are heat, drought, and even cold tolerant.
OTHER USES	The mucilage may be used as an earthen or lime plaster additive, which adds water resistance to plaster. Spine-free prickly pear pads make nutritious and juicy animal fodder. Spines are used for tattooing.

Cutting off areoles/glochids from Opuntia ficus-indica *pad*

Photo: Brad Lancaster

Burning off glochids and soft spines from Opuntia ficus-indica *pad*

Photo: Brad Lancaster

NOPAL

Calabacitas con Nopalitos Fritos

Photo: Jill Lorenzini

Ⓥ

NOPALITO PAKORAS

Contributed by Kusuma Rao

DRY INGREDIENTS:

1/2 cup chickpea flour

1/2 cup of rice flour

1/2 teaspoon asafoetida

3/4 teaspoon turmeric

1 teaspoon cayenne powder

1 1/2 teaspoons cumin seeds

WET INGREDIENTS:

Oil for frying (preferably sunflower, grapeseed, or peanut oil)

3 jalapeños, cut into long strips

1/3 cup chopped cashews

3 medium nopales, spines removed, cut into 3- to 4-inch strips

20 curry leaves, chopped (optional)

2-inch piece of ginger, julienned

1 teaspoon salt

During the summer monsoons my father would always request something indulgent and deep-fried. While my mother insisted on cooking healthy meals throughout the year, she would make a special exception on a rainy monsoon day with a cup of masala chai and pakoras for the family. My recipe is a different take on her fritters, adding the comforting, earthy feel of nopales and a little crunch with nuts. The spices in this recipe take me back to relaxing Sundays with my parents. My addition of nopales in place of the traditional onions tugs at my desert heartstrings. It is one of my favorite uses of the nopal.

In a medium bowl, whisk dry ingredients until thoroughly combined. Heat oil in a frying pan (cast iron with high sides is best) to about 325° F. You will want at least 2 inches of oil in the pan. Have a pair of heatproof tongs or a spider strainer on hand ready to go.

PREP YOUR PAKORAS:

In a large bowl mix wet ingredients except the salt with your hands until thoroughly combined. Sprinkle the salt over the mixture. Mix with your hands again. Work quickly—the longer that salt has contact with the nopales, the more moisture pulls out of the pads. Add the dry ingredients to the vegetable mixture. Toss quickly until evenly coated.

FORM PAKORAS:

When your oil is to temperature, form pakoras by gathering with your hands about 1/4 to 1/3 cup of mixture. Clump together by squeezing gently with your hand to form ovoid shape. It's okay if there are nopales sticking out here and there. Drop into the oil 3 to 4 at a time. Fry until golden brown with a slightly reddish hue. Remove from the fryer and drain on a paper towel. Serve with a sweet and tart chutney.

MAKES 25 to 30 PAKORAS.

(GF) (S) (V)

NOPALITO JERKY

Contributed by Barbara Rose, Bean Tree Farm

This is a chewy, crunchy, smoky, spicy nopalito snack. It makes a great addition to trail mix, salad, stews, etc. If you burn the glochids off the small pads, the jerky will have a smoky flavor. If you do that over a mesquite wood fire, even sweeter!

Position solar oven or preheat conventional oven to 300° F. Clean pads by burning and/or scraping off spines and glochids, and remove perimeter edge/skin around pad. Slice pad crosswise into 1/4-inch slices. Toss in spice mixture. Spread thinly on cookie sheets. Slow-roast or solar-dry in your solar oven until chewy/crunchy (40 minutes, depending on temperature). Store in airtight containers. Great in a trail mix!

MAKES 2 to 3 CUPS.

4 to 5 young, tender nopales, about the size of your hand, cleaned

1/4 cup spice mixture: equal parts cumin, chile powder, coriander, garlic powder, oregano, and salt

GF

DESERT TEPARY BEAN SALAD WITH NOPALITOS

Contributed by Elizabeth Mikesell

1/2 cup finely chopped red onion

2 garlic cloves, minced

2 to 3 tablespoons Key lime juice and zest from 1 lime

1/3 cup sun-dried tomatoes, rehydrated in hot water, or 2 cups chopped fresh tomatoes

1 teaspoon dried or 2 tablespoons fresh oregano or oreganillo, chopped

1 tablespoon olive oil

1 1/2 to 2 cups cooked tepary beans

1 1/2 cups chopped lemon basil or cilantro

2 tablespoons thyme or lemon thyme

1 1/2 cups chopped, marinated, and grilled nopalitos

1 serrano chile, seeded and minced

Salt and fresh-ground pepper to taste

1/4 cup feta cheese

1/2 cup avocado, chopped

2 tablespoons pine nuts

*MARINADE:

1/4 cup lime juice

1 teaspoon garlic powder or 2 garlic cloves, minced

1 tablespoon olive oil

Sea salt and fresh-ground pepper to taste

Our arid desert offers up a plateful of nutritionally dense, palate-pleasing options. Different colors of tepary beans are always in my pantry and I use whatever I have on hand: white, brown, red, or a mix of all three. In springtime, tender young prickly pear pads are perfect for marinating or pickling to add interesting crunch to this salad. When summer arrives, the lemony-crunchy purslane takes the place of nopalitos. Herbs change seasonally too: cilantro in the cool season, basil in warm season.

Soak onions and garlic in lime juice. Toss tomatoes and herbs in oil. Toss together tepary beans, lime zest, basil or cilantro, thyme, nopalitos, chile, salt and pepper, onion/garlic mixture, and tomatoes; taste and adjust seasonings. Sprinkle with feta, avocado, and pine nuts. Splash lime juice over avocado and salad. Serve at room temperature or chilled.

*NOTE: For more flavor, marinate nopalitos 24 hours or more before grilling using this recipe.

VARIATION: Use 1 cup purslane for nopalitos.

MAKES 4 SERVINGS

GF V

NOPALITOS EN ESCABECHE

Contributed by Amy Valdés Schwemm, Mano y Metate

Escabeche is the Spanish word for "pickle," which is a wonderful way to eat nopalitos. Makes a wonderful garnish or side dish or you can put a whole pickled pad in a quesadilla!

Slice nopalitos or leave whole. Cook in boiling water for 5 minutes, or until drab green and tender. Drain and rinse. Place brine ingredients in a saucepan and bring to a boil. Turn off heat and add nopalitos, onion, carrot, and garlic. Let cool then eat or store in the refrigerator. If all pieces stay submerged in the brine, it will keep for quite a while.

A few pads of young nopales, cleaned

1 slice onion (optional)

1 carrot, sliced (optional)

2 cloves garlic, sliced

BRINE:

1 cup distilled vinegar

1 cup water

1/2 teaspoon salt

Oreganillo and/or Mexican oregano to taste

Chiltepin to taste

GF V

NOPALITOS PIPIÁN

Contributed by Amy Valdés Schwemm, Mano y Metate

1 tablespoon oil

1/2 tin Mano y Metate Mole (Pipián Rojo or Pipián Picante)*

1/2 cup broth, veggie or meat

2 pads nopales, cooked and sliced

Salt to taste

Many people tell me they don't like nopalitos, but then they are won over by this dish! It is one of my favorite ways to show off some of the mole powders I make, Pipián Rojo (mild) or Pipián Picante (medium spicy). The sauce improves the texture of the nopalitos (by hiding the slime many object to) and the nopalitos thicken the sauce nicely. Cholla buds also work well here, and you can substitute a good red chile sauce for the pipián.

In a saucepan, gently heat oil. Add mole powder, stirring to prevent scorching. When the paste is fragrant and a shade darker in color, add broth. Stir and simmer until the sauce thickens. Add nopalitos and simmer until heated, thinning the sauce with more broth if it becomes too thick. Salt to taste. Serve with hot tortillas, beans, and salad.

*NOTE: Mano y Metate Mole is a product of freshly ground whole spices, nuts, seeds, and chiles. It's an easy way to use the celebrated Mexican sauces. You can buy it locally in Tucson and Southern Arizona or order it online (ManoyMetate.com).

SERVES 2 to 4.

SOUTHWESTERN VEGETARIAN-SAUSAGE GUMBO

Contributed by Patty West

I worked for many years in a restaurant that made gumbo and came to enjoy the flavor combinations. This recipe takes advantage of the naturally mucilaginous nature of nopales in a mix of flavors from Louisiana, adapted to the desert.

Make a roux.*

On stovetop: In a frying pan, heat flour until it turns a golden brown and then add oil, stirring until blended.

In microwave: Mix flour and oil in a heat-resistant glass dish and heat 2 minutes at a time, stirring between heating. After about 10 times of this heating and stirring the mixture should turn the color of peanut butter. This is when it is ready.

Add 2 cups of broth to roux and stir until creamy and even. In a large pot, sauté onion, garlic, zucchini, celery, and dried spices in butter over medium heat. Once vegetables are soft, add the rest of the broth to the vegetables. In a separate skillet, sauté soy sausage; add canned and fresh tomatoes, Worcestershire sauce, rice, nopales, and hot sauce and cook for 10 minutes. Add sausage/tomato mixture and roux to vegetable pot and stir over medium-low heat. Serve hot and garnish with fresh herbs.

*NOTE: A roux is a mixture of butter (or oil) and flour, cooked until bubbly. It can be browned very deeply, then used as the basis for etouffe and brown sauce.

MAKES ABOUT 20 CUPS.

1 3/4 cups all-purpose flour

1 cup canola or peanut oil

10 cups vegetable broth (or bouillon)

2 onions, chopped

4 cloves garlic (chopped finely or pressed)

1 zucchini, chopped

3 stalks celery, chopped

1 teaspoon cinnamon

3 teaspoons oregano or oreganillo, dried

3 teaspoons basil, dried

Salt and pepper

4 tablespoons non-dairy butter or margarine

1 package soy sausage

1 can (28 ounces) of diced or crushed tomatoes

5 diced fresh tomatoes

4 tablespoons Worcestershire sauce (vegetarian)

4 cups cooked rice

2 to 3 cups diced cooked nopales

Hot sauce of your choice

1/3 cup fresh basil or cilantro (optional)

(GF) (V)

NOPALES CABBAGE SALAD WITH TAHINI DRESSING

Contributed by Rani Olson

SALAD:

4 cups cooked potatoes

4 cups cooked nopales

1/2 head purple cabbage, shredded fine

1/2 cup currants (or raisins)

1 crisp apple, chopped

1/2 cup toasted pepitas (or walnuts or sunflowers)

DRESSING:

1/4 cup tahini

Zest of 1 lemon

1/4 cup lemon juice

1/4 cup water

1/2 teaspoon salt

1 teaspoon cumin

1/8 teaspoon cayenne

1 teaspoon honey or sugar (optional)

Black pepper to taste

This delicious, nutritious salad celebrates the freshness of nopales in a tangy tahini backdrop with a good surprise of crunch and sweetness.

Bring two pots of water (with a little salt) to boil. Chop potatoes into 1- to 2-inch cubes and boil in one pot until tender and fully cooked, 15 to 30 minutes depending on the potato. Do not discard water when potatoes are done cooking. Keep the water boiling.

Meanwhile, remove spines from nopales. Rinse nopales to assure all spines are removed. Chop into 1-inch strips and then chop strips into 1/2-inch pieces. Put nopales into second pot of boiling water and boil for 5 to 6 minutes on a rolling boil. Remove and rinse to remove "babas" (slime). Discard this slimy water. Put once-boiled nopales into the pot of boiling potato water and boil for 5 to 6 minutes on a rolling boil. Remove, rinse, and put aside. Discard water.

With a whisk or blender combine dressing ingredients.

FOR A COLD SALAD: Combine all salad ingredients except pepitas. Toss salad with dressing and garnish with pepitas.

FOR A ROASTED SALAD: Roast shredded cabbage in the oven with a splash of olive oil for 15 minutes. Combine all salad ingredients except pepitas. Toss salad with dressing and garnish with pepitas.

MAKES 6 to 8 SERVINGS.

EASY NOPALITO SALSA

Reprinted with permission from Carolyn Neithammer's
The Prickly Pear Cookbook (Rio Nuevo Publishers, 2004)

This is a great recipe to introduce people to nopalitos. Starting with your favorite commercial salsa and canned beans lets you put this dish together in a hurry. Serve this salsa with chips or as a topping for chicken, fish, or grilled steak.

In a large skillet, heat oil on medium heat. Add nopalitos and sauté until they are slightly shriveled and turn olive green. In medium bowl, combine all other ingredients. Add nopalitos and stir.

MAKES ABOUT 1 1/2 CUPS.

1 tablespoon oil

1/2 cup cleaned prickly pear pads diced in 1/4-inch pieces

1/2 cup prepared or homemade salsa

1/2 cup canned black beans, rinsed and drained

1 tablespoon chopped fresh cilantro

1 tablespoon fresh lime juice

GF

CALABACITAS CON NOPALITOS FRITOS

Contributed by Jo Schneider, La Cocina Restaurant

I made this dish for a Desert Harvesters benefit at the restaurant. Someone brought me some freshly harvested local squashes so I thought of calabacitas and then added the fried nopalitos. I did them gluten-free with polenta, which gives them a really nice crunch! They can also garnish any salad or southwestern dish.

TO MAKE CALABACITAS:

1/4 cup olive oil

1 yellow onion, diced

1 cup corn

2 poblano peppers, diced

3 tomatoes, quartered

1/2 pound zucchini, sliced

1/2 pound yellow squash, sliced

2 garlic cloves, minced

Salt and pepper to taste

1 teaspoon oregano

1/3 cup of cotija cheese

1/4 cup Nopalitos Fritos

In a large skillet, heat oil on medium-high then add onion, corn, and poblanos. Stir occasionally and cook for 15 minutes or until the onion becomes translucent. Reduce heat to medium. Add tomatoes, zucchini, squash, garlic, salt and pepper, and oregano to the skillet and cook for 25 more minutes. Once all the vegetables are tender, remove from heat. Top with Cotija cheese and Fried Nopalitos.

TO MAKE NOPALITOS FRITOS:

2 nopales, cut into 1-inch squares

1 cup gluten-free flour

2 cups milk

2 cups dry polenta or cornmeal

1/2 cup canola oil

In medium bowl, dust the nopalitos with flour and let sit for 2 minutes. Shake off excess flour. Dip nopalitos in milk enough to wet them, then toss or roll in polenta or cornmeal. In a medium skillet, heat oil on medium-high heat. When oil is hot, fry battered nopalitos for 2 minutes. Flip and continue cooking for 2 more minutes. Remove with a slotted spoon and place on a dry paper towel to absorb excess oil. Use as a garnish or eat as a snack!

MAKES 4 to 6 SERVINGS.

MEET
CHOLLA

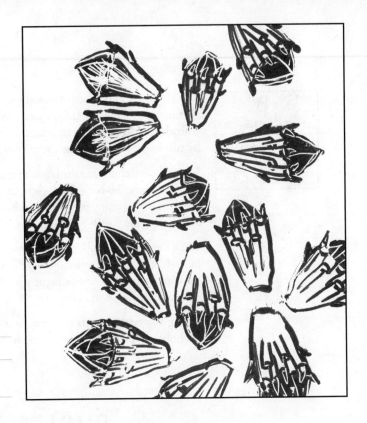

Cylindropuntia spp.

O'odham: *ciolim*

Spanish: *cholla, tasajo (buckhorn); siviri, clavellina (pencil)*

The largest cactus genus is Opuntia, which includes

cholla and prickly pear cactus. Whereas prickly pear grows flat roundish pad segments, cholla grows elongated cylindrical stem segments. Cholla vary in size, shape, and character: There are buckhorn, staghorn, pencil, cane, chain fruit, jumping, Christmas, diamond, teddy bear, and silver cholla, among others. They sure sound harmless, even fun. But watch out for the spines! Cholla spines are sheathed and barbed. Getting them out can hurt more than getting them in. Got tweezers? Don't leave home without 'em.

Cholla cacti are one of the most widespread and successful cacti and epitomize the juicy succulence of the warm Sonoran Desert, sometimes called a lush or dry-tropical desert. Cholla spread by dropping their segments or when segments get stuck to hides of animals and are transported to a new location. Also, during rainy seasons in summer and winter, when the soil gets saturated and cholla swells with rain and weight, whole sections break off and fall. What appears to damage the cactus actually benefits it: Anyplace cactus segment areoles touch the ground they can sprout roots and re-establish. In this way, cacti move!

One of the first foods available in early spring, cholla is valued for its tasty and nutritious flower buds. Cholla bursts out with plentiful buds and new segment growth starting in early March and continuing progressively into April and May, and even June, July, and August, depending on the species. Cholla sometimes blooms a second time in late summer if rains are plentiful and well timed. Once open, cholla flowers display a huge spectrum of colors, from yellow, pink, maroon, and magenta to green, bronze, cream, orange, and more.

The trick to harvesting the edible parts of cholla cacti is to find flower buds that have not yet opened. Harvesting is most easily done on cholla varieties with the least number of spines and glochids, the largest buds, and the most plentiful number of buds per plant. Staghorn (*Opuntia versicolor*), buckhorn (*Cylindopuntia acanthocarpa*), and pencil cholla (*Cylindropuntia ramosissima* and *Cylindropuntia arbuscula*) are favored species for edibility and ease of harvest.

Tongs, gloves, and other cleaning tools help speed up the harvest and make it less spiny. Remove spines and glochids from cholla buds before picking by using a stiff brush, a sprig from a nearby plant, or tweezers. Spines can also be removed after harvesting by burning them off or by rubbing cholla buds on a screen or in sandy dirt.

Cleaned cholla buds require blanching in boiling water before freezing or thoroughly drying for later use. Buds may also be pickled after blanching as a way to store and transform flavors. Rehydrate dried buds by soaking in water until buds plump to original size. Thaw frozen buds. Cook fresh buds in boiling water for 10 to 20 minutes. To reconstitute dried buds, cook for 45 minutes to two hours.

Cholla buds taste similar to artichoke, another unopened flower bud that we eat. But cholla buds, like many cactus foods, have a somewhat slimy texture component. They are desert substitutes for okra or asparagus tips. Pickle, sauté, or roast them, or add them to stews, soups, salsas, casseroles, nori rolls, and pizza.

Eating flowers and buds is a treat in itself, but eating the flower buds of a cactus as formidable as cholla is a peak culinary experience!

- Jill Lorenzini

CHOLLA BASICS

FLOWER BUD & BLOOM SEASON	SPRING I DRY SUMMER I WET SUMMER – March through August.
PARTS USED	Flower buds.
HARVESTING TIPS	Easiest to harvest from cholla species with the least number of spines, such as staghorn, buckhorn, and pencil cholla. Make a small stiff "paintbrush" from yucca fibers, a creosote branch, or sticky-leafed triangle-leaf bursage and brush spines off bud while it is still attached to the cactus. Use long tongs to remove the "clean" bud with a quick twist.
CAUTION	Spines!
PREPARATION/ STORAGE	After spines are removed, buds can be boiled for 10 to 20 minutes before freezing or drying. A solar oven works well for drying, with door left open a bit to vent released moisture and moderate temperature. Remember to only dry buds, not cook them. Buds can also be dried on a screen out in the open in direct sun. If fully dry when jarred, buds keep well for a long time. Frozen buds last for at least a year.
NUTRITION	Rich in calcium and magnesium, and other nutrients and slimy mucilaginous polysaccharides that help regulate and stabilize blood sugar levels.
PLANTING TIPS	Best to grow from cuttings, as it is much easier and quicker than growing from seed. Plant with summer rains, when plant is plump from moisture, in terrace or top zone of rain garden. Note: If growing cacti in nursery pots, let soil dry out between each watering. Small pots and seed trays drain better than large pots.

REVIVING TRADITIONS: TERROL DEW JOHNSON AND TOHONO O'ODHAM COMMUNITY ACTION (TOCA)

by Brad Lancaster

Wheat flour makes me sick! I think it has no strength. But when I am weak, when I am tired, my grandchildren make me gruel out of the wild seeds. That is food.

- Maria Chona, from Ruth Underhill's *The Autobiography of a Papago Woman* (1936)

Small actions can grow great things. This is what Terrol Dew Johnson, a young renowned basket weaver, and his artistic friends discovered in 1996 when they pooled their passions and community along with a $2,000 grant to create a summer program for Tohono O'odham youth on the reservation west of Tucson.

Each week Terrol and other artists introduced young people to a new art form—basketry, photography, or painting. Food was integrated with the programming, as grandmas and mothers volunteered to cook. Kids helped elders with the food prep, learning to harvest from gardens and surrounding wild food plants, such as sweet pods from the mesquite and nutty acorns from the Emory oaks.

The program became Tohono O'odham Community Action (TOCA), a non-profit organization dedicated to creating a healthy, culturally vital, and sustainable community on the Tohono O'odham Nation through food systems, wellness programs, and cultural revitalization.

TOCA's co-founder and director, Terrol holds no formal degree. Rather, his community has been his university and his library. Many of his early lessons came from his grandfather, a healer, and his grandmother, an herbalist, who showed him that people could heal with what grew around them. "They taught me that if you see a need, you just do it," he said.

Terrol Dew Johnson

Photo courtesy of TOCA

This concept became one of TOCA's principles for enhancing community assets: "See our resources, not just our needs."

TOCA helps reinforce traditional methods of harvesting, hunting, and cooking of seasonal foods by providing transportation so students and teachers can travel across several districts of the Tohono O'odham Nation to exchange knowledge. Elders are able to bring monthly demonstrations and tastings of wild and traditional domesticated foods to children from kindergarten to high school.

"Singing traditional songs, sharing traditional foods, or harvesting those foods with kindergartners leads to a growing pride, desire to learn, and willingness to share," Terrol said.

Today, schoolchildren are harvesting healthy foods from school gardens on the reservation, and full-time cultural teachers (some of them alumni of TOCA's programs), are helping to incorporate wild food harvests into the school curricula. "Young people—all people—want to feel connected to something," Terrol said.

As the teachings spread, students have become hungry for traditional foods like tepary bean quesadillas and tepary bean chile stew, preferring them to school cafeteria pizza, Terrol said.

This is significant given the high rates of diabetes among O'odham people. According to TOCA, 76 percent of O'odham sixth, seventh, and eighth graders are overweight or obese due to the consumption of highly processed (junk) foods. Such conditions make these young people more susceptible to diabetes, Terrol said.

But research has found that native foods such as tepary beans, mesquite pods, acorns, and cholla buds can help regulate blood sugar and significantly reduce both the incidence and effects of diabetes.

On a larger scale, TOCA also grows traditional foods on Terrol's grandfather's traditional farm, bringing back passively harvested rainwater and runoff to irrigate. These methods enabled the O'odham to turn the tepary bean into the world's most drought-tolerant domesticated bean—a wonderful example of fitting the crop to the land, rather than fitting the land to the crop.

To share the tastes and nutrients of traditional foods with the public, TOCA began a catering service and sold prepared foods at the Desert Rain Café in Sells, Arizona. Up to 75 percent of the ingredients come from tribal farms and wild food foraging, and each dish contains at least one traditional food, Terrol said.

Cholla Bud Pico de Gallo (p. 230), for example, is made from the de-spined flower buds of the cholla cactus. The buds are harvested by community members, and each year the café buys up to $30,000 worth for its own dishes and to sell to other restaurants.

In addition to providing business opportunities for tribal members, the café also re-introduces foods that were once common on family tables, but have dropped out of custom, such as wild spinach.

TOCA educates through its publications as well. The book *From I'itoi's Garden: Tohono O'odham Food Traditions* shares stories and photos on how to harvest, process, and cook many traditional O'odham wild and domesticated foods in both traditional and modern settings. Its magazine, *Native Foodways*, spotlights stories about people who are reviving, continuing, and evolving their food, artistic, and storytelling traditions.

Terrol said sharing with youth and fellow members of the Nation in this way strengthens cultural pride. "The resources and connections of others are added to ours, and ours to them. More people get interested, and the circle grows."

NOTE: The Desert Rain Café in Sells closed its doors in April 2017. At the time of this book's publication, TOCA was seeking a new location for the café in Tucson, Arizona.

Learn more about Terrol Dew Johnson and the work of TOCA at TOCAonline.org.

CHOLLA

Vegetable and Cholla Bud Skewers

Photo: Christian Timmerman

GF V

CHOLLA BUD PICO DE GALLO

Reproduced with permission from *From I'itoi's Garden: Tohono O'odham Food Traditions*
by Tohono O'odham Community Action (TOCA) with Mary Paganelli Votto and Frances Manuel

1/2 cup dried cholla buds

1/4 cup minced red onions

1/4 cup minced red bell peppers

1/3 cup diced tomatoes

2 tablespoons fresh chopped cilantro

2 tablespoons lime juice

2 teaspoons minced jalapeño peppers

1 teaspoon sea salt

This delicious and colorful salad is full of flavor and crunch and a favorite dish at TOCA's wonderful Desert Rain Café.

In a large saucepan bring dried cholla buds in water to a boil. Reduce heat to a simmer and simmer until buds are soft (about 1 1/2 to 2 hours). Drain cholla buds, chill, and chop. Combine all remaining ingredients with chopped cholla buds and toss together.

MAKES ABOUT 2 CUPS.

(GF) (V)

CHOLLA PICKLES

Reprinted with permission from Carolyn Niethammer's
The Tumbleweed Gourmet: Cooking with Wild Southwestern Plants (University of Arizona Press, 1987)

Cholla pickles are a great way to enjoy these little desert nubs of nutrition. If you use cholla buds that have been fully dried and then soaked and cooked, there will be no gumminess in the buds. You can also use fresh buds that have been cooked and partially dried.

Sterilize a half-pint jar and lid by boiling for 15 minutes. Freshen dried cholla buds by soaking for at least 3 hours and then boiling for 30 minutes. Drain. If using cleaned fresh cholla buds, boil for 20 minutes then partially dry in the sun for a couple of hours until lightly shriveled. Pack hot cholla buds in prepared jar with the peeled garlic clove and the chile. Heat the vinegar with the sugar or honey and cloves until the sugar or honey is completely dissolved. Fill the jar with the liquid and cover with the lid. Cool, then store in refrigerator at least 1 week before eating.

1 cup dried and freshened cholla buds or fresh buds

1 clove fresh garlic

1 small red chile

1/2 cup vinegar

1 tablespoon sugar or honey

3 or 4 whole cloves

MAKES ABOUT 1 CUP.

GF V

VEGETABLE AND CHOLLA BUD SKEWERS

Contributed by Wendy Garcia, Tumerico

3 ounces of cleaned, dried cholla buds

8 wooden or bamboo skewers, soaked in water for 10 minutes

1 zucchini cut into 1-inch slices

2 yellow squash, cut into 1-inch slices

1/4 pound whole, fresh mushrooms

1 cup olive oil

3 tablespoons lime juice

1/2 teaspoon salt

1/8 teaspoon ground black pepper

3/4 cup chopped fresh cilantro

These fun springtime skewers are a great way to celebrate the tasty and nutritious cholla bud. Lots of flexibility in this recipe as you can skewer lots of vegetables of your choice!

Cover the cholla buds in water and soak for 12 hours before assembling.

When ready to cook, preheat oven to 350º F and soak skewers for 10 minutes. On soaked wooden skewers, alternately thread cholla buds, zucchini slices, yellow squash slices, and whole mushrooms. Place skewers on greased pans. Whisk together olive oil, lime juice, salt, and black pepper. Brush mixture over vegetable skewers, reserving some to drizzle over cooked skewers when they are ready to serve. Bake skewers on center oven rack for 10 minutes. Turn and bake for 10 minutes more. Remove skewers from the oven and let sit a few minutes. Drizzle with reserved marinade and sprinkle with fresh, chopped cilantro. Serve warm or cold.

MAKES 8 SKEWERS.

CHOLLA BUD SALAD

Contributed by Janos Wilder, Downtown Kitchen+Cocktails

This recipe from one of Tucson's favorite chefs features a creative combination of spicy, sweet, and citrus with the delicious texture of cholla buds. Well worth the harvesting effort!

Either fresh or reconstituted cholla buds work well here. Their artichoke-heart-like flavor lends them to many dishes from stews to salads, sautéed or simply pickled. This recipe combines them with some other ingredients from the region. Verdolagas are a nutritions, fresh, wild salsa green; citrus is one of the modern staples hereabouts; queso fresco, available in most grocery stores, is a simple and mild white cow's milk cheese. Pumpkin seeds add great crunch to the salad. As an alternative, seed savers might want to toast up seeds from other calabazas they have harvested in the fall. Barely blanched green beans add a snap to the salad and the mushrooms a luxuriousness and texture, which mimics that of the cholla buds. Jalapeño orange vinaigrette provides a bit of acidic bite and heat while the orange supremes and sweetness add a pop of contrasting and reinforcing flavor.

Place the cholla buds and water into a 6-quart pressure cooker over high heat until regulator starts to rock. Adjust heat down so that regulator rocks evenly and gently. Cook 20 minutes then remove from heat; cool until air vent/cover lock has dropped. Remove and drain the cholla buds. Reserve for a multiple of other recipes. To store for a longer period of time, pickle the cholla buds.

TO PREPARE SALAD:

In a large bowl, gently mix prepared cholla buds, green beans, mushrooms, and verdolagas together. Season with salt and pepper. Toss in the jalapeño orange vinaigrette (directions below) and garnish with the pumpkin seeds, queso fresco, and orange supremes.

JALAPEÑO ORANGE VINAIGRETTE:

In a blender puree the jalapeño, scallions, garlic, cilantro, and orange juice concentrate. With the motor running whip in the olive oil in a slow steady stream. Adjust seasoning with salt and very finely ground pepper.

MAKES 4 SERVINGS.

TO PREPARE CHOLLA BUDS:

1 1/2 cups dried cholla buds

12 cups water

TO PREPARE SALSA:

1 cup fresh or reconstituted cholla buds

1 cup fresh, tender, blanched, trimmed green beans bias-cut into 1/3-inch pieces

1 cup sliced mushrooms

3/4 cup fresh, raw verdologas (purslane), picked over

Salt and pepper, divided

1 jalapeño, seeded and chopped

1/3 cup scallions, chopped

1/2 teaspoon fresh crushed garlic

1/2 bunch cilantro

1/4 cup orange juice concentrate

3/4 cup olive oil

1/4 cup toasted pumpkin seeds

1/2 cup queso fresco, crumbled

1/2 cup orange supremes

GF

CHOLLA BUD FENNEL PEAR SALAD

Contributed by Ian Fritz

1 cup cholla buds

1 medium fennel bulb

1 medium Asian pear, chilled

5 cups young arugula

1/3 cup grated Parmesan or other hard cheese

Olive oil

Sherry vinegar

Sea salt to taste

This simple salad combines the earthy flavor of cholla with the sweetness of pear. It's a great springtime Sonoran Desert complement to Cholla Bud Bisque (p. 235).

De-spine and blanch cholla buds for 60 seconds and drain. Trim the fennel bulb, quarter it lengthwise, and slice it into paper thin slivers. Quarter and core the Asian pears and cut them into thin slices. Combine all ingredients and toss with oil and vinegar and salt to taste.

MAKES 4 to 6 SERVINGS.

GF

CHOLLA BUD BISQUE

Contributed by Ian Fritz

This soup is ripe with delicious complementary flavors and full of springtime zest against the delicious asparagus-like flavor of cholla. It's especially good if you make your own vegetable stock.

De-spine and blanch fresh cholla buds for 60 seconds and drain. In a large skillet or soup pan, melt butter and cook the leeks over medium heat for 8 to 10 minutes until soft. Add cholla buds, fennel, lemon zest, rice, salt, and 3 cups of water. Bring to a boil then lower heat and simmer for half an hour or until all vegetables are tender. Add 2 cups of vegetable broth, dill, and a pinch of pepper and cayenne to taste. Puree the soup in a blender in batches or using an immersion blender. Stir in lemon juice. Add salt and pepper as needed. Add cream if you wish.

MAKES 5 to 6 CUPS.

1 1/4 pounds (about 3 cups) cholla buds, fresh

2 tablespoons butter

2 medium leeks, chopped

1 large fennel bulb, chopped

Zest and juice of 1 lemon

3 tablespoons Arborio rice

1 1/2 teaspoons sea salt

2 to 2 1/2 cups vegetable broth

1/2 cup fresh dill, finely chopped

White pepper to taste

Cayenne to taste

2 to 3 tablespoons heavy cream (optional)

GF S

SOLAR POLENTA PIZZA

Reprinted with permission from Barbara Rose and Jill Lorenzini's *Wild Recipes: Seasonal Samplings* (2008)

This is a simple and hearty wheat-free alternative to traditional pizza. Desert toppings make it visually unique and super tasty.

POLENTA:

2 cups polenta (replace 1/2 cup polenta with mesquite flour if you want a sweeter taste)

6 to 8 cups salted water or broth

1/4 to 1/2 cup butter, oil, grated cheese, or combination

Herbs and spices as desired

ASSORTED TOPPINGS:

• Tomato sauce

• Sky Island Pesto (p. 289)

• Cheese of your choice.

• Desert foods such as halved cholla buds, sautéed nopalitos and onions, wolfberries, bean tree sprouts, etc.

• Grilled veggies

• Bacon

• Hard-boiled egg, sliced

Cook polenta in water in solar oven about 1 hour or until thick, or stir on stovetop for about 45 minutes until soft and thick. Stir in butter, oil, or grated cheese and herbs if desired. Remove from heat before polenta begins to firm, and spread about 1/2 inch thick in 1-inch deep pans. Let cool. Any extra polenta can be shaped, sliced, and fried for another meal.

Top polenta with tomato sauce and/or Sky Island Pesto and sprinkle with cheese. Then add your choice of seasonal desert and other ingredients and toppings. Be creative! Drizzle with oil before baking/browning in a hot solar oven, or broiling in a regular oven until cheese is melted and toppings sizzle. Remove immediately. Serve warm or at room temperature. You'll need a knife and fork to eat this pizza.

MAKES TWO 11- x 9-INCH POLENTA PIZZAS

GF

CHOLLA-CHILAQUILE BREAKFAST BAKE

Contributed by Jill Lorenzini

This hearty breakfast (or brunch) gets you off to a solid start, starring calcium-rich cholla buds and some familiar Southwest flavors in garlic, green chiles, coriander, and cilantro.

Preheat oven to 350º F. In a large skillet, heat half the oil, then lightly cook both sides of each tortilla. Set aside to drain on paper towel. Heat rest of oil in skillet and sauté onion, garlic, and salt and pepper until soft. Add cholla buds, 2 chopped green chiles, and ground coriander. Simmer 5 more minutes. To assemble chilaquiles, lay a few tortillas in bottom of a greased 11- x 17-inch glass baking/roasting/casserole pan. Spoon cholla bud/onion mixture over that. Add cheese layer. Repeat layers until all ingredients are used. End with a cheese layer and arrange long strips of green chile over top. Carefully pour beaten egg into dish (best to pour slowly in a corner of pan so as not to upturn layers). Bake 20 to 30 minutes, until egg is cooked through. Test with toothpick. Serve hot or warm with salsa and avocado.

MAKES ABOUT 12 SERVINGS.

3 tablespoons oil

12 medium corn tortillas

1 large onion, chopped

4 cloves garlic, sliced

Salt and pepper to taste

8 ounces blanched or rehydrated cholla buds

3 green chiles, roasted, seeded, peeled; 2 chopped, 1 cut into long strips

1 cup cheese (cheddar, pepper jack, etc.), grated

3 eggs, beaten

Salsa

Avocado

1 teaspoon ground coriander

(GF) (R) (V)

SALT-CURED CHOLLA BUDS

Contributed by Jill Lorenzini

2 cups fresh or blanched cholla buds, spines and glochids thoroughly removed

2 to 3 cups coarse sea salt

Using salt to dry-cure olives inspired this recipe for preserving cholla buds after the harvest. Salt draws moisture out and imparts flavor into the buds for a unique treat. After curing, cholla buds can be stored, pickled, marinated, or used in your favorite or new dishes.

Thinly cover the bottom of a 9-inch glass pie plate with salt (about 1/8 inch thick). Place cholla buds close together on plate then cover with remaining salt. Set in a cool, dry place to cure for 2 to 3 days. Test after 1, 2, and 3 days to check progress. Buds will shrink to about half their size when completely cured and be dry but chewy. They can also be stored in salt until needed.

MAKES 2 CUPS.

MEET
DESERT CHIA

Salvia columbariae

O'odham: *da:pk*

Spanish: *chia, salvia*

Early spring comes in February in the Sonoran Desert as
warmer temperatures and lengthening days stir seeds to germinate and begin their annual cycles of growth. One of these seeds is desert chia. Chia's beautifully textured and fragrant leaves grow close to the ground along sandy bajadas and wash margins, where seeds from previous seasons were scattered from wind-blown seedheads.

In March and April, chia sends up a singular flower stalk along which flowers grow in ring-like clusters. The tiny, blue-purple flowers are exquisitely beautiful and quite tasty for their size. Each pollinated flower produces a tiny chia seed, which ripens fully in May and June to a gray or brownish color. The whole plant dies back when the growth cycle is complete. The flower cluster dries, seed pods open, and wind and animals disperse the plant's seeds. They lie dormant through the heat of summer and the cold and waning light of fall and winter. After ample winter rain, spring arrives and the cycle resumes.

Chia has been a prized food source for thousands of years. It was sacred to ancient Aztec, Incan, Toltec, Mayan, and other cultures, cultivated it widely and valued it as an energy source, a hydration helper, a ceremonial seed, an item of tribute and exchange, and a powerful plant ally. In the Mayan language, chia means strength. In the desert Southwest, the Tohono O'odham and others have used desert chia for food and medicine, relying on its hydrating qualities through dry, hot seasons.

Chia seeds are hygroscopic: When put in water, they swell up and a layer of mucilage builds up around the seed. This gives the seeds super-hydrating and super-food qualities. Chia contains loads of iron, fiber, oil, calcium, protein, omega-3s, and antioxidants too!

- Jill Lorenzini

DESERT CHIA BASICS

FLOWER BUD & BLOOM SEASON	SPRING – February through April.
FRUIT/SEED HARVEST SEASON	SPRING | DRY SUMMER – March through June.
PARTS USED	Seeds, flowers, sprouts.
HARVESTING TIPS	Desert Chia seedpods clusters are a bit prickly so use the sturdy stem to harvest and tap when collecting seedheads and seeds. Ripe, dry seeds are super tiny and may stick to moist hands so harvest into a small bowl or onto a folded piece of paper that then can double as a funnel for pouring seeds into a storage jar. Pick tiny flowers carefully and use them as a dainty garnish or snack.
BEST HARVESTING PRACTICES	Note locations of vigorous chia plant growth in late winter to early spring and return to patches when they are flowering and setting seed.
CAUTION	Only sprout chia seeds on non-toxic, food-grade surfaces such as glass, dinner plates, or terra cotta foodware. Avoid terra cotta chia pets or flower pots that are not food-grade certified.
NUTRITION	Packed with protein, oils, fiber, calcium, and other nutrients, chia is a super-food, and a super-hydration food as well. Like several other desert foods, the mucilage it produces slows digestion and absorption of starches in the body, thereby stabilizing blood sugar levels and providing other health benefits.
PLANTING TIPS	Plant in loose sandy soils that receive ample moisture but drain well.
OTHER USES	Body care products. Medicinal.

DESERT CHIA

Prickly Pear Chia Gel-O

GF R V

DESERT CHIA SPROUTS

Contributed by Jill Lorenzini

2 to 3 tablespoons desert chia seeds

Purified water

These fresh sprouts are easy to make and give you a nutritious living part of the desert to eat. Unlike other sprouted seeds that you just rinse and drain, chia seeds have to be consistently hydrated in order to sprout. This is how the famous Chia Pet works. Water seeps through the porous clay of the animal-shaped pot and keeps the chia seeds consistently moist. When the seeds sprout, the animal grows its "fur." This method also illustrates the time-tested use of garden ollas, a water-holding clay reservoir used as an efficient, slow-watering tool. Sprouting seeds for eating in a Chia Pet, however, is NOT recommended, because the container is not food-grade. I use a food-grade terra cotta saucer and a pie dish, or a glass plate and a wet, cotton bandana.

TERRA COTTA SAUCER METHOD:

In a small bowl, mix chia seeds with just enough water to cover. Let sit 5 minutes. Fill a pie plate half full of water. Spread soaked chia seeds evenly in the bottom of a terra cotta saucer. Place the terra cotta saucer in the pie plate. Pour enough water into pie plate to reach just below rim of the clay saucer. Cover pie plate to hold in moisture. Check regularly and add water as needed until seeds sprout and grow. Using a spray bottle, mist sprouts to moisten as needed during growth days.

GLASS PLATE METHOD:

Moisten a cotton bandana and fold it to fit on a glass dinner plate. Sprinkle chia seeds evenly over the bandana. Cover with another plate. Using a spray bottle, mist bandana and seeds to moisten as needed during the 3 to 4 days it takes for seeds to sprout and grow.

When spouts grow stems and green leaves, harvest them by trimming them off with scissors. Serve on salads, sandwiches, and burritos, or use as a garnish.

(GF) (R) (V)

SPICY CHIA SEED BLEND

Contributed by Jill Lorenzini

Local seed/spice blends can be used as a condiment on almost any food and are an easy way to bring a little bit of the desert into every meal! This one is both spicy and nutritious.

In a spice grinder or mill, grind seeds into a powder to your desired coarseness. Sprinkle blend over salads or vegetable roasts or use as a rub. Store in jar in refrigerator.

EQUAL PARTS:

Barrel cactus seeds

Desert chia seeds

Wild mustard seeds
(or greens, dried)

Chiltepin to taste

(GF) (R) (V)

HYDRATING CITRUS-CHIA SUMMER SALSA

Contributed by Barbara Rose, Bean Tree Farm

2 to 3 cups assorted sectioned citrus with juice (pith and section fiber removed, to taste)

1/4 cup chia seed, more as needed

1 cup kombucha or prickly-pear vinegar

1 cup chopped onion (I'itoi's, red, white, green, or combination)

1 cup cilantro or a mix of preferred wild greens, mint, herbs, chopped

1/4 cup chopped fresh garlic and fresh ginger mix, to taste

1/4 cup barrel cactus seeds

Salt and pepper, to taste

Chiltepines (fresh or dried) OR hot red and green chiles, chopped, to taste

This recipe acknowledges the sweet, sour, spicy, salty, and saucy qualities of salsa, but substitutes Arizona citrus for tomatoes and adds the nutritious desert chia and barrel cactus seeds, along with chiltepin fire. Great for pairing with chips, guacamole, or to top off your topopo! Make it as chunky, smooth, or soupy as you like.

Over a large bowl, remove pith and section fiber from citrus. Chop citrus into bite-sized pieces and add to citrus juice. Soak chia in kombucha or vinegar to soften. Lightly pre-salt chopped onion if strong-flavored. In large bowl, combine all ingredients and let mingle for 15 to 30 minutes. Adjust seasoning and serve or store in fridge. Addition of probiotic kombucha means salsa will keep longer than you expect, and improve with age… if it lasts that long!

MAKES ABOUT 5 CUPS.

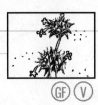

GF V

ALEGRIA AMARANTH BARS

Contributed by Jill Lorenzin. Adapted from Wayne Coates's
Chia: The Complete Guide to the Ultimate Superfood (Sterling, 2012).

These ancient popped amaranth candy bars are popular in Mexico and Central America. Adding chia gives them a special desert crunch!

Preheat skillet over high heat. Add amaranth seeds, 1 tablespoon at a time, and heat until they pop. Transfer seeds to a bowl. Lightly toast chia seeds in skillet. Transfer to bowl. Coat 9- x 11-inch baking pan with oil. In saucepan, combine oil, honey, molasses, salt, and vanilla and heat over high heat until just boiling. Reduce to medium heat and stir constantly for another 10 minutes or until mixture thickens. Remove from heat and stir in seeds. Spread firmly and evenly into pan(s). Cool thoroughly and cut into bars.

MAKES 24 BARS.

6 tablespoons amaranth seeds

1/4 cup chia seeds

1/4 cup coconut or olive oil, plus more for greasing pan

1/4 cup honey, flavored agave, prickly pear, or mesquite syrup

1/4 cup molasses

1/2 teaspoon vanilla

Salt to taste

(GF) (R) (V)

DESERT CHIA PUDDING

Contributed by Jill Lorenzini

1 1/2 cups pourable coconut milk

Dash of salt and cinnamon

Fresh grated ginger, to taste

3 tablespoons chia seeds

ADD-INS (YOUR CHOICE):

• 1 teaspoon barrel cactus seeds

• 1 teaspoon saguaro seeds

• 1 tablespoon sunflower seeds

• 2 tablespoons wolfberry, hackberry, golden raisins, or currants

How can something so simple taste soooo great? Rich, oily coconut milk plumps chia seeds, fruit, and other seeds in this recipe, for a filling and nutritious breakfast, snack, or fancy dessert.

Pour coconut milk into a small bowl. Add salt and spices and mix well. Add chia, all other seeds, and fruit. Stir well. Allow pudding to sit for 15 to 20 minutes until it thickens. Cover and refrigerate, or serve and eat. Great warmed, too.

MAKES 3 SERVINGS.

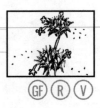

GF R V

CHIA AGUAS FRESCAS

Contributed by Rachel Morningstar

This refreshing agua fresca features hydrating chia seeds to help keep you energized. Chia balances blood sugar and provides sustained energy.

Mix all ingredients in a pitcher. Wait a few minutes then mix again. Serve over ice.

1/4 cup fresh lemon or lime juice

1/4 cup agave nectar

1/4 cup chia seeds

10 cups water

MAKES 5 SERVINGS.

(GF) (R) (V)

PRICKLY PEAR CHIA GEL-O

Contributed by Jill Lorenzini

8 ounces prickly pear fruit juice concentrate

2 tablespoons raw agave syrup (or more)

4 to 6 tablespoons chia seeds

Barrel cactus seeds to garnish

This colorful snack or light dessert is loaded with crunch and nutrition and helps keep the body hydrated in hot, dry summer conditions.

In a medium bowl, mix prickly pear juice and agave syrup. Add chia seeds to thickness desired. Divide mixture into 4 small glasses or wine glasses (about 2 ounces per glass). Refrigerate at least 30 minutes or until chia seeds absorb liquid and create a gel. Soaking for 2 to 3 hours or even overnight will result in a thicker gel. Garnish with crunchy barrel cactus seeds.

MAKES 4 SERVINGS.

MEET
PALO VERDE

Parkinsonia spp.

O'odham: blue: *ko' okma ki*; foothills: *kuk chehedagi*

Spanish: *palo verde, medezá, dipúa*

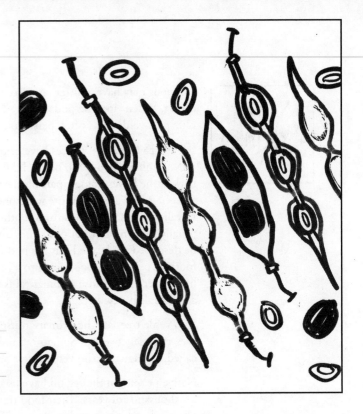

Two native species of palo verde tree grow in the Sonoran Desert: blue palo verde (*Parkinsonia florida*) and foothills or littleleaf palo verde (*Parkinsonia microphylla*). These desert legume trees are valued for their drought tolerance and for their striking green bark. Their cheerful yellow flowers bloom profusely from mid-April through May, and can be seen for miles! Blue palo verde blooms first, followed shortly thereafter by foothills palo verde. The flowers are edible. They have a fresh pea-like flavor and add seasonal tastiness to an early summer hike, or local color and flavor to your favorite springtime recipes and beverages.

Green seeds develop inside pods from around mid-May into June after bees, birds, and flies pollinate flowers. When green pods swell, you can pick and snack on the fresh bright green seeds inside. Or harvest a bunch for the larder or freezer. Blanch seeds still in the pod to keep them green, then cool them in cold water, remove seeds from pods, compost the pods, and eat the seeds or freeze them for later. You can also remove the seeds first, then blanch them, thoroughly dry them, and store for later use. Rehydrate them, cook them, or grind them into flour.

If you miss the flowering or green seed stage, don't fret. You can also harvest ripe, dry, dark brown seeds off the trees before the winds and rains of summer seasonal storms do. Separate seeds from pods, and freeze or toast them to reduce insect damage before storing.

Dry, ripe seeds may be soaked and sprouted, just like alfalfa or other seeds. After palo verde seeds swell up with soak water and seed coats crack open, squeeze seeds out of seed coat and compost seed coats. Use buttery-sweet sprouted seeds raw or cooked.

BLUE PALO VERDE trees have blueish-green bark, as the namesake describes, with small curved spines along the branches. Older trees may develop grayish, textured bark at the lowest, oldest part of their trunks. They are less widespread than foothills palo verde and prefer wash margins and warm, frost-free locations. Seedpods from blue palo verde are broad and flat, usually holding two to three flat, lima-bean-like seeds that are bright green and shiny. When green,

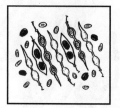

seedpods may have a bitter taste, so wash your hands after picking and shelling, and before eating. When ripe, the pods change from green to straw-colored. Lucky for harvesters, mature blue palo verde pods often persist on trees into the next flowering season.

FOOTHILLS PALO VERDE trees have bright green bark. There are no spines on the branches but they terminate in a sharp point. Like blue palo verde, older trees may develop grayish, textured bark at the lowest, oldest part of their trunks. But foothills palo verde are more drought tolerant than blue and are thus more widespread. They thrive in various habitats, from rocky foothills to valley floors. Seedpods from foothills palo verde constrict tightly around plump oval seeds, usually three to four per pod. They also have a "tail" at the end that tapers to a point and can be described as "beaded," as the pod thins between seeds, resembling a string of beads. Green foothills palo verde pods ripen to a brownish-red color and often drop en masse and dehisce, or burst open, just before summer rains begin, giving seeds the best chance to germinate, survive, and establish new trees.

Palo verde trees are the primary nurse plants for saguaro cactus; their ranges across the Sonoran Desert closely overlap. Sometimes the Arizona Upland subdivision of the Sonoran Desert is called the saguaro/palo verde forest because of this interconnectedness.

Native peoples of the region have used leguminous desert tree foods like palo verde seeds for thousands of years. Their food traditions inform current harvest and use practices. Honor the tradition and enjoy the deliciousness!

- Jill Lorenzini

Foothills palo verde flowers

Photo: Jill Lorenzini

PALO VERDE BASICS

LEAF DROP	Any leaves still on trees yellow and drop in mid March, preceding new leaf and flower bud growth starting around the spring equinox.
FLOWERS BLOOM	SPRING – Late March, April (early April for blue, mid-April for foothills).
GREEN SEED HARVEST	SPRING – Late April, May.
DRY RIPE SEED HARVEST	DRY SUMMER – June, early July before or between summer rains.
HARVEST TIPS	Harvest pods by hand into buckets or baskets, and watch for spines within blue palo verde branches and thorns at ends of foothills branches. Be very careful if bending branches while harvesting as they break easily.
PROCESSING TIPS	Blanch green seeds in pods, remove from pod then eat, use in a recipe, or freeze for later use. Blanched green seeds may also be completely dried and ground into flour. Soak and sprout dry ripe seeds or use in recipes, store for later use, or dry and grind into flour.
NUTRITION	Seeds are gluten-free and provide protein and dietary fiber.
PLANTING TIPS	Plant with summer rains in the terrace or top zone of a rain garden. Seed scarification: Nip the side, not the tip, of the seed coat with toenail clippers just enough to get through hard outer seed coat.
OTHER USES	Produces fodder for honey bees/pollinators, desert tortoise, sheep, and cattle. Medicinal.

FROM FOOD FOREST TO KITCHEN:
BARBARA ROSE AND BEAN TREE FARM

by Kimi Eisele

If you thumb through the recipes in this book, sooner or later you'll start to see patterns. One of those patterns is "Contributed by Barbara Rose, Bean Tree Farm." Indeed, Barbara is a master desert harvester and culinary creatress, living and working on a 20-acre saguaro/ironwood tree forest north of Tucson called Bean Tree Farm.

Barbara first arrived on the land as a caretaker in 1985. But over the years, she rooted herself amidst the trees and cactus, built rammed earth residences and a barn, and transformed the place into a permaculture community that hosts workshops, tours, and feasts, with the aim of inspiring others to live and work with the desert ecosystem and eat from its abundant food forest. The farm takes its name from the hundreds of ironwood and palo verde trees—along with a few mesquites—that live there, trees offering perennial beans she uses in salads, soups, salsas, and sprouts.

For Barbara, both permaculture and cooking invite a common practice of noticing and finding patterns.

Permaculture principles encourage agriculture with minimal waste, labor, and energy input, mimicking natural patterns in the landscape to create fertile, life-giving food systems. Such systems lead to projects like food forests, which are designed ecosystems that offer food for people while maintaining healthy habitats for wildlife. They are different from more mainstream and commercial agricultural systems based on stripping land of natural habitat to grow a single crop. "We make the ground bare and throw one crop in and we are surprised year after year when it doesn't grow well," Barbara said.

Barbara Rose

Photo: Brad Lancaster

The natural ironwood/palo verde/saguaro forest at Bean Tree was already such a food forest. Barbara worked to enhance it with additional food-bearing trees like pomegranate, fig, jujube, and olive planted near building structures to gather rain runoff and household greywater.

Barbara sees cooking and recipes in terms of patterns as well. "There's a kimchi pattern, a posole pattern, a stew pattern," she says.

Once you take note of these patterns, she says you understand how things work and you can start experimenting and innovating. Which is how she discovered that ironwood and palo verde seeds could be sprouted, like other beans.

She was reading about local ethnobotany and had seen that packrats and rabbits ate the seeds. She knew how to soak and sprout mung beans and sunflower seeds, so she thought, "Why not sprout these? Let's see what it does."

It worked, and both seeds produced delicious edible sprouts. Later she noticed palo verde seeds sprouted naturally from the ground after the rain. "You can pick those tender little things and they taste like peas."

Growing up in southwest Florida on the Gulf of Mexico, her grandmother had avocado and citrus trees in the backyard. As a young adult in New England Barbara loved reading about food foraging in books like Euell Gibbons's *Stalking the Wild Asparagus* and going out to harvest in the lush eastern woodlands.

But when she moved to the Sonoran Desert, it took Barbara a few years before she began to see that the desert, too, was full of food. Early on, someone told her that saguaro fruit was edible. She picked one and found it white and hard and not very tasty. "Why would anyone eat that?" She later learned it hadn't been ripe.

Barbara soon met other desert dwellers like Brad Lancaster, who took his first permaculture class in her living room. Both were experimenting with eating from the desert thanks to what they were learning from Tohono O'odham friends like Stella Tucker (see The Saguaro Fruit Harvest, p. 116), who for several years taught saguaro fruit harvesting at Bean Tree Farm.

"Little by little I started to see, oh my God, you can eat everything here," Barbara said.

Among the foods in Bean Tree Farm's forest are legume trees, cactus fruits and pads, berries, and herbs from which Barbara and others make small-batch, artisanal products, including chutneys, sauces, rubs, kimchi, herb salts, tinctures, salves, and more.

Barbara cooked for a living on and off after leaving home—at day-care centers, a college, and Head Start. But she says her inspiration to be creative in the kitchen came from her father, a fisherman who loved to cook.

Although they often differed on what a woman in the 1950s and '60s should be doing, she said, "I just remember his pleasure and his creativity when he was in the kitchen. He messed around—he never used a recipe, and it was always really good."

Barbara has taken that experimental spirit into her creations with desert foods. Again, her understanding of patterns has given her confidence to try new things based on what she already knows.

"If food is a whole bunch of flavors and colors and textures and sweet, sour, salty, umami, and bitter and you understand the patterns of what makes food taste good to you and your family, then you can experiment," she said.

That's how she came to create a local, place-based version of borscht, the dark pink beet soup of her Ukrainian ancestors. "I just thought, what's sweet, sour, wet, salty, fermenty, and pink? Oh, prickly pear! Let's try it."

She replaced beets, which require more water to grow in this desert climate, with prickly pear fruit, abundant atop *Opuntia* varieties every summer. Her Prickly Pear Borscht (p. 159) marries the colors and texture of the traditional soup with a new, fresh desert tang.

It all came from paying attention to the food forest in her midst. "That's what I was trying to distill into the borscht experience, that sense of observation, experimentation, and place," Barbara said.

Indeed, Barbara thinks of her offerings not as "education" but as "inspiration," a way to foster a love for a place and its flavors. "You can learn about desert foods and see if you like them," she said. "Then you can take care of the land that produces them and play with them and see what you get."

And now, with so many of Barbara's recipes to inspire, there's nothing stopping you.

Learn more about Barbara Rose and Bean Tree Farm at BeanTreeFarm.com.

PALO VERDE

Three-Bean Salad with ironwood blossom garnish and green foothills palo verde seedpods on side

(GF) (R) (V)

PALO VERDE SPROUTS

Contributed by Barbara Rose, Bean Tree Farm

Collect dry palo verde seeds in late May or June. Store in freezer or in jars in a cool dry place.

Wonderfully crispy, these sprouts add flavor and seasonality to any dish.

TO SPROUT THE SEEDS:

Soak seeds in warm water with a splash of vinegar for 24 hours. Remove any seeds that float. The next day rinse seeds and check for plumpness. Rinse and drain well several times a day, not allowing seeds to dry out or sit in water. Repeat for 2 to 3 days. Check daily for sprouting to begin. Seeds will plump and root will begin to break through. Remove any off-color or slimy seeds daily. When root is length of seed, rinse again and begin to harvest! Usually seeds don't all sprout at once (great survival strategy!), so you will have sprouts maturing for several days. Slip off seed skins before adding to salads, stir-fries, salsas, soups, or using as a garnish.

VARIATION: You can use this same method to sprout ironwood seeds. Try mixing palo verde and ironwood seeds in a single batch for fun!

1/2 CUP DRY SEEDS YIELDS ABOUT 3/4 CUP SPROUTS.

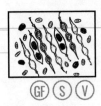

SONORAN DESERT HUNZA MIX

Contributed by Jill Lorenzini

This is a desert twist on the energy-boosting Hunza trail mix using ingredients not from the Hunza Valley in Pakistan but from the lush Sonoran Desert. Wolfberries instead of goji berries, dried green palo verde beans instead of pistachio nuts, Arizona pecans instead of cashews, piñon nuts instead of cacao nibs, and dried saguaro fruit instead of mulberries.

In a large bowl, combine all ingredients. Transfer to jar and store in refrigerator.

MAKES 4 1/2 CUPS.

1 cup blanched, dried, and toasted green palo verde beans

1 cup air- or solar-dried wolfberries

1 cup Arizona pecans, chopped coarsely

1 cup crumbled dried saguaro fruit pieces

1/2 cup dried chopped piñon nuts

GF V

THREE-BEAN SALAD

Contributed by Barbara Rose, Bean Tree Farm

2 cups fresh green beans, cut into 1-inch pieces, steamed or stir-fried, cooled

1 cup blanched green palo verde beans, removed from pods, cool

1 medium red onion, minced

3 cloves garlic, minced

Desert and garden herbs and spices, to taste

Salt and pepper, to taste

Hot chile peppers, minced, to taste (optional)

Olive oil and vinegar or lemon juice for dressing

2 cups seasoned, cooked white tepary beans, cooled

Nothing says summer like Three-Bean Salad and here's a variation on the standard recipe featuring unique wild and native-cultivated ingredients, full of nutrients and flavor.

In a large bowl, combine green beans, palo verde beans, onion, garlic, herbs and spices, salt and pepper, and chiles. Add in oil and vinegar to dress salad and toss. Add tepary beans and toss. Allow to marinate in fridge at least 1 hour. Serve chilled with chips and salsa, warm tortillas or quesadillas, or mesquite crackers.

MAKES ABOUT 6 CUPS.

POSOLE CON FRIJOLES DE PALO VERDE

Contributed by Aaron Wright

Posole is a traditional Mexican stew that pre-dates the Spanish conquest. There are numerous regional variants, but the core ingredient is hominy. Hominy is corn that has been "nixtamalized" by soaking in a calcium-based solution (such as lye or wood ash). As well as softening the kernels, this process adds calcium and increases the amount of niacin absorbed from the corn. Posole usually contains chiles, meat (typically pork), lime, and seasonal vegetables. This vegan version substitutes the hulled beans of foothills palo verde for the meat. As a result, this recipe fuses New Mexican (green chiles) and Sonoran (palo verde) ingredients into a refreshing take on an indigenous staple.

Puree the green chiles in a food processor. Add oil to a large soup pot and sauté onion and garlic for about 2 minutes over medium heat. Add vegetable broth, chopped tomato, oregano, and salt, and simmer. Add hominy and palo verde beans and return to a boil, then reduce heat and simmer for 10 minutes. Add the green chile puree and lime juice. Stir. Serve warm. Pairs well with mesquite tortillas, sopapillas, or fry bread.

MAKES 6 SERVINGS.

4 to 6 green chiles, roasted, peeled, and chopped (New Mexico Hatch chiles are ideal)

2 tablespoons oil

1 onion, diced

6 cloves garlic, minced or pressed

6 cups vegetable broth

1 tomato, chopped and roasted

1 tablespoon dried oregano

2 to 3 teaspoons salt

3 cups hominy (rinsed and drained)

2 cups hulled foothills palo verde beans

1/4 cup lime juice

(GF) (V)

SONORAN SUCCOTASH

Contributed by Jill Lorenzini

1/4 cup oil

1 medium onion, chopped

4 cloves garlic, minced

1 large jalapeño or 3 to 4 chiltepines

1 red bell pepper, chopped

1/4 cup chopped basil

2 teaspoons dried thyme

1/2 teaspoon dried sage

Salt and pepper to taste

1 1/2 cups green palo verde seeds* or Ironwood Edamame (p. 135)

2 cups white, brown, or black tepary beans

3 cups corn

2 tablespoons vinegar

1 pint cherry tomatoes, halved

* You can use either freshly picked green palo verde seeds, or those that were picked fresh then blanched, frozen, and thawed.

A delicious Sonoran Desert version of the filling and healthful dish created by first peoples bringing together various wild and cultivated food staples (primarily corn and beans).

In a large skillet, heat oil over medium heat. Add onion, garlic, and peppers. Sauté until onions are translucent. Season with herbs and salt and pepper, and simmer a bit longer. Add palo verde or ironwood, tepary beans, corn, and vinegar. Mix to coat all ingredients. Toss in tomatoes. Garnish with avocado slices. Serve hot or room temperature.

MAKES ABOUT 6 CUPS.

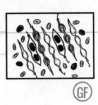

GF

YUCCA FLOWER AND PALO VERDE BEAN FRIED RICE

Contributed by Amy Valdés Schwemm, Mano y Metate

Coming home from a road trip last spring, I stopped to check out the ripening pods on a foothills palo verde tree. I harvested the few pods that were still tender, leaving the rest to fully mature. Next to it was a soap tree yucca (Yucca elata) in flower so I harvested a few of those. Even if I don't have time to look for, harvest, and process a large quantity of something, I can always make a simple dish more special with a handful of beans found along the way!

In a cast iron or nonstick pan, heat oil over medium heat. Cook onion briefly then add cooked rice. When rice is heated, add palo verde beans and egg, stirring briskly to scramble egg into rice. Once the egg is cooked, remove from heat and stir in yucca flower petals. Season with salt or soy sauce to taste, and serve.

1 splash cooking oil

1 l'itoi's onion or 1 tablespoon of white onion, diced

1 cup leftover steamed rice

2 tablespoons fresh foothills palo verde beans, boiled and shelled

1 egg

4 soap tree yucca flowers, petals only

MAKES 1 to 2 SERVINGS.

MEET
DESERT
FLOWERS

Cholla (*Cylindropuntia* spp.)

Chuparosa (*Justicia californica*)

Creosote (*Larrea tridentata*)

Desert Chia (*Salvia columbariae*)

Desert Lavender (*Hyptis emoryi*)

Desert willow (*Chilopsis linearis*)

Desert Ironwood (*Olneya tesota*)

Lyreleaf jewelflower (*Streptanthus carinatus*)

Octopus Agave (*Agave vilmoriniana*)

Ocotillo (*Fouquieria splendens*)

Oreganillo (*Aloysia wrightii*)

Palo verde (*Parkinsonia* spp.)

Prickly pear (*Opuntia* spp.)

Wild onion (*Allium* spp.)

Yucca (*Yucca* spp.)

Please don't eat the daisies! But please do eat the palo verde, desert ironwood, desert chia, chuparosa, yucca, oreganillo, Lyreleaf jewelflower, and wild onion flowers. And please use desert willow, prickly pear, cholla, ocotillo, and other desert flowers in teas, infusions, tinctures, fragrances, and salves.

Desert flowers mostly bloom in spring and summer, in response to two rainy seasons—one in summer, from around late June through August; the other in winter, from roughly November through January. (These rain cycle schedules are approximate; ongoing drought and changing climate conditions affect cycles as well.)

Flower color and fragrance attract pollinators that forage for abundant pollen and nectar, and

make possible the production of delicious and nutritious edible fruits and seeds in their seasons of harvest. Many intimate and interesting relationships have developed between desert flowers and their pollinators, from bats to birds to bees to moths. To respect the busy and beloved pollinators and avoid the heat, harvest desert flowers in the cool mornings and early evenings.

Flowers are a great and simple way to connect to place seasonally. Pluck some during a late winter hike for a sweet bright snack, and suddenly flowers are part of fond hiking memories. Flower fragrances have close associations with different seasons, like the sultry-sweet desert willow of summer. Sounds do too, like the low buzz of thousands of bees foraging palo verde, ironwood, and mesquite trees, heavy with flowers, in late spring and the beginning of dry summer.

Desert flowers are delightful when eaten fresh, but also may be dried, candied, ground into flour, brewed into teas, and used medicinally in various formulas.

- Jill Lorenzini

DESERT FLOWERS BASICS

FLOWER BUD & BLOOM SEASON	SPRING	WET SUMMER – February through April and July through August.
PARTS USED	Flowers, buds, petals.
HARVESTING TIPS	Flowers are delicate and easily bruised so use care when handling. Snip off at stem with scissors or pruners and hold by stem to avoid touching flowers. Air-dry small flowers.
BEST HARVESTING PRACTICES	Harvest into a basket lined with cloth or into a wooden bowl.
CAUTION	Watch for foraging bees and other pollinators while harvesting and avoid disturbing them.
NUTRITION	Different flowers contain different healing and medicinal qualities.
OTHER USES	Press dry and use in art projects.

DESERT FLOWERS

Chiltepin Beet Hummus with palo verde blossom garnish

Photo: Christian Timmerman

(GF) (R) (V)

CREOSOTE CAPERS

Contributed by Jill Lorenzini

2 cups creosote flower buds (unopened flower; some yellow showing is okay), fresh air-dried at low temperature

1/4 cup wolfberries or hackberries, toasted

Herbs and spices of your choice: ground peppercorns, coriander, dill, garlic, mustard seeds, desert lavender, oreganillo, etc.

3 tablespoons lemon zest

1 1/2 to 2 cups lemon juice

A desert twist on a classic Mediterranean condiment. Creosote bushes can bloom multiple times throughout the year, depending on rain and other factors. Using lemon juice is a great way to preserve surplus buds and flowers for use during seasons when creosote is not flowering.

In a small bowl, combine creosote buds, toasted berries, and your choice of herbs and spices. Add lemon zest and juice, and mix well. Store in a jar in the fridge and allow flavors to blend for about a week. Flavors will continue to mature; lemon capers keep well. Serve as a pungent condiment or topping that invokes flavors associated with rain and the desert.

MAKES ABOUT 2 1/2 CUPS.

(GF) (V)

DESERT BLOOM GRANOLA

Contributed by Lia Griesser for EXO Roast Co.

Granola is a perfect way to incorporate textures that might normally feel too crunchy or dry by softening them with milk (or a milk substitute). This recipe celebrates so many natural desert flavors. You can add fresh flowers when in season or use dried flowers to brighten your morning all year long. At EXO, our ingredients vary depending on what's in season and what wild-crafted goodies we're able to source. We've created a recipe where substitutions can be easily made by keeping the main ratios in balance. Think of granola as a fun way to work with what you have. Most ingredients can be modified or substituted without upsetting the overall effect.

Preheat oven to 350º F. In a large bowl, combine all "Baked Ingredients." Lightly chop any larger nuts and seeds so you don't end up with a sore jaw. You can keep your granola sugar-free by using date syrup, mesquite syrup, or honey, or add piloncillo (unrefined cane sugar) to amplify sweetness and transform the mix from more of a muesli to a clumping granola. Spread mixture on a rimmed baking sheet in an even layer. Bake for 30 to 45 minutes, stirring every 10 minutes, until golden brown. Transfer granola to a large bowl. Add "Raw Ingredients," tossing to combine.

If storing for longer than a week or so, keep granola in the freezer to help keep nuts and seeds from going rancid.

*NOTE: To dry flowers, lay on racks or baskets with an open weave that allows fresh air to circulate around their tender forms. Throw out any flowers that develop mold, which can happen especially in tight buds that have not fully opened and retain their moisture. Separate the flowers from their twigs, or petals from their calyx, depending on the sharpness of their structure.

MAKES 6 to 7 CUPS.

BAKED INGREDIENTS:

6 cups gluten-free oats

2 cups nuts and large seeds (bellotas, pine nuts)

2/3 to 1 cup small seeds (saguaro, barrel cactus, evening primrose, cocklebur, chia, wild sunflower)

1 cup shredded coconut

1 teaspoon salt

1 teaspoon fresh or dried citrus zest

1/2 teaspoon cardamom

1/2 teaspoon cinnamon

1 teaspoon black pepper

1 teaspoon vanilla extract or 1/2 of a vanilla bean

2/3 cups date syrup (locally harvested from Iskashitaa Refugee Network in Tucson)

1/3 block of piloncillo (optional)

3/4 cup olive oil (makes for the crispiest result, but you can substitute other oils/fats)

RAW INGREDIENTS:

1/4 cup or more dried flowers*: petals of ocotillo, ironwood, cholla, prickly pear (break up if large), palo verde, elderberry, chamomile, desert willow, wild sunflower

1 cup or more dried fruit: wolfberry, hackberry, saguaro, candied barrel cactus, Mexican elderberry, jujube, graythorn berry

1/4 cup mesquite flour, powdered manzanita berry, or pinole

GF V

OCTOPUS AGAVE FLOWER FLOUR

Contributed by Jill Lorenzini

2 cups fresh or partially dried
flowers from octopus agave

My father gifted me a handful of bulbils from an octopus agave plant (native to southern Sonora), and I gratefully planted them around my homestead. About 10 years later, all at once, they bloomed! Each plant sent up a magnificent, 12-foot-tall flower stalk that grew and changed daily, and was soon completely covered in flower buds. Flowers then bloomed yellow starting at the bottom of the stalk and spiraling up to the top in beautiful patterns. It was every pollinator's dream! The flower-laden stalks swayed and buzzed through the season. Soon after, flowers gave way to tiny bulbils, miniature versions of the mature plant that bore them, all over the stalk. For weeks after that the bulbils grew heavily and densely together on the stalk. Eventually, their collective weight cracked the stalk, sending it to the ground. Right about that time the bulbils had grown small roots, just in time for summer rains. So the cycle began anew.

Add a little of this light tasty flour to tortilla or other doughs, batters, soups, sauces, and seasoning mixtures, or use as a garnish on desserts, salads, and beverages. The ultimate flower power!

Pick by hand fresh, or shake mostly dried flowers off stalk of agave into a basket or a cloth sheet below. Out of full sun and heat, air-dry flowers thoroughly in a basket or wooden bowl covered with a cloth. Toss or shake daily so flowers dry evenly and don't spoil. Once fully dry, store lightly packed flowers in jars in a cool dark place for later use. Or grind flowers into a flour, by hand or with an electric grinder. Sift as desired for finer texture.

MAKES ABOUT 1 CUP.

GF R V

FLORAL ICE CUBES

Contributed by Jill Lorenzini

Spruce up any summer drink with the flavors and colors of the wild desert with these easy-to-make ice cubes.

Fill ice cube tray 3/4 full of water. Put in freezer until water becomes slushy but not solid. Place flowers into each cube of slushy water, use chopstick or small tongs to arrange evenly, then fill tray completely. Freeze. Pop colorful cubes out of trays and use in water, iced tea, lemonade, or juice for festive, flowery drinks.

MAKES 12 ICE CUBES.

1 cup seasonal flowers (ocotillo, palo verde, ironwood, chuparosa, creosote, desert willow, etc.)

Water

GF R V

CANDIED FLOWERS

Contributed by Barbara Rose, Bean Tree Farm

1 egg white, beaten

1/8 cup water

1/4 cup superfine sugar

About 100 desert flowers: your choice of ironwood, palo verde, ocotillo, octopus agave, desert willow, and the petals of barrel cactus, cholla, and prickly pear flowers, etc., fresh-picked and clean

Beautiful crystallized edible desert flowers up the "wow" factor of any food. Harvest desert flowers throughout the year to add local and seasonal color to plates and menus.

Beat egg whites together with water. Put sugar on a small plate. Put wax paper over a baking sheet. Use tweezers to hold each flower. Use paintbrush to brush egg-white mixture onto each flower. Cover prepared flowers with superfine sugar and place on waxed paper to dry. If needed, sprinkle more sugar on flowers on tray. Let dry about 3 to 4 hours in a warm place and make sure all egg white has dried completely before using. Or, let dry until flowers are completely dehydrated and crisp. Store in jars in a cool dry place.

TO MAKE VEGAN:

Replace egg with 1/2 cup sugar and 1/4 cup water. Combine sugar and water and heat on medium heat, stirring regularly, until mixture boils. Reduce heat and simmer until all sugar is dissolved, stirring often. Remove from heat and cool to room temperature. Use tweezers to hold flowers and dip into sugar water. Let drip off, then dip into bowl of superfine sugar. Set prepared flowers on wax paper on baking sheet. Sprinkle more sugar on flowers if needed. Let dry 2 to 3 hours before using. Or let dry 2 to 4 days until flowers are crispy. Store in jars in cool dark place.

MAKES 100 FLOWERS.

(GF) (V)

PICKLED YUCCA BLOSSOMS

Contributed by Jill Lorenzini

Delicately flavored pickled yucca blossoms are an exquisite accompaniment to savory desert meals. They also make great accent garnishes. Try on tacos, in salads, in nori rolls, or with hummus.

Make sure yucca blossoms are clean and insect-free. In a small pot, bring vinegars to a low boil, then reduce heat and add garlic, salt and pepper, and coriander seeds and simmer about 10 minutes. Remove from heat. Let cool. Put slice of lemon on bottom of 24-ounce canning jar. On top of lemon add layer of yucca blossoms (about 4) and then a layer of palo verde beans. Continue layering, lemon then yucca then palo verde, until jar is nearly full. Carefully add vinegar-spice mixture until filled to 1 inch below rim. Clean rim and seal with lid. Refrigerate for a few weeks before serving.

24 yucca blossoms

20 ounces rice vinegar and/or apple cider vinegar

3 cloves garlic, sliced

Salt and pepper to taste

Fresh coriander seeds

1 small lemon, washed, seeded, and thinly sliced

1 cup green foothills palo verde beans

24-ounce canning jar and lid

MAKES 12 SERVINGS.

BANANA YUCCA (*Yucca baccata*) also has edible fruit, but they can be tricky to procure in the wild. Many animals (vertebrate and invertebrate) like to eat these tasty treats. Some years there are not sufficient quantities for the wildlife and humans, in which case it's better to leave the fruit for the critters. But in a good year plants will have multiple fruits, healthy and thriving. Collect fruit when they are mostly green, turning yellow on the edges. Ripen them in a sunny window. (They rarely get to the ripe stage in the wild because they get munched first!) Unripe, the fruit can be somewhat caustic, so sample cautiously, ensuring all is sweet and ripe before consuming more. Yucca fruit can be fried, baked, or roasted and added to stir-fries and baked goods, or just enjoyed with a little butter.

Since the fruit is rare to find in sufficient quantity, be sure to savor the treat!

-Patty West

Banana yucca in fruit

Photo: Brad Lancaster

(GF) (V)

STUFFED YUCCA FLOWERS

Contributed by Jill Lorenzini

8 ounces chèvre or ricotta or crumbled tofu

4 ounces fresh herbs of your choice: aloysia, desert lavender, parsley, cilantro, garlic greens, chives, marjoram, thyme, etc., chopped fine

Salt and pepper to taste

1/2 cup walnuts, ground into a coarse nut butter

1/4 cup toasted barrel cactus seeds

1/4 cup fine mesquite flour

This is a delightful and impressive desert flower snack with the sweet hint of mesquite and desert herbs.

In a small bowl, mix crumbled chèvre (or ricotta or tofu) with herbs, salt, pepper, nut butter, and barrel cactus seeds. Put mesquite flour on a small plate. Scoop out 1 to 2 tablespoons of cheese or tofu mixture and roll (or dab) in mesquite flour. If this proves too difficult (cheese and tofu work differently), mix mesquite flour directly into filling. Carefully stuff clean yucca blossoms with filling.

MAKES 12 BLOSSOMS.

MEET
WILD GREENS & DESERT HERBS

NATIVE	NON-NATIVE/NATURALIZED
Amaranth (*Amaranthus* spp.)	Epazote (*Dysphania ambrosioides*)
Aloysia/Oreganillo (*Aloysia wrightii*)	Canadian fleabane (*Conyza canadensis*)
Cudweed (*Pseudognaphalium canescens*)	Lamb's quarter (*Chenopodium* spp.)
Chinchweed (*Pectis papposa*)	Malva (*Malva neglecta*)
Desert chickweed (*Stellaria media*)	Shepherd's purse (*Capsella bursa-pastoris*)
Desert lavender (*Hyptis emoryi*)	Sow thistle (*Sonchus* spp.)
Estafiate (*Artemesia ludoviciana*)	Tumbleweed (*Lechenaultia divaricata*)
Miner's lettuce (*Claytonia perfoliata*),	Verdolagas/Purslane (*Portulaca oleracea*)
Monkey flower (*Erythranthe guttata*)	Wild mustard/London rocket (*Sisymbrium irio*)
Peppergrass (*Lepidium* spp.)	Yerba santa (*Eriodictyon californicum*)
Wild oregano (*Monarda* spp.)	
Yerba mansa (*Anemopsis californica*)	

The Sonoran Desert is often referred to as a lush desert, since not just one

but two rainy seasons bring water to the landscape. Winter rains are mostly gentle, originating from northern Pacific Ocean storm patterns. Summer monsoons blow surges of wet tropical air from the Gulf of Mexico into the sweltering Sonoran Desert heat, creating huge cumulus clouds that deliver intense lightning and thunderstorms, strong winds, and flash flooding.

The result of these seasonal drenching rains is a variety of fresh annual greens and perennial and annual herbs that provide nutrition, unique tastes and textures, and support for our bodies in transitioning from season to season. Familiar, introduced, and naturalized greens—better known as weeds—are also available to desert foragers.

Greens have always been welcomed by native cultures as a fresh food after long winters, when stored foods dominate the menu and hunger looms in the background. Spring greens epitomize this season of renewal as they burst forth from the earth in response to increased light and warmth, and a strong sense of potential.

Summer greens can survive aridity, extreme temperatures, violent storms, and nibbling from hungry native animals. When summer monsoon rains arrive to baptize this season of restoration, summer greens thrive. Eating summer greens helps get us through the final months of hot, humid weather, and opens the view to milder seasons of harvest ahead.

Summer rains produce light, juicy, tart, cooling native greens and herbs like amaranth and miner's lettuce, and non-natives like epazote, tumbleweed, malva, and verdolagas. Winter rains produce hearty, spicy, often warming native spring greens and herbs like peppergrass, yerba mansa, monkey flower, desert chickweed, desert lavender, and aloysia, plus non-natives like wild mustard or London rocket, shepherd's purse, sow thistle, and lamb's quarter.

Greens and herbs are versatile in the kitchen. They may be used fresh in salads, salsas, and pestos; cooked like other greens; and added to soups, casseroles, kimchi, stuffings, hummus, sauces, and smoothies. They also may be dried or frozen and stored for later use. If kale can be made into chips, certainly wild greens and herbs can be too!

- Jill Lorenzini

WILD GREENS & DESERT HERBS BASICS

HARVEST SEASON	SPRING	WET SUMMER – February through April and again from late June through September.
PARTS USED	Tender growing tips and leaves.
HARVESTING TIPS	Pinch back new growth to increase subsequent harvests.
BEST HARVESTING PRACTICES	Since greens usually grow close to the ground, make sure harvest areas are toxin-free, and watch for snakes in summer.
CAUTION	Make sure to accurately identify all wild greens and herbs before consuming.
NUTRITION	Vitamins and minerals.
PLANTING TIPS	Plant with summer rains. No scarification needed for most greens and herbs.
OTHER USES	Fodder for chickens and other animals.

MEALS OF THE MOMENT:
AN HERBALIST FORAGES FOR BREAKFAST

by Kimi Eisele

If you go to the back room of EXO Roast Co. on any given morning, you're likely to see Lia Griesser hard at work in the small, open kitchen. She scurries from pan to plate to jar, looking up to greet customers who come to watch.

Behind her on a high kitchen shelf are jars. Lots of jars. And inside them, dried green, gray, lavender, and orange herbs and flowers, which she uses in several of the cafe's breakfast offerings. One dish is the Herb Egg Sandwich, made with whipped chévre, sweet limes, barrel cactus fruit, and a variety of seasonal herbs on a homemade sourdough English muffin.

"I wanted to bring wild harvested foods into a kitchen," Lia said.

Before she became the kitchen manager of EXO Coffee, Lia worked at the Tucson Herb Store. She was studying herbalism and had a regular practice of ethically harvesting regional plants for other practicing herbalists. She had also spent years working in restaurants and wanted to finally merge her two lives, she said.

When EXO's owners Amy and Doug Smith expanded the coffee shop and opened a kitchen, they had already been experimenting with desert foods like chiletepin and mesquite (see Sweet and Spicy, p. 193). Their breakfast menu also includes the Wild Waffle, a gluten-free mesquite waffle served with prickly pear/chia jam.

But Lia's meals added a host of desert herbs and flowers many Tucson eaters might never have heard of. She links her choices closely to the season and the wild offerings.

In salad dressings, the Herb Egg Sandwich, and seasoning for pickles, she uses yerba santa, desert

Lia Griesser

Photo: Robert Anthony Villa

lavender, pectis, monarda, oreganillo, cudweed, estafiate, or "whatever else is currently sprouting new growth," in place of more conventional choices like thyme and mint.

Lia's Sky Island Pesto (p. 289) is made using "whatever greens are most bountiful." EXO works closely with small farmers in the region, and modifies their menu to encompass only what farmers have at the time. Today it's mustard greens, tomorrow maybe purslane.

The café's Desert Bloom Granola (p. 267) is also adaptable to whatever's in season. "It has a lot of ingredients! But you don't need perfect ratios, so I add whatever I have in at the time. If we're out of ironwood flowers I'll use ocotillo, and so on," Lia said.

One challenge has been keeping up with the necessary quantities. While Lia is the primary harvester, she depends on help. "We'd run out if it were only on me. It wouldn't be sustainable," she said.

The café also has to rely on external vendors to supply the kitchen. "It's a top priority that the goods coming to us are ethically harvested with the plant's best interest in mind," she said.

Lia acknowledges that she has a special skill set, one she's learned from many regional teachers and living indigenous traditions. "More and more people are learning how to do this," she said. "It's wonderful to see a community grow up around it."

She also hopes customers will continue to be open to new flavors. "Not many people have nostalgic or comforting associations with these foods. The flavors can be odd and unfamiliar."

But if you're willing to be a little adventurous, she said, there's always a fresh herb from the Sonoran Desert waiting to win your heart.

Learn more about Exo Roast Co.'s evolving kitchen at ExoCoffee.com.

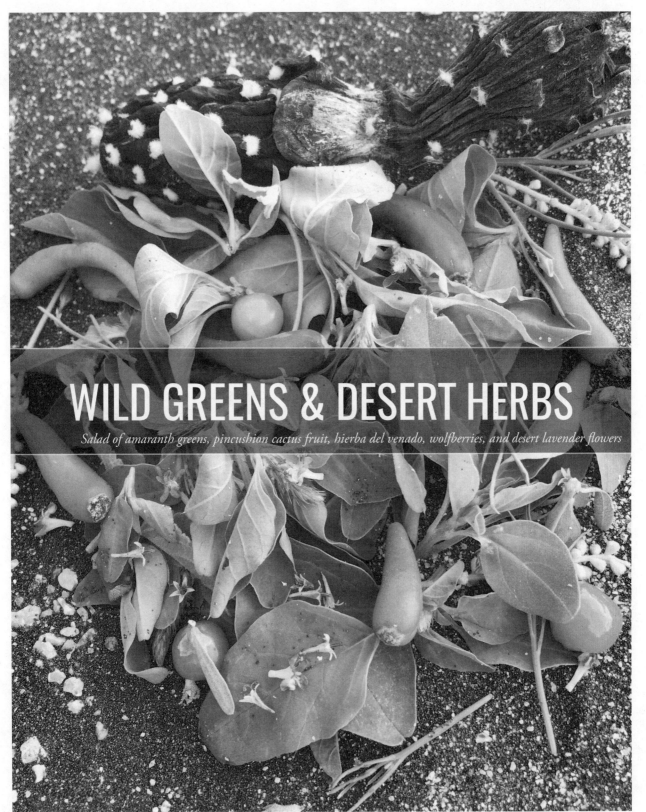

WILD GREENS & DESERT HERBS

Salad of amaranth greens, pincushion cactus fruit, hierba del venado, wolfberries, and desert lavender flowers

Photo: Jill Lorenzini

GF R V

DESERT HERB SPICE BLEND

Contributed by Jill Lorenzini

Equal parts:

Saltbush, dried

Desert lavender, dried

Oreganillo, dried

Lemon basil, dried

Pinch of hierba del venado, or damiana (*Turnera diffusa*)

Local seed/spice blends can be used as a condiment on almost any food and are an easy way to bring a little bit of the desert into every meal! This one is both soothing and nutritious.

In a spice grinder or mill, grind plants into a powder to your desired coarseness. Sprinkle over salads or vegetable roasts or use as a rub. Store in jar in refrigerator.

Ⓡ

CUCUMBER PURSLANE SOUP

Contributed by Elizabeth Mikesell

A refreshing summer soup mixing the earthy flavor of purslane, also called verdolagas, with the crisp cool of cucumbers.

Put all ingredients into a blender and blend until smooth. Taste and adjust seasonings as needed. Add water if too thick. Chill and serve in tumblers or just drink it straight out of the jug, in front of the fridge, in the middle of the night.

MAKES 2 SERVINGS.

2 1/2 cups Persian cucumbers (about 3), not skinned, chopped roughly

1 green tomato, roughly chopped

1 medium young onion, chopped

3 garlic cloves, peeled

1/2 cup tender purslane leaves

1 small green chile

3/4 cup Greek yogurt

2 teaspoons sherry vinegar

1/2 teaspoon sugar

1/2 stale pita bread, broken into bits

2 tablespoons extra virgin olive oil

Pinch of salt, to taste

TIPS ON CHOOSING THE TASTY PURSLANE

There are two types of purslane commonly growing wild in the Sonoran desert: the tasty one (when eaten raw) – true or common purslane or verdolagas (*Portulaca oleracea*), and the not-as-tasty one – horse purslane (*Trianthema portulacastrum*), which, while edible, is much less palatable and may irritate the throat. Here are a few tips to tell them apart:

• COMMON OR TRUE PURSLANE has more teardrop-shaped leaves, yellow flowers and, typically, more succulent stems.

• HORSE PURSLANE has rounder leaves and lavender to pink flowers.

GF R V

PICKLED VERDOLAGAS

Contributed by Jill Lorenzini

10 chiltepin peppers

3 pounds fresh clean tender verdolagas, coarsely chopped

1 head garlic, peeled and sliced

2 Meyer lemons, seeded, sliced, and quartered

Salt and pepper, to taste

1 gallon raw apple cider vinegar

This is a great way to use a surplus of spicy summer verdolagas. Easy no-cook pickling.

Wash, sterilize, and dry ten 12-ounce, wide-mouth jars and lids. Put one chiltepin in each jar. In a large bowl toss together verdolagas, garlic, and lemon. Season to taste with salt and pepper. Pack verdolagas mixture loosely into jars. Cover verdolagas in jars with vinegar to 1 inch from top of jar. Press verdolagas down to remove air bubbles; add more vinegar if needed. Clean rims and seal tightly. Refrigerate for at least a month then sample to see if verdolagas have absorbed vinegar and seasoning flavors. Serve on tacos or add to salsas, chutneys, salads, soups, sauces, gazpacho, or hummus.

MAKES TEN 12-OUNCE JARS.

GF V

VERDOLAGAS POTATO SALAD

Contributed by Paula Verde

Potato salad is a mainstay at summer picnics! This recipe highlights a nutritious and tasty green called verdolagas or purslane that thrives after summer rains in the desert, and is plentiful for harvesting. The lemony taste of fresh verdolagas complements the sweet and earthy taste of yams and potatoes. This salad is also colorful and festive with all the different kinds of potatoes and yams.

Wash and dice yams and potatoes. In large pot, boil potatoes in water until tender but still firm. Drain and cool. In large bowl, combine potatoes and yams, verdolagas, celery, onion, garlic, carrots, cilantro, lemon juice and zest, oil, and spices. Toss to mix well. Taste and adjust seasonings as needed. Chill for several hours or overnight before serving.

MAKES ABOUT 20 SERVINGS.

3 garnet, jewel, and/or Japanese yams

2 Yukon gold potatoes

2 red potatoes

2 purple potatoes

2 cups verdolagas, chopped

4 stalks celery, sliced

1 small red onion, chopped

2 cloves garlic, minced

3 carrots, grated

1/2 cup cilantro, chopped fine

Juice and zest of 1 large lemon (or more, to taste)

1/2 to 3/4 cup olive oil, to taste

Salt and pepper to taste

1/2 teaspoon celery seeds

1 teaspoon smoked paprika

GF R V

VERDOLAGAS SLAW

Contributed by Jill Lorenzini

1 medium purple cabbage, cored and sliced thin or chopped

2 carrots, grated

2 scallions, sliced thin

1 1/2 cups coarsely chopped fresh tender verdolagas

1 clove garlic, minced

Fresh grated ginger to taste

3 tablespoons olive oil

Fresh lime juice to taste

Barrel cactus seeds

1/2 teaspoon smoked paprika

1 teaspoon dried desert lavender

Salt and pepper to taste

Cayenne pepper (optional)

Crispy, juicy, tart, spicy, and sweet, this summer slaw has it all! Colorful, hearty, and healthful, this dish was a favorite at one of the Desert Harvesters demonstration events at the Santa Cruz River Farmers' Market.

In a large bowl, combine cabbage, carrots, scallion, verdolagas, garlic, and ginger. In a smaller bowl, whisk together oil, lime juice, barrel cactus seeds, and seasonings. Add dressing to slaw and mix well. Chill for 2 hours then serve.

MAKES ABOUT 6 to 8 SERVINGS.

GF V

VERDOLAGAS FRITTERS

Contributed by Paula Verde

Everyone loves a fritter! Especially these earthy ones, made from the abundant and nutritious greens known as verdolagas or purslane.

In a medium bowl, combine verdolagas, onion, garlic, carrots, chia seeds, herbs, salt, and pepper. Let sit 10 minutes. Add cornmeal and toss lightly to mix. Heat oil in skillet to medium heat. Spoon verdolagas mixture the size of small pancakes onto skillet. Brown well on one side then flip and brown the other side. Set on plate (with paper towel, if desired). Continue until all mixture is used. Enjoy warm or cool or re-heat and serve as a side dish or main course, great with salsa, guacamole, or pesto.

MAKES 6 SERVINGS.

8 ounces (1 cup) cleaned verdolagas, chopped small

1 small onion, minced

2 cloves garlic, minced

2 carrots, grated

1 tablespoon chia seeds

1/4 cup fresh minced herbs

Salt and pepper to taste

1/2 cup blue or yellow cornmeal

Cooking oil

(GF) (R) (V)

VERDOLAGAS SALSA

Contributed by Paula Verde

2 large ripe red tomatoes, chopped (about 2 cups)

2 large ripe yellow tomatoes, chopped (about 2 cups)

1 medium red onion, chopped

2 cloves garlic, minced

2 cups verdolagas, chopped

1 cup pomegranate kernels

3 scallions or l'itoi's onion, sliced

1 jalapeño, seeded and minced

2 limes, juiced and zested

2 tablespoons olive oil

Salt and pepper to taste

1/2 teaspoon cumin

1/2 teaspoon coriander

1/4 teaspoon epazote

Sizzling summer temperatures require hydrating and cooling summer foods like spicy salsa, made even juicier with verdolagas (aka purslane), a succulent summer green that thrives after seasonal rains soak the ground and trigger growth. The lemony taste of verdolagas enhances other flavors in this salsa and adds a nice crunch.

In a large bowl, combine all ingredients. Let marinate for a few hours or overnight before serving.

MAKES ABOUT 10 CUPS.

GF V

TUMBLEWEED TEMPEH TACOS WITH WATERMELON SALSA

Contributed by Jill Lorenzini

Even tumbleweed is edible! Tempeh takes flavors well and makes a great taco, chimichanga, or burrito filling. These tacos take advantage of that pesky but famous tumbleweed, a plant that germinates with summer rains, making its tender tips available for harvest in late summer. Add to them, a delicious and refreshing watermelon salsa, and you get the hot and cool of summer all at once!

In a large skillet sauté onion, tempeh, and garlic in oil over medium heat until tempeh is browned and soft. Stir in grated carrots and tumbleweed tips and simmer a few more minutes, until carrots and greens soft. Season with coriander and salt and pepper. Lightly heat corn tortillas in an oiled skillet. Fill each soft taco shell with tempeh mixture. Top with lettuce and pepitas.

For watermelon salsa, combine all ingredients in a medium bowl. Serve over tacos.

MAKES 4 TACOS.

1 medium onion, chopped

1 block tempeh, cubed small

3 cloves garlic, minced

Toasted sesame oil

2 carrots, grated

3 cups tender tumbleweed tips

1 teaspoon ground fresh or dried coriander

Salt and pepper to taste

4 corn tortillas

Romaine lettuce, shredded

Pumpkin seeds (pepitas), toasted

WATERMELON SALSA:

1 cup watermelon, diced or chunked

1 purple onion, chopped, or 3 scallions, chopped

1 to 2 garlic cloves, minced

Lemon juice

Jalapeño, minced, to taste

1 cup tomatoes, chopped

Cilantro, chopped, to taste

Salt and pepper to taste

OFF-GRID GREENS TART

Contributed by Amanda Bramble

CRUST:

1/3 cup mesquite flour, sifted

1+ cup whole wheat flour or use a portion white flour

1/2 teaspoon salt

1 stick butter

3 tablespoons cold water

FILLING:

2 bunches kale, chard or equivalent wild greens like amaranth, lamb's quarter, or mustards

1 smallish onion

3 or more cloves garlic, minced

1 bunch garlic chives, chopped

Pepper and whatever other herbs or spices you like

1/4 cup sunflower seeds

TO ADD LATER:

1 egg (or more if you have chickens)

1 cup grated Asiago, Parmesan, or Feta cheese, if well drained and crumbled (optional, but if leaving cheese out, you may need to add more salt)

This recipe is inspired by all the wild greens that are available to forage at the same time that my garden greens are also producing. I want to eat them all! This greens tart has a mesquite-flour crust. For this greens tart, you can use wild amaranth, lamb's quarter, and mustards, as well as the chard and kale and orach from your garden—or whatever greens you have! The mesquite-flour crust gives it a special sweet and desert flavor.

I live off the grid without a freezer, a food processor, or a conventional oven. I cook in solar ovens (see Tending to the Sky, p. 308). I have both a hot parabolic reflective cooker and a slow-cooking box oven. I recommend using these "beyond fossil fuel" appliances for our sunny bioregion. This recipe is written with that in mind. You can, however, adapt this recipe easily to a standard fossil-fuel kitchen.

MAKE THE CRUST:

In a large bowl, mix the dry ingredients and then cut the cold butter into bits. Mix in the butter by hand by rubbing the bits of butter and flour very quickly between your fingers, picking it up, rubbing it, and dropping it. If the mixture begins to feel greasy, refrigerate for a few minutes before proceeding. Sprinkle cold water over the mix. Mix with wooden spoon and gather into a ball. Smoosh into a patty and refrigerate again for at least 10 minutes in a container or plastic bag. Then roll out the crust with extra flour preventing sticking. Oil and flour an 8-inch pie pan and lay the crust into the pan, forming it to the sides.

Cook the crust first. I like to put it on the parabolic solar cooker for 15 to 20 minutes, turning three times, or less if you use a cast iron pan to distribute the heat better. The parabolic cooker reflects all the light to a central cooking area. It's hot and will burn one side of your dish if you don't rotate the pot. Use an oversized lid that overhangs the baking dish to let any condensate drip off of the crust. This is how to get a crispy and toasted crust. You can also cook the crust in a slow-cooking solar oven. It may take an hour and a half, depending on your weather. Moisture may evaporate onto the inside of the glass of the slow-cooking solar oven. If so, open the door and wipe off condensate, then cook for longer. Cook the crust until it's done and it pulls away from the pan a little.

MAKE THE FILLING:

Chop the greens and take out any really large stems, which can throw off your recipe because they take longer to cook. (Don't let stems go to waste. I like to ferment them with some spices.) Chop onion and cook with smaller chopped stems with oil for a bit, then add the rest of the chopped greens, garlic, herbs, and seeds. Cook in a dark-colored pot with a lid for 10 minutes or so on parabolic or a half hour or more in box cooker. Cook until the greens are bright and cooked, but not mushy. Bigger chunks of onions and kale/chard stems should be mostly cooked. If there is water on the bottom of the pot, drain it.

In a small bowl, whisk the egg and add grated cheese. Add this mixture to the cooked and drained greens. Pour filling into crust. Cook in a slow-cooking box solar oven with no lid. Moisture may evaporate onto the inside of the glass of the solar oven. Wipe off condensate once or maybe twice. I cook this tart at 260° F for 1 1/2 hours. Let cool. Slice into wedges and serve.

MAKES 6 to 8 SERVINGS.

GF V

TEPARY BEANS 'N' GREENS

Reprinted with permission from Barbara Rose and Jill Lorenzini's *Wild Recipes: Seasonal Samplings* (2008)

1 bunch I'itoi's onions, chopped

2 to 3 cloves garlic, minced

2 to 3 tablespoons olive oil

1 cup dry tepary beans, sorted, soaked, cooked, and seasoned to taste

1 1/2 cups tender new growth of lamb's quarter, amaranth, or other seasonal greens, chopped small

Salt and pepper

Simple and solid, this dish packs a punch nutritionally with protein, fiber, vitamins, and minerals on the plate. Plus, they're tasty and versatile and make great leftovers, and travel or picnic food. Tepary beans are known for their sensational flavor, drought tolerance, and high-protein qualities.

In a large skillet, sauté onion and garlic in oil over medium heat until soft. Add cooked tepary beans, mix well, and heat through. Add greens and toss until wilted, 1 to 2 minutes. Remove from heat and adjust seasonings as needed. Serve with warm mesquite tortillas or corn chips, and top with salsa, guacamole, sour cream, and olives. Or use in burritos, tacos, tostadas, chimichangas, etc.

MAKES ABOUT 3 CUPS.

GF R

SKY ISLAND PESTO

Contributed by Lia Griesser for EXO Kitchen

Our pesto recipe is designed to fluidly handle the pressure of seasonally changing ingredients, based on availability. The trick is to build up complementary flavors of our region that reflect the season. When we ran out of basil in the fall, we transitioned to a combination of arugula, thyme, onion, and monarda (wild oregano) in the winter, ingredients that help warm the body, strengthen the lungs, and circulate the blood. Making pesto is also an easy way to eat raw heartier or spikier wild harvested greens that would normally need to be cooked, such as various thistles, stinging nettles, and squash leaves. Fair warning, this recipe makes a healthy portion. Freeze it for later or reduce by half or quarter the amount.

In a food processor blend Parmesan, nuts, seeds, garlic, salt, and olive oil until smooth. Add greens 2 to 3 cups at a time (they won't all fit in the food processor at once). When measuring, pack greens down into the cup to fully fill. It takes A LOT of greens! Use the pulse setting so as not to overprocess/overheat and wilt the greens. When using sour verdolagas in the spring and summer, omit the sumac. To balance the zing of spicier greens like London rocket (wild arugula), substitute a couple cups of spinach, kale, or chard in your total amount of greens used.

MAKES ABOUT 2 CUPS.

1 cup grated Parmesan

1 cup mix of nuts and/or seeds: pine nuts, bellotas, chia, barrel cactus, wild sunflower

4 garlic cloves

2 teaspoons salt

1 cup olive oil

8 cups greens:

- Spring/Dry Summer: amaranth, verdolagas/purslane, and lamb's quarter

- Wet Summer/Early Fall: basil

- Late Fall/Spring: arugula or mustard greens

OPTIONAL FLAVORFUL ADDITIONS:

1 to 2 tablespoons wild herbs: oreganillo, chinchweed, wild oregano, Canadian fleabane, estafiate, yerba santa, cudweed

1 teaspoon ground black pepper

1 teaspoon ground mustard seed

2 teaspoons sumac; we use the local lemonade berry (also called lemonade sumac, *Rhus integrifolia*)

1/2 to 1 cup onion (wild onions, l'itoi's, leeks, garlic scapes, or anything with a similar flavor)

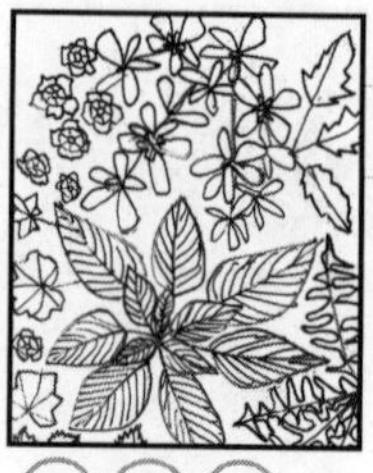

(GF) (R) (V)

INFUSED DESERT GREENS VINEGAR

Contributed by Jill Lorenzini

1 quart organic raw apple cider vinegar

3 cups seasonal desert herbs and greens: desert chickweed, aloysia, wild mustard, desert lavender, etc.

This vinegar tonic is a great way to celebrate the wild herbs and greens of the desert. Plus it makes a lovely gift for your favorite foodies.

Pack herbs and greens loosely into wide-mouth quart jar. Fill to top with vinegar and cap. Store in a cool dark place for 3 weeks. Vinegar may change color as the essence and nutrition of the plants infuse into the vinegar. Strain and bottle for use on salads and in sauces, salsas, and soups. Add small fresh sprig of herb or green to vinegar bottle to show what flavored it.

MAKES 1 QUART.

GF R V

FLAVORED AGAVE SYRUP

Contributed by Jill Lorenzini

Agave syrup may be used in many ways in various recipes. The light syrup makes visible the beautiful herbs and spices infusing it with their flavors.

Add flowers and spices of your choice to a pint jar of agave syrup. Cover tightly and shake well. Let flavors infuse into syrup at least 2 weeks before using. Flavorings become candied when saturated with agave syrup, so may be eaten as a special treat. Use syrup over ice cream and other desserts, on oats, in hot tea or cold beverages, in baking, or as is for a tonic.

MAKES 16 OUNCES.

2 tablespoons flower and herb options: desert lavender sprigs, chuparosa, desert willow, ocotillo

Lemon zest

Ginger, grated

1 tablespoon spice options: cinnamon stick, cardamom pods, dried chiltepin, etc.

16 ounces light agave syrup

(GF) (V)

DESERT TEA

Contributed by Amanda Brown, Tucson Herb Store

1 heaping tablespoon dried ocotillo flower

1 heaping tablespoon dried globe mallow leaf and flower

1/2 teaspoon yerba buena (spearmint)

This is a simple, tasty, and nutritious tea to make from local desert plants. The flavor is earthy and lightly floral with a touch of mint, and the flowers themselves are delightfully beautiful. We sometimes offer Desert Tea at the Tucson Herb Store and it is definitely a customer favorite. I like to prepare it warm in the colder months and make a sun tea and serve it chilled in the hotter months. I like to sit with the steeping plants while they infuse into the water and admire what the desert offers.

Pour 2 cups of boiling water over plants. Let steep for 10 minutes. Strain plants, drink and enjoy!

NOTE: Harvest ocotillo flowers just before they open up so you don't have to contend with as many insects when drying them. When harvesting globe mallow, pick plants far away from sidewalks. Globe mallow is a favorite plant for dogs to relieve themselves on during walks.

MAKES 2 CUPS.

GF V

RED BEER WITH ALOYSIA

Contributed by Barbara Rose, Bean Tree Farm

Experience the unique tastes of desert herbs and seeds in this flavorful refreshing beer!

Muddle aloysia in citrus juice. Wet tops of glasses in juice, then dip in salt/cactus seed mix. Pour in beer, prickly pear juice, chile sauce, and herbed citrus juice. Serve over ice if desired.

MAKES 18 OUNCES.

1 sprig aloysia

Juice of 1/2 lime, sour orange, or grapefruit, fresh or from frozen

Salt and roasted barrel seeds for glass rims

16 ounces locally brewed beer

1 ounce prickly pear juice or prickly pear ice cube

1/2 to 1 teaspoon hot chile sauce

(GF) (V)

DESERT LAVENDER TEQUILA

Contributed by Jill Lorenzini

8 ounces (1 cup) fresh desert lavender, in bloom if possible

64 ounces high-quality tequila

This simple recipe combines a well-loved agave spirit with the taste of desert lavender. Enjoy it responsibly and gift generously to friends.

Make sure desert lavender is clean and free of bugs. Drop sprigs of lavender into full bottle of tequila. Re-cap and store in a cool, dark spot for about 4 weeks. Tequila may change color and desert lavender will fade as essence and flavors infuse into the alcohol. Strain into 64-ounce pitcher, then pour into smaller bottles or refill original rinsed jar. Compost used herbs. Add small sprig of fresh desert lavender to individual bottles to show what flavored it.

MAKES 64 OUNCES.

GF V

CREOSOTE BITTERS

Contributed by Barbara Rose, Bean Tree Farm

This recipe takes advantage of the desert's best-smelling herb, creosote (Larrea tridentata), also called Reina del Desierto. Creosote is a very potent traditional medicinal herb and should be used VERY sparingly. It should not be ingested regularly without research and/or a health care professional.

Harvest creosote cutting top 5 to 10 inches of growth, when vibrant, shiny, and in bud and bloom. Dry in paper bag until crumbly, then strip off stems and branches. Macerate leaves in enough alcohol to cover herbs and store in a dark cool place for a month or more, which will yield a full-strength tincture. Strain and add equal amount (or more) of water to make an 80-proof bitter, about 40 percent alcohol. The higher the alcohol content, the longer it keeps. For a truly local bitter, add to macerating step a bit of Seville orange rind, brittlebush, brickelia, yerba mansa, or mesquite sap. Store tincture in a dark glass bottle in a cool place.

As a flavor or bitter, add ONLY a couple drops of full-strength tincture per drink. The flavor will be there even with this small amount!

You can also add a few drops to a spray water bottle to cool off and "smell the rain" when it's hot!

1 part creosote, dried and finely chopped or ground

1 to 2 parts 190-proof grain or other food-sourced alcohol, to cover and more

1/10 part additional spices and herbs of your choice, crushed or ground (optional)

MEET
MEATS &
INSECTS

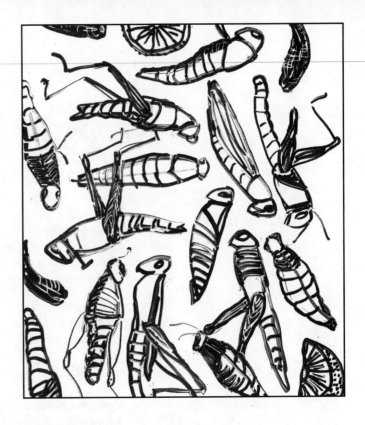

If small game is fair game, this section proves it! Meats and insects add to the diet much-needed protein, fat, and other essential nutrients, although acquiring and processing them takes time and some special skills and tools. Along with the amazing nutrient-dense plant foods of the Sonoran Desert, animal foods are also abundant and varied. Some game animals traditionally hunted in the Arizona Upland include rabbits, javelina, deer, and various birds. The clearinghouse for all hunting information, rules, and regulations may be found at Arizona Game and Fish at AZgfd.com.

- Jill Lorenzini

Pot of processed packrats

Photo: Barbara Rose

Processed packrats marinating in Bean Tree Farm mesquite/chile barbeque sauce and coconut oil

Photo: Barbara Rose

MEATS & INSECTS BASICS

HARVEST/HUNTING TIMES

Contact your state's Game and Fish department for local hunting seasons and regulations.

NOTE: We only include some small game in this book, since the hunting of small game is often less impactful on the ecosystem than the harvest of larger game. Additionally, around the home small game such as packrats and grasshoppers are considered pests. Eating them transforms these "pests" into local harvests.

CAUTION

There are sometimes outbreaks of septicemic and bubonic plague in rabbits and rodents such as packrats, squirrels, and prairie dogs. The disease can be transmitted to humans via fleas that carry the bacteria. Fleas seek out another living, warm-bodied host when their original host dies and its body cools. Some ways to reduce the risk of such transmittance of fleas include:

- Drown the host animal and its fleas before processing the carcass.
- Before the host body cools, burn off its hair and fleas over a fire prior to processing.
- Wear gloves when you field-dress the animals to prevent the plague bacteria from entering the body through open cuts or abrasions in the skin.

See your health care provider immediately if you contract any unexplained illness involving a sudden and severe fever. Make sure they test for the plague. With early diagnosis and antibiotics, this disease is easily treatable.

Avoid the use of poisons that could be absorbed or ingested by potential harvests.

MEATS & INSECTS

Chapulines con Mole

Photo: Amy Valdés Schwemm

GF

PACKRAT:
HOW TO CATCH AND EAT ONE

Contributed by Bill Cunningham

Why would you even want to eat a packrat? It's pretty simple, really. These little animals are plentiful, and tasty, and usually very clean. They are not to be confused with the "city rats" that live on garbage. Packrats are vegetarian and live on nutritious cactus, desert plants, and seeds. I live out of town in the desert, and to me, hunting and eating them is not only for food but part of "pest control," because they can do a lot of damage and propagate very fast. There is hardly ever a shortage of this animal on my 5 acres. I like to think of them as a resource rather than a big problem. I probably catch a couple dozen of them in a typical year, and have been doing this for many years now.

CATCHING PACKRAT:

Packrats can easily be caught in a live trap, which means that you will kill and prepare them when you find them. I usually set the trap at night, using an apple core with some peanut butter as bait. Even better bait is prickly pear fruit or saguaro seeds. I put the trap out around my house where I have seen their droppings or midden/nest. Once you catch one, an easy and quick way to kill it is to put the trap in a large container of water—such as a large trash can of rainwater—to drown it. This should happen quickly, in a minute or two. If you trap one in the traditional "kill trap," you won't know how long it's been dead and should not trust the safety of the meat.

PROCESSING PACKRAT:

Start by cutting off the feet, head, and tail. I use a sharp kitchen or hunting knife and a short block of 1 x 6 plank as a cutting board. Carefully cut the belly fur/skin without puncturing the gut, and pull off the fur coat. It usually comes off in one piece, and can be saved to make a small purse or bag, as the fur is quite soft. After you have "helped it off with its coat," it's time to open up the gut and pull out the innards. I usually leave intact the heart and lungs—everything above the diaphragm—as those parts are good to eat and it saves a little time to just leave them in. I keep two bowls of clean water on my work table to rinse the knives and meat as I work. Discard innards. This process is very similar to cleaning a small fish we called "pan fish." Once cleaned, rinse the packrat well.

COOKING PACKRAT:

Sometimes I "age" the meat in the fridge for a couple of days to let the meat "relax" before adding it to a Ziploc bag of other packrats in the freezer. It takes more than one to make a meal or dish of them. But if I happen to be making soup that day, I'll add the meat to the soup to add flavor and protein. Packrat is delicate and will totally fall apart if cooked more than a couple of hours. Due to the numerous small bones, this makes it harder to enjoy the meat, so it's best not to overcook them. You can also roast them over a fire/barbecue, fry, steam, boil, or bake packrat. They have a delicate flavor and can be spiced with your favorite herbs and spices.

GF

PACKRATS WITH GRAVY

Contributed by Patty West as told by Elizabeth Rocha,
an Apache elder and teacher whose passion is maintaining traditions and language

*The Apache word for packrat is "lŏs clooe." We would hunt packrats in the fall
when the snakes weren't out. We would all go out hunting together, my mom and
dad and all my brothers and sisters. Dad would decide what day and cut branches
of cottonwood and willow and make bats from the wood. We did it on the weekend
because they worked. Mom would wake us up early and say, "Get up we're going to
get rats." We would get excited because we would know it would be fun. Took a long
time to get there … there was lots of cactus and mesquite where the nests were. Used
to be lots of packrats but now you don't see them. Maybe we killed them all. The nests
look like a pile of sticks, but it's a nest. My mom wore high-top tennis shoes and camp
dress tucked in front like a sumo wrestler. My dad and brothers would tie their pants
at the bottom so the rats wouldn't crawl up.*

*My dad would poke a large stick—about 8 feet long—into the nest and shake and poke until the packrats came out. You have to be
fast because they run right under you. The kids would run and jump. Those rats were everywhere. They would run everywhere and
we'd get some, and some would run off. We'd hit them right on the head. You had to make sure they were dead—they will bite you if
you don't hit them right.*

*Dad scolded my younger brother and he'd go get the gunnysack, until Dad would say I think we have enough. Then my mom would
pull her dress back out and get decent. We'd all get in the car and Mom said, "I guess I did look funny."*

*The kids would gather wood and one of those big cooking pots with boiling water. We'd add more wood to keep the fire going while
it cooked for about 2 hours. Mom would cut the head and feet off and slit the skin and pull it off with the innards and toss it to
the dogs. We always had dogs. Whatever we cleaned they ate the insides and head and feet. My mom and dad would eat the rats
wrapped in a tortilla or bubble bread and pulling the meat off the bones and dip the tortillas and bread in a bowl of the gravy. We
just liked the gravy with bread.*

- Elizabeth Rocha

4 to 6 packrats
(depending on size)

1/2 to 1 cup acorn
(or wheat) flour

Salt to taste

4 to 6 tortillas or
bubble bread (ash bread)

Catch packrats. Process and clean packrats. Boil 1 gallon of water in a large pot. Place packrats in water and boil
on low for 1 to 2 hours. Blend acorn flour (or other flour) with a small amount of water until it's the consistency
of pancake batter and then add to the pot. Season with salt to taste. Serve on tortillas or bubble bread, dipping in
remaining gravy from the pot.

MAKES 4 to 6 SERVINGS.

GF

PRICKLY PEAR MARINATED MESQUITE QUAIL

Contributed by Abe Sanchez

1 or 2 lemons or limes

6 dressed quail, whole or butterflied (may substitute chicken or any firm fish fillets)

Salt and pepper

2 cups prickly pear juice

1/4 cup olive oil

1 cup mesquite flour

Oil for baking sheet or frying

This recipe marries the sweetness of mesquite with the tartness of prickly pear to season the small desert quail. Serve with steamed quinoa drizzled with the drippings, rice and beans, or on a salad bed of wild greens like arugula or verdolagas.

Squeeze lemon juice over birds and season with salt and pepper. Marinate birds in prickly pear juice for 2 hours or overnight in refrigerator. The dark red or orange prickly pear juice may stain the meat the color of the fruit, but goes away when cooked.

TO BAKE:

Preheat oven to 350º F. Remove birds from marinade, pat dry, and brush with olive oil. Rub birds with mesquite flour and place on a lightly greased baking sheet. Bake for 45 minutes or until brown and crispy. Butterflied birds will cook faster than whole birds.

TO FRY:

Remove birds from marinade, pat dry, and brush with olive oil. Rub birds with mesquite flour and place in pan with hot cooking oil and cook until golden brown on each side. You may need to occasionally scoop out the loose mesquite flour in the pan since it will burn, and the bitter, charred flour may stick to the birds.

MAKES 6 SERVINGS.

GF

CHAPULINES (GRASSHOPPERS) CON MOLE

By Nicole Francis and Amy Valdés Schwemm

Catch grasshoppers with verve, vigor, lots of friends, and lots of laughter. Keep them in a container to let their digestive tracks clear. Put the whole container in the refrigerator to slow them down or in the freezer to kill them. Fry in oil until crispy and drain on paper towels to absorb excess oil. Season with salt and Mano y Metate Mole powder. Eat as a snack or grind up into a meal to use as a seasoning. The small ones fry up very crispy but take so many to make a meal. The larger ones are meatier, but the legs and wings get stuck in your teeth, so remove them before eating.

Grasshoppers (as many as you can catch!)

Oil for frying

Salt to taste

Mano y Metate Mole*

*NOTE: Mano y Metate Mole is a product of freshly ground whole spices, nuts, seeds, and chiles. It's an easy way to use the celebrated Mexican sauces. You can buy it locally in Tucson and Southern Arizona or order it online (ManoyMetate.com).

PART III
LIVING AND EATING IN PLACE

Chiltepin Salsa

Photo: Christian Timmerman

by Jill Lorenzini

WHY I WANDER: DEVELOPING INTIMACY WITH PLACE

I like to move and be moved. Especially out in the natural world. In this part of the Sonoran Desert, that means hiking through towering cactus forests, savoring the smell and gift of seasonal rains, and enduring sweltering heat in exchange for summer's sweet harvests. And without even trying, stumbling across little miracles and staggering beauty: a foraging desert tortoise, rain-filled rock mortar holes, tidy coyote beds under ironwood trees, silvery saguaro skeletons, winter javelina scat speckled black with shiny barrel cactus seeds, the frothy wavefront of a summer stormwater flow. It also feeds a familiar and deep need in me to have a meaningful relationship to place, to home.

Books and study provide delicious and craved intellectual fare, and an ordered structure upon which to pin the details of personal experience. Rides and drives through desert landscapes, especially protected and mostly intact ones, satisfy broad curiosities and offer a sense of general understanding. But only walking into and through a place reveals the sensuous contours and the hidden spaces, the plant personalities and specific human traces. It slows the pace to one that encourages exploration and immersion, not separation, and uncovers the depth and details that dissolve myths and misconceptions. Step by step, it delicately exposes what the road passes by, and what words and books sometimes fall short of conveying. The desert allows this.

When I'm there, I let it move me. Plants grow in prescribed patterns, and the spaces in between create meandering natural pathways that invite wandering. Beauty or eye-catching oddities move me, too, beckoning me in their direction—and on the way, to the surprise of early spring wildflowers. Sometimes my legs and feet go their own curious way. I disengage my busy mind and follow, listening, observing, sniffing the air, poking around. Other times, I let my open heart guide me, and discover things I never set out to find: crystals, arrow points, potsherds, saguaro boots. I find insights too, reaching for one thing and grasping another.

All the wandering—the miles, the terrain, the seasons, the weather, the years, each step—is recorded like a story on my muscles and in my body, a map of my physical relationship with this desert place. I feel its cool washes and undulating bajadas in my bones, the thin air and dizzying vistas of Sky Islands like butterflies in my stomach. I harbor the bliss and brace of desert swimming holes, the salty-white, sweat-stained remembrance of trails. Just a memory away: dust devil disruptions, a belly full of saguaro fruit, pounding summer storms and deluges. And the tone and ache of covering so much ground: always inside me. This is the desert's unique personality—its "there-oir," its placeness—imprinted on my body, my life.

My appetite leads the way too. I like to taste where I am, to eat from place. Especially wild, native, and cultivated foods that define the essence of the place in which they grow, and express a specific flavor profile—a terroir—that captures it. If we are what we eat, then I'm thrilled to be part mesquite, saguaro, cholla, ironwood, wolfberry, amaranth, and aloysia.

Knowing the edible native plants of a place, their traits and tastes, their growth and harvest seasons, and the intricate indigenous wisdom that informs their use is a tasty way to further develop connection to place. It empowers stewardship too, long-term care for the living systems that sustain our health, our souls, the environment, our survival. Snacking on yellow palo verde flowers makes a spring hike memorable. Searching sandy washes in muggy-moody late summer increases the likelihood of finding wolfberries and desert hackberries plumped by rains. Touching sticky saguaro fruit to the heart before eating is an act of reverence honoring native traditions and life-giving wild foods. Mouth-watering mesquite memories fuel thorny harvests at one of the hottest, most intense times of year.

By eating and celebrating these seasonal desert foods, we invite the desert into our lives—literally, as food that feeds our bodies, and, figuratively, as a deep rootedness to a place we love. What could be more intimate than that? One of the longest and most rewarding relationships I've ever had is with this special Sonoran Desert place, and with the amazing plants and perennial foods that bring it to life.

Relating this way to place requires more than connection. It requires commitment and abiding love, like any lasting relationship. It demands that we show up, consistently and creatively, and act as good observers and listeners, offering our whole selves, open to learning and change. It also requires reciprocity, the glue that holds everything together. In a reciprocal relationship, we don't just take, we also give generously. We don't just harvest, we plant. We don't just learn, we share what we know. We don't just remove, we replace, restore, and regenerate. We don't just observe and direct, we interact and strive for understanding. We don't just relish, we toil. We don't just take for granted, we honor with reverence. I wander with these things in mind.

If it's solace I'm seeking, I visit the elders, the saguaros, the ancient ironwoods. Somehow being near them, greeting them like old friends, and lying down underneath them restores my well-being and inspires patience and constancy. It heals me like creosote salve does. I climb to saddles and ridges where the wind freely roams and let it blow through me, permeate my wounds, my being. I take that feeling back home with me, like pretty stones in my pocket, something to hold on to.

When I'm overwhelmed and needing quiet (what I call "Q-deficient"), I know where to go. Vastness isn't loud. Sometimes it's actually melodic. The wide-open desert reminds me that quiet is not the absence of sound, but of noise, of din. Animal calls, wind in spines, my feet crunching in the sand—these are quiet sounds. I listen carefully. At times I end up talking to the plants and the place, breaking the silence, telling it like it is, heart on my sleeve. The desert, that ideal listener who never needs to respond or advise or analyze, doesn't mind.

by Amanda Bramble

TENDING TO THE SKY:
SOLAR COOKING AS CONNECTION

When I harvest the plants that grow on the land where I live, I feel a sense of connection and contentment. I'm embodied in my own animal nature. I'm the creature that grazes on tender new leaf growth and digs into the earth to find a cool place to rest, the animal who instinctively rubs aromatic herbs on her skin.

Making meals with the food of the land allows me to be the kind of human I want to inhabit this beautiful earth. I can't help but have a deep sense of gratitude and respect for the fruits, leaves, buds, and seeds that provide such delight and nourishment. Every morsel is precious. Living with this gratitude and respect is as good as it gets for me. If I have an attitude of appreciation, I have a great life.

I have the same sense of respect and wonder for the sunlight that makes our desert what it is. We can harvest the sun to make these desert foods into luscious meals. Solar cooking has a long list of benefits. For starters, it keeps heat out of your house in the summer, reduces your use and expense of fossil fuels, and keeps the atmosphere cleaner. What attracts me is the giddy joy I get from watching my food bubbling away with the heat of the sun, and eating delicious concoctions that have been such a literal and direct collaboration with the cosmos.

When you cook with the sun, you point the solar oven toward the east in the morning. If you are cooking all day, you will end up tracking the entire course of the sun through the sky. You will notice our local star rises at a different place on the horizon as the seasons change, as does the sun's noonday location. You will see just how many hours of sunlight we lose during the winter and gain in summer.

Solar cooking helps us to track natural patterns of our environment, which can then inform other actions such as where to plant trees (to provide needed shade or winter sun access) or how best to cool and heat our homes with added awnings or vegetation. For me, it's another layer of learning to become the kind of human

animal that lives in balance with her environment. And it has an immediate payoff: delicious food!

You can put a meal in the solar oven, forget about it, and come back in a few hours to steaming dinner. It's quite easy. You just have to be willing to pay attention to a few things:

THE OVEN:

Buy a solar oven. Or make one! There are many oven designs, but I suggest a sturdy, weather-resistant oven you can station outside your door or nearby. You can install it onto an old table or swivel chair in a convenient location that gets sun throughout the day.

TEMPERATURES AND COOK TIMES:

Cooking in a solar oven takes longer than cooking in a conventional or "fossil-fuel-consuming" oven. So you'll have to make adjustments if you're adapting a recipe. You'll get the hang of it after some experimentation.

Foods start cooking at 180° F (82° C). My solar box oven doesn't get above 275° F (135° C), which makes it an excellent slow cooker (Fig. 1). In this type of oven, I can forget about my food and it won't burn at these lower temperatures.

EASY DISHES AND SMALL AMOUNTS:

Start with easy dishes like stews, casseroles, lentils, sweet potatoes, and quinoa. Most of the energy that goes into cooking something goes toward getting the entire dish to cooking temperature. So start with small amounts and cook early in the day, once the sun has risen a bit (say, 9 am). Chop food into small pieces. The more surface area it has, the faster it will cook. Use a dark pot with a tight-fitting lid. Put a thermometer in your oven to help track temperature. After you have had some success move on to breads, pies, black beans, and all the local wild-harvested ingredients you can gather!

Figure 1. *A low-temperature, slow-cooking, solar box oven. In this style, you don't need to tend to food much, as it will not burn. This oven is cooking Amanda's Off-Grid Greens Tart.* Photo: Amanda Bramble

Figure 2. *A high-temperature, fast-cooking, parabolic solar oven. To keep food from burning in this style of oven, you must carefully tend it, as Andy shows here. This oven can be used on mildly overcast days or colder winter days when a lower-temperature, slow-cooking, box oven would not perform well.* Photo: Amanda Bramble

PARABOLIC COOKERS:

You could dive right into hot solar cooking with a fast cooker, also called a parabolic cooker (Fig. 2). These can cook at much higher temperatures, which means you have to be careful not to burn food. You will have to learn quickly how often to turn the pot, as it needs to stay long enough in one place to cook, but not so long that it burns.

Wind, clouds, the seasonally changing angle of the sun, and outside air temperature are all factors in the crafting of your meal as they will all affect the temperature within your solar oven. This is just the kind of relationship so many of us need to bring balance into our lives.

Solar cooking invites us to pay attention to our environment at a very immediate level. Staying put and belonging to a place has many rewards. A big one is giant proud smiles at working with the wonders of nature, including the sun. Another, of course, is dinner cooked solely with the heat harvested from our local star.

Note: See Amanda's solar recipe for Off-Grid Greens Tart (p. 286). Other solar recipes in this book are marked with this icon: (S)

See the index (p. 333) for a list of solar-cooked recipes.

Amanda Bramble and her solar ovens   Photo: Andy Bramble

PLANTING RAIN, FERTILITY, WILD FOODS, AND COMMUNITY

Everything we need is already here. We just need to learn to see it, get to know it, and collaborate with it.

My family moved to the drylands when I was three. As I grew up playing in the desert, I often wondered, "How do people live here without food from the store?" Our suburban desert home was surrounded by an incredibly diverse natural native food forest, but I hadn't learned to see it yet.

Through play, I discovered I could chew on mesquite pods and eat prickly pear fruit. And the Boy Scouts introduced me to desert hackberries. But I was still missing so much.

As I got older I read stories by regional ethnobotanists like Gary Paul Nabhan and Carolyn Niethammer about wild food plants. I started to get to know these plants in the yard, the open desert (plant identification books in hand), and botanical gardens like the Arizona-Sonora Desert Museum and Tohono Chul Park. The more plants I got to know, the more connected I felt to this place.

When I met Stella Tucker, a Tohono O'odham elder who grew up harvesting from and collaborating with the desert, I learned that I, too, have a role in these wild food forests.

We all do.

I visited Stella's camp in Saguaro National Park West where her family has harvested saguaro fruit for generations. One hot June morning, Stella showed me how to separate the skin of the saguaro fruit from its pulp. She then placed the empty shell of the fruit at the base of the saguaro open and facing up to the sun "to help bring on the summer rains."

Life in the Sonoran Desert would not exist without those rains. They break the intense dry heat, germinate seed to turn brown lands green, and spark a flurry of birds, insects, and other life to sing. Stella's action transformed an extractive harvest into a reciprocal one: Returning part of the harvested fruit and its nutrients back into the soil and root zone of the saguaro would help the saguaro grow and produce still more fruit.

Reciprocal relationships with place are core to Desert Harvesters' work (and play). The following four tenets guide our work in planting the desert's bounty.

1 ▶ PLANT THE RAIN

"Plant the rain" means creating water-harvesting earthworks, basins, or rain gardens that capture and infiltrate rainfall and runoff in the soil and roots, rather than wastefully drain it away. Planting the rain also flushes harmful salts out of the plants' root zone; adds fertility (rainwater is naturally salt-free, and contains beneficial nitrogen and microorganisms); reduces downstream flooding; mitigates erosion; and helps "bring back the water," as Petey Mesquitey sings (see A River of Abundance, p. 317), recharging our groundwater, wells, springs, creeks, and river flows.

Planting the rain first creates a foundation for plants to grow and thrive solely, or at least primarily, with on-site rainfall and captured runoff. Rain is free! No costly pumped, imported, or extracted waters are needed or taken (see Figs. 1a, 1b).

Learn more about planting the rain at HarvestingRainwater.com.

Figure 1a. Sick landscape wastefully drains the rain, runoff, and fertility away to be replaced with costly irrigation systems and imported fertilizer. Arrows depict stormwater flow. Illustration by Joe Marshall; reproduced with permission from Rainwater Harvesting for Drylands and Beyond, *Volume 1, by Brad Lancaster.*

Figure 1b. Healthy landscape resourcefully plants the rain, run-on, and fertility for free. Arrows depict stormwater flow. Illustration by Joe Marshall; reproduced with permission from Rainwater Harvesting for Drylands and Beyond, *Volume 1, by Brad Lancaster.*

CAPTURING STREET RUNOFF

It turns out that over *a million gallons of rain per mile per year* falls on Tucson's neighborhood streets before it goes down the storm drain! That is enough water to provide all the irrigation needs of native shade trees lining, and shading, both sides of the streets—if we direct it there.

We can direct that street runoff to the trees by planting within or beside water-harvesting earthworks then cutting or coring street curbs so water can enter the basins (see Figs. 2, 3). We can also direct runoff from roofs, patios, and raised paths to adjoining sunken planting basins (see Fig. 1b).

Worried about toxic heavy metals from the street? Fear not. Studies by Mitch Pavao-Zuckerman at the University of Arizona found that the woody perennial vegetation does not take up toxic heavy metals from the street runoff into its edible parts. Annual crops like leafy greens or tubers, however, do take up such heavy metals and should not be planted in or harvested from areas watered by street runoff.

Figure 2. Street runoff directed to street-side tree basins via curb cuts enables the street to irrigate the street trees for free. Illustration by Joe Marshall; reproduced with permission from Rainwater Harvesting for Drylands and Beyond, *Volume 1, by Brad Lancaster.*

Figure 3. *Vaughan Lancaster plays near rain garden filled with street runoff. Reproduced with permission from* Rainwater Harvesting for Drylands and Beyond, *Volume 1, by Brad Lancaster.*

2 ▶ PLANT THE PLANTS

Planting endemic plants means planting plants that have co-evolved with the unique climate, soils, and wildlife of a place over millennia. A native mesquite tree in its native bioregion supports far more native pollinators and other wildlife, than a non-native mesquite tree in that same landscape.

PLANTING FROM SEED:

The cheapest and easiest way to plant vegetation is from seed when both the seed and rain are falling. Collect seed from the plants with the characteristics you seek, such as best flavors, most bountiful fruit sets, and best ripening times (though keep in mind that plants grown from seed can differ in some characteristics from the mother plant). Plants grown *in situ* from seed are more drought hardy and grow faster than those planted from nursery stock because their roots were never bound in a pot or cut, and they were not dependent on regular irrigation. Plant seed when the rains begin in its ideal rain garden zone within water-harvesting earthworks, or within all three zones (bottom, terrace, and top zones), and let the seed decide which zone it prefers (see Fig. 4).

Plant at least three seeds in a growing area to improve chances of germinated seedlings. As they grow they can be thinned out, leaving the most vibrant specimens with the best harvest characteristics. Protect seedlings from hungry rabbits and other critters by using chicken wire fencing or hardware cloth. Hard seed (palo verde, mesquite) typically needs to be scarified to enhance germination (see Fig. 5).

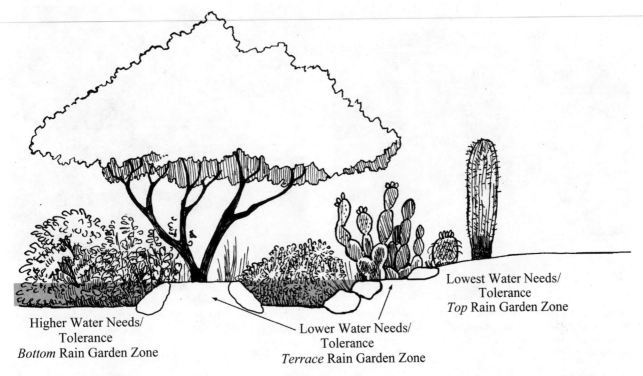

Figure 4. *Planting according to plants' water needs and tolerance determines their ideal rain garden zone. Here water captured in a storm has filled up to the terrace level. It will all infiltrate into the spongey soil in less than 12 hours, likely less than 1 hour. Illustration by Joe Marshall; reproduced with permission from* Rainwater Harvesting for Drylands and Beyond, Volume 1, *by Brad Lancaster.*

In figure:

Lowest Water Needs/
Tolerance
Top Rain Garden Zone

Higher Water Needs/
Tolerance
Bottom Rain Garden Zone

Lower Water Needs/
Tolerance
Terrace Rain Garden Zone

Figure 5. *Palo verde seed scarified after nicking side of hard seed coat with toenail clippers. See the Planting Tips section of the Basics sidebar at the beginning of each wild food ingredient chapter for its seed scarification tips.*

PLANTING FROM NURSERY STOCK:

Buying plants from local nurseries means your money stays in your community. Such nurseries are often more receptive to growing the native plants you request. One- to five-gallon-sized plants are cheaper and less likely to be root bound, since they haven't been constrained by pots as long as bigger plants. Once in the ground, these smaller plants tend to grow faster than larger ones and outsize them after just a few years of growth.

Plant each plant in an ideal rain garden zone (see Fig. 4). Irrigate to get new plantings established, usually one to three years. In the hot months, irrigate every other day for the first three weeks after planting, then cut back to a good watering once a week. Eventually water once a month, until established. To avoid the cost, leaks, and hassle of a drip irrigation system, you can water by hose, drip bucket, or water trailer until the plant is established (see Figs. 6, 7).

Figure 6. Neighborhood foresters watering desert ironwood tree (within water-harvesting basin lower than street) just after planting. Mulch was added moments later. Street curb will later be cut to direct street runoff into basin.

Figure 7. Drip bucket (try to get the ones with strong, metal handles). Drill a hole 1/8 inch (3 mm) in diameter near bottom of 5-gallon bucket, fill with water, and place beside plant as needed. Reproduced with permission from Rainwater Harvesting for Drylands and Beyond, Volume 2, *by Brad Lancaster.*

PLANTING FROM CUTTINGS:

Cactus such as prickly pear and cholla are easy to propagate from cuttings, which produce clones of the mother plant. Choose a healthy pad from a prickly pear or a cane from a cholla. Mark what side of the pad or cane faces south before you cut it from the mother plant. Plant it cut-side in the ground keeping mark south-facing to avoid sunburn. As with seed, the cutting will do best when planted within or beside a water-harvesting basin during the rainy season. *Note: Staghorn and buckthorn cholla have an amazing range of flower colors. You can select and propagate cuttings based on edible flower-bud quality and flower color.*

3 ▶ PLANTING AND CYCLING FERTILITY

Gravity pulls everything downhill for free. Designed as the low spots in the landscape, rain gardens naturally collect and hold leaf drop, mulch, and other fertility. Beneath the canopy of their mother plant, fallen leaves create a sheltering, sponge-like mulch. Fallen fruit, unharvested mesquite pods, cut-up prunings, and bird manure also make good, nutritious mulch (see Fig. 8). This mulch moderates temperature extremes, helps water infiltrate the soil, prevents evaporation, cycles nutrients back into the soil and plant, and provides habitat and food for beneficial microorganisms (see Fig. 9).

Raking up or blowing away leaves and other nutrient-rich material strips fertility out of a landscape. As we like to say, leaves are called "leaves" because we are supposed to leave them. Leaves and other organic matter will decompose and cycle back into the soil life much faster with additional moisture captured in the water-harvesting earthworks. Make sure the top of the mulch remains lower than the inlet to the earthwork/basin, so water can continue to flow into the basin.

Figure 8. Capturing leaf drop and cut-up prunings in water-harvesting basin beside tree.

Figure 9. Fertile, sponge-like mulch of organic matter and microorganisms harvested within runoff-harvesting basin.

4 ▶ PLANTING, HARVESTING, AND STEWARDING TOGETHER TO GROW COMMUNITY

Enjoying these activities with friends and neighbors enhances human health and builds community while improving neighborhoods and watersheds. For example, volunteer neighborhood foresters have planted over 1,400 native food-bearing trees in Tucson's Dunbar/Spring neighborhood since 1996 in annual community planting events designed to share the labor and get to know neighbors (see Figs. 6 to 12). Community stewarding is further enhanced by other events, forester hangouts, and trainings, including free twice-a-year pruning workshops keeping public walkways and bikeways shaded and accessible. Certified arborists supervise volunteer forester crews working throughout the neighborhood. A chipper/shredder trailer follows the crew, turning the prunings into mulch to protect and build soil around the trees. Visit DesertHarvesters.org for workshops, plantings, a sample native tree list, and a "call to neighbors."

Figure 10. Dunbar/Spring Neighborhood Foresters logo by neighbor Marina Cornelius.

Figure 11a. Before. Barren public right-of-way before the planting of rain, native food plants, and fertility. Reproduced with permission from Rainwater Harvesting for Drylands and Beyond, *Volume 1, by Brad Lancaster.*

Figure 11b. After. Neighborhood food forest and more life after the planting of rain, vegetation, and fertility. All is freely irrigated solely with passively harvested rainwater and street runoff. Reproduced with permission from Rainwater Harvesting for Drylands and Beyond, *Volume 1, by Brad Lancaster.*

Figure 12. Happy harvest with friends and neighbors.

A RIVER OF ABUNDANCE

Thanks in large part to the ecology of the Santa Cruz River, the Tucson area has the longest continuous history of farming in what is now the continental United States—over 4,000 years. Tucson owes its existence to the Santa Cruz River. It was the foundation for wild abundance (including the now gone Great Mesquite Forest) and continuous indigenous and resettled cultures.

I arrived in Tucson too late to see the river alive and instead experienced the barren results. Around 2004 or 2005, Petey Mesquitey shared a song about the Santa Cruz on his weekly radio show "Growing Native" on KXCI 91.3 Community Radio. The song helps me to see and feel what was lost, and what could be regained if we changed our ways. This motivates my work. It is why I plant the rain.

SANTA CRUZ RIVER SONG

I've been reading all these stories about a dry river bed,
How it ran a hundred years ago, at least that's what I've read
There were cottonwoods and ash trees and mesquite bosques
With willows and elderberries back in those olden days

There were marshes and meadows not far from the banks
Where you'd find frogs and turtles in quiet little tanks,
There were fish in the water, there were birds in the trees,
And the shade on the river made for a cool desert breeze

Bring back the water, bring back the flow
To the river that crossed the desert so long ago.
Sometimes I tell you it just gives me the blues,
When I think of that river we call the Santa Cruz

That was a long time ago and it might be hard to find clues
Of the plants and the animals along the old Santa Cruz
Oh I missed it all and though I wasn't even there
When I think of the river it just don't seem fair

Bring back the water, bring back the flow
To the river that crossed the desert so long ago.
Sometimes I tell you it just gives me the blues,
When I think of that river we call the Santa Cruz

It was a long time ago and it'd be hard to find clues
Of the plants and the animals along the old Santa Cruz
There were fish in the water, there were birds in the trees
And the shade on the river made for a cool desert breeze

There were fish in the water, there were birds in the trees
And the shade on the river made for a cool desert breeze

Hear Petey Mesquitey singing the song at DesertHarvesters.org.

- Brad Lancaster

by Richard Stephen Felger and Neil Logan

THE DESERT IS FOOD

Impoverished places with a scarcity of healthy foods are called food deserts. But Apache elders say, "The desert is where the food is."

The Sonoran Desert is a hundred thousand square miles surrounding the northern Gulf of California (see map, p. 24) and supports 2,500 species of seed plants. Native Americans used 450 for food—some as staples and others as snack foods. Our interest is drawn to the staples, diverse and intriguing: desert tree legumes, cactus fruits, seawater grain and other perennial grains, desert goji berry, and desert fan palm.

The Sonoran Desert is an ideal place for economically viable native food crops, especially long-lived perennials for no-till agriculture. Some water is needed, although minimal compared to non-desert crops, and poor-quality water is okay, while harvested rainwater is excellent. The fruit from organ pipe cactus (*Stenocereus thurberi*) is used for beverages including superior wines, preserves, flavoring, and more. It's one of the world's best fruits, almost as good as pitaya agria from Baja California, another cactus suitable for developing or hybridizing. Native desert fan palm (*Washingtonia filifera*) has large yields of small date-like fruits. It's a high water user but only a small area needs irrigating and wastewater will do. Mesquite (*Prosopis* spp.) trees and their pods are ideal for farming the future. Foothills palo verde (*Parkinsonia microphylla*) has high-protein seeds. Desert wolfberry is in the same genus (*Lycium*) as goji berry, and can be used similarly. Nipa (*Distichlis palmeri*) is a grain growing with seawater at the delta of the Río Colorado. And there are more. Hedge your bets, intercropping food plants for farms as well as home gardens. You'll get high nutrition, taste, and local food resiliency—and growing markets exist for local foods. It's a drying world.

Yet modern food production in arid regions today is largely based on consumptive systems imported from more humid regions. We propose wild arid foods as crops to fit the environment. We do not approve of changing the environment to fit the crop. And if you harvest from plants in the wild, leave plenty for renewal and for the animals.

MESQUITE – *PROSOPIS*

World hunger can be addressed by developing mesquite as an arid-land crop. Mesquite offers agricultural independence for arid and semi-arid regions and can be the world's first major new crop since soy.

Mesquites are hardwood, nitrogen-fixing members of the legume family in a group of species of the genus Prosopis and native to arid regions of the Americas. Six species from North America known as mesquite, and about two dozen in South America often called *algarrobo*, are significant. Some of these species are now naturalized in distant parts of the world.

The roots harbor nitrogen-fixing bacteria and powerful fungal allies enabling *Prosopis* to grow in harsh environments like lava in Hawaii or the saline, hyper-arid coastal deserts of Peru. The pods are non-toxic, gluten- and soy-free, high-fiber, and protein-rich food. The pods do not split on ripening (so contents do not fall away), an efficient feature for harvesting. The usual method of preparation involves sun drying or fire parching to reduce moisture content, control insects, and make processing easier. Dry pods are then ground into flour, or steeped in water to make drinks. The flour is hygroscopic (readily absorbs moisture from the air, and becomes a hard mass when exposed to humid air), so it should be stored in dry conditions.

The bulk of the pod, the pulp (mesocarp) is rich in calories/carbohydrates with a balanced amino acid profile. Within the mesocarp each pod contains hard, protein-rich seeds encased in a tough, leathery endocarp. There is much variation in pod size and taste—some have an apple-like flavor and others contain important phytonutrients like the anthocyanin pigments in blueberries. The husk (exocarp) and endocarp are not digestible, but can add dietary fiber to the flour. By-products of pod processing can be feedstock for mycoculture and aquaculture systems, thereby increasing the protein output through biological conversion. Other products include honey, ethyl alcohol from the pods, and bio-energy from the wood.

Tropical species such as *P. limensis*, native in Peru and naturalized in Hawaii, can produce three or more crops of pods per year. Others, in deserts and arid lands at higher latitudes, such as *P. velutina* in Arizona, tend to produce one large crop in early summer and additional pods into the fall.

The mesquites and *algarrobos* in North and South America served native peoples, agriculturalists, as well as hunter/gatherers as part of everyday life. People knew of trees or groves with sweeter pods and superior yields. The sweet pods provided nutritional foundation for civilizations in the Americas thousands of years before maize (corn) was developed. The wood is a high-quality, clean-burning fuel, preferred for cooking and widely used for charcoal, construction, and numerous other products. The gum and black sap have been widely used for medicine and dye.

People went out to mesquite groves to harvest the pods in early summer—a time of plenty and for socializing. The pods were variously dried and toasted, stored or not, pounded in a bedrock or wooden mortar with a large, wooden pestle, and the flour sorted by winnowing. The flour could be consumed as an *atole* (porridge), made into tortillas or cakes, or fermented into alcoholic beverages called *aloja*.

Mesquite honey has become economically important since introduction of honeybees from the Old World. Kiawe white honey from *Prosopis pallida* in Hawaii is considered one of the finest and most expensive gourmet honeys in the world. Currently, countries in the South American "Chaco" are developing *Prosopis* to produce organic ethyl alcohol to extract and preserve herbal medicines to create medicinal programs and alleviate costly importations.

Field tests of different mesquites are under-way in various regions of the world. The agricultural potential rivals that of the major modern crops. High-yielding, pest-resistant, flavorful candidates exist in test plots and remnant forests. Studies indicate annual pod yields of 2 to 4 tons per hectare in the colder-tolerant species like *P. velutina* from the Northern Hemisphere, or *P. alba* in the Southern Hemisphere, while the tropical species *P. pallida* may yield up to 10 tons per hectare. Mesocarp-flour yields are in the range of 1 to 5 tons per hectare per year depending on the species and environment. Centuries-old trees in South America, Hawaii, and the southwestern U.S. are still yielding large quantities of pods annually. *Prosopis limensis* established in Hawaii (native to coastal Peru) may sequester as much as 1.2 to 8.9 tons of carbon per hectare/year, the range based on soil type.

If total available food value of the *Prosopis* tree is used, depending on the species and environment, 1 hectare of land may provide food calories for 4 to 44 people annually. At these rates only 0.5 percent of the available terrestrial landmass of the planet could provide calories for 4.5 billion people.

THE FUTURE OF PROSOPIS IS NOW

Due in large part to human activity, our warming planet currently has an atmospheric CO_2 level of 400 parts per million (ppm). Interestingly, the last time the planet had 400 ppm of atmospheric CO_2 coincided with *Prosopis* expansion of the late Miocene. About 15 million years ago atmospheric carbon levels ranged between 300 and 500 ppm, temperatures were 3 to 5 degrees Celsius hotter than the beginning of the Industrial Revolution, and sea levels were 100 to 200 feet higher (Greenop et al. 2014). As the inland seas on the North and South American continents receded, they left vast saline deserts. These became the domain of *Prosopis*, from which many of the present-day species evolved. These rapid-growing, nitrogen-fixing, C3 organisms transpired endlessly, pumping fresh water into the atmosphere while breathing in the carbon floating in the air to create new soil.

Megafauna of that era helped spread trees through their manure after eating the abundant, sweet, nutritious pods. In South America, the spectacled bear and camelids such as the guanaco are notable as later (Pleistocene) dispersal agents. This epoch molded and shaped the species that early people came to cherish as a veritable "tree of life" while migrating through the Americas. As early as 10,000 years ago *Prosopis* pods formed the nutritional foundation of some of the first human populations along the Pacific Coast of South America. In what is present-day Peru, people whose staple was *Prosopis*, built pyramids, smelted gold, and recorded their cultures on pottery thousands of years before the advent of corn (*Zea mays*).

Today, corn is the dominant crop, but there is a key difference between corn and mesquite. Corn is entropic, requiring consistent, high water input and heavy fertilization and depletes the soil. *Prosopis* is biogenic, enriching the soil through nitrogen fixation and leaf litter, increasing humidity through the action of its canopy, and encouraging the creation of ecosystems: "99 years of mesquite for 1 year of corn."

We need to remove stumbling blocks to make *Prosopis*-based foods widely available. First, *Prosopis* has a reputation as a thorny invader. Second, not all *Prosopis* are created equal. Arturo Burkart (1976: 522) points out that in Argentina "trees with straight trunks 8 to 10 meters tall occur, but these are becoming extremely rare, from being cut in preference to the other shorter ones. Thus a negative, artificial selection is taking place, which should be counteracted by genetic up-building of the best lines in experimental plots."

We can overcome negative "artificial selection" by utilizing what we know of historical dispersions and creating small-scale, controlled naturalizations. These controlled naturalization events can spread one paddock at a time in a manner similar to traditional crop rotation, such as in the Andes. First, a crop of corn is grown inside a paddock surrounded with a fence or traditional animal control barrier (hedges of agaves and cactus, etc.). After the corn is harvested, cows are brought into the paddock

to eat the corn stubble supplemented with rations of *Prosopis* pods selected from trees with desired attributes (delicious pods, good growth form, climate hardiness, etc.). The cows poop and stomp the *Prosopis* seeds into the mud, creating temporary feedlot conditions that serve to suppress competitor weeds and fertilize the plot. After the cows are removed, the seeds germinate with the next rainfall and a *Prosopis* thicket arises.

The thicket creates competition for light among the young trees, forcing them to reach higher. Later, the thicket is pruned of thorny plants and horizontal stems, leaving tall trees with wide spacing. As the tree canopies fill, they begin to bear fruit. Further selection can be made for disease-resistant trees with abundant tasty pods and few or no thorns. What is left is a productive orchard of superior trees. The seeds can be used to start a new paddock and the process repeated.

This low-tech strategy has financial and functional advantages. Neil Logan's survey of *Prosopis* orchards in Latin America and Hawaii has turned up a crucial factor: Development of the radicle (taproot) is one of the most important indicators of successfully established, highly productive orchards. Cattle planting *Prosopis* as described above gives rise to a phenotype best suited to the site. Perhaps most important, the taproot is not disturbed, as it would be if transplanted. This enables the young tree roots to find deep underground water reserves vital to abundant pod production in the desert during drought.

Taco, as the mesquite tree is known to the Quechuas of the southern Andes, is an unfailing crop providing abundance when and where it is too hot and dry for other crops. It's not that *Prosopis* grow without water; rather it is their ability to tap water that few other trees can reach. Algarobia species have a dimorphic root system consisting of a deep taproot essential for reproduction and shallow lateral roots largely supporting vegetative growth. The foliage can help precipitate ambient moisture, misty rains, fog, or high humidity, which falls to the ground and becomes available to shallow roots. However, summer heat may evaporate moisture droplets before they reach the ground. The deep taproots are anchored in cool subterranean water-bearing soil, which facilitates fruit production. In the case of *El Rey del Desierto* (*Prosopis limensis*), this seasonal fluctuation in the availability of water may relate to presence or absence of thorns.

By honoring lessons of the past, we can integrate them into a positive future. The ancient mesquites are here again to help navigate the task of feeding people under challenging conditions generated by climate change. *Prosopis*: The past is our present and future.

REFERENCES AND FURTHER READING

Burkart, Arturo E. 1976. A monograph of the genus Prosopis: (Leguminosae Subfam. Mimosoideae). *Journal of the Arnold Arboretum* 57 (3): 219–249; 57 (4) 450–525.

Felger, Richard Stephen. 2007. Living resources at the center of the Sonoran Desert: Native American plant and animal utilization. Pages 147–192 in Felger and Bill Broyles, editors, *Dry Borders: Great Natural Reserves of the Sonoran Desert*. University of Utah Press, Salt Lake City.

Felger, Richard Stephen, and Mary Beck Moser. 1985, reprinted 2016. *People of the Desert and Sea: Ethnobotany of the Seri Indians*. University of Arizona Press, Tucson.

Greenop, Rosanna, Gavin L. Foster, Paul A. Wilson, and Caroline H. Lear. 2014. Middle Miocene climate instability associated with high-amplitude CO_2 variability. *Paleoceanography* 29: 845–853. (doi:10.1002/2014PA002653)

Hodgson, Wendy C. 2001. *Food Plants of the Sonoran Desert*. University of Arizona Press, Tucson.

Nabhan, Gary Paul. 1985. *Gathering the Desert*. University of Arizona Press, Tucson.

Pearlstein, S. L., R. S. Felger, E. P. Glenn, J. Harrington, K. A. Al-Ghanemd, and S. G. Nelson. 2012. Nipa (*Distichlis palmeri*): A perennial grain crop for saltwater irrigation. *Journal of Arid Environments* 82: 60–70.

Rea, Amadeo. 1997. *At the Desert's Green Edge: An Ethnobotany of the Gila River Pima*. University of Arizona Press, Tucson.

Russell, Sharman Apt. 2005. *Hunger: An Unnatural History*. Basic Books, New York.

Richard Stephen Felger
University of Arizona Herbarium
Tucson, AZ 85721
rfelger@email.arizona.edu

Neil Logan
Forest Agriculture Research Management Center
PO Box 551754
Kapa'au, HI 96755
neil@farmcenter.org

by John Slattery

MEDICINAL USES OF EDIBLE PLANTS OF THE SONORAN DESERT

An elder vaquero friend of mine in Sonora named Bernardo once told me that tres espinas (three spines) from the mesquite grande tree boiled in water and drunk in a three-cup dosage over three days eliminates parasites. Fortunately, I haven't needed to apply this remedy, but I trust Bernardo's experience.

I have used mesquite medicine on other occasions, however. Once I fell into a giant saguaro cactus while trying to reach for a ripe fruit. I came down with such force that I was left with a face and arm full of dirty cactus spines. Once the shock wore off (and great humility set in), I put some leafing branches of mesquite from my yard into a pot and set it to boil along with some chaparral. I soaked in this tea throughout the afternoon cleansing my aching wounds and relieving the pain gradually into the night. Next morning: no pain, no swelling. How simple these remedies are, I thought. I needn't look any further than what lay before me.

Foraging has seen a recent upsurge in popularity, but it's nothing new. Regardless of our heritage, all of our ancestors knew this experience to some degree. Walking the earth to gather one's food and medicine, we can nourish both the spirit and the body and create a deeper sense of place. Not only that, but we can diminish the degree of separation between our food and medicine. This integrated experience activates various levels of our awareness as we move within nature registering and decoding patterns with all of our senses and engages us in the process of healing. Following nature's rhythmic, seasonal flow draws us toward a state of wholeness, while informing us of our present needs (nutritional or otherwise). This was a large aspect of wellness for our ancestors, I believe, and it ties into the integral nature plants have as healing agents within our lives.

Although we tend to view medicinal herbs as useful for particular ailments or conditions, understanding their *context within place* is key to understanding all the ways they present us with healing opportunities. As you begin to explore integrating wild, indigenous foods into your diet and home landscape, also consider that many of these plants have valuable and specific medicinal applications as well.

Here is a selection of useful medicinal applications for a sampling of Sonoran Desert plants.

MESQUITE (*PROSOPIS SPP.*)

All parts of mesquite—leaves, pods, flowers, inner bark, thorns, and sap, or *chucata*—offer simple home remedies for a variety of ills.

The pods, leaves, or flowers can be used to make an eyewash to treat inflamed conjunctiva, sore eyes, or pink eye. This medicine could be of great help to diabetics who frequently incur eye inflammation due to poor circulation.

Chewing mesquite leaves and swallowing the juice was commonly done to help indigestion. Eating fresh leaves helped inhibit dysentery or diarrhea. A tea of the leaves was used to treat headache, stomachache, and fever. Held in the mouth, the tea was used to lessen painful gums. The leaves and flowers have a mild sedative effect used as a tea, relaxing an overactive mind and relieving hot conditions.

The Apache and Tewa used a cold tea of the pods for earache. Additionally, the "molasses," or syrup, made from cooking a concentrated tea of the pods over low heat for many hours can be a soothing aid to convalescing patients, providing nutrition and soothing irritations in the digestive tract. I have used this syrup as a replacement for sugar or honey when creating medicinal syrups. The flavor is far less sweet, yet it still aids in preservation. The flour made from the pods is highly nutritious, gluten-free, digestible without cooking, and high in insoluble fiber which makes for a very low glycemic load. The O'odham people of Southern Arizona have the highest rates of diabetes in the world. While mesquite was once one of their main traditional foods, it is largely absent from the diet now.

An infusion of the bark was given to children to stop bedwetting. The O'odham used the inner bark of *kúi* as a tea for indigestion as well as an emetic or cathartic, and it could be used as a food when necessary. The powdered, inner bark from the screwbean mesquite (*Prosopis pubescens*) was applied to wounds or rashes, and the root tea was used for menstrual irregularities.

The black sap, called *choohoo viduj* in Tohono O'odham, can be used to heal cataracts. One of the premier medicines from mesquite is made from the clear sap, or chucata (*oo'shuk* in O'odham), which contains mucilage. The medicine is made by dissolving the sap in warm water (3:1, water to sap), straining it, and adding glycerin to preserve it. This is a wonderful remedy when recovering from an intestinal illness, abdominal surgery, painful sore throat, laryngitis, or peptic ulcers. It can also be used topically for wounds, sores, sunburn, and sore eyes. Simply holding the clear sap in one's mouth as it dissolves can also relieve a sore throat.

DESERT IRONWOOD (*OLNEYA TESOTA*)

As the heat picks up in late spring, the subtle pink and white pea blossoms of the ironwood form a sort of haze over this tremendous tree when viewed from a distance. Desert inhabitants have long used *palo fierro* blossoms as an infusion, serving as a tonic for the heart and lungs. More specifically, this tea can be used to treat a chronic cough, even whooping cough, or to allay the ache of an emotional wound to the heart. A decoction of the bark (mashed and boiled in water) is also used to treat diabetes.

PALO VERDE (*PARKINSONIA* SPP.)

The legume in the desert foothills joining saguaro and cholla in abundance is our yellow palo verde (*Parkinsonia microphylla*). While yellow palo verde is used predominantly in local folk medicine, the blue palo verde (*P. florida*) and Mexican palo verde (*P. aculeata*) also have applications. Yellow palo verde bark is employed as a diabetes and kidney remedy in the villages of Sonora. The bark is stripped

from the branch, dried, and decocted into a tea drunk three times a day to aid in kidney function, relieving inflammation in the kidneys, and bladder, while relaxing the kidneys and enhancing the flow of urine. While I don't dispute this remedy, I believe a diet that incorporates abundant low-glycemic, high-fiber wild desert plant foods in place of highly processed, denatured foods will greatly help diabetics suffering from insulin resistance, the root cause of the disease.

Although widely underappreciated in the Sonoran Desert, Mexican palo verde (*Parkinsonia aculeata*) is now found naturalized on every continent except Antarctica. It has been studied for its usefulness in jaundice, urinary tract infections, and melanoma. Specifically, the apigenin content of the leaves is believed to affect melanoma tissue culture, which is an exciting possibility. Flower and leaf liniments from Mexican palo verde have been used to relieve rheumatism, and decoctions of the leaf and stem can help treat malaria.

WOLFBERRY (*LYCIUM PALLIDUM*)

One species of Sonoran Desert wolfberry is used for medicine. It often grows in small clusters at roadsides. A tea or tincture prepared from the leaf and stem are used as a decongestant. This plant works well in a hay fever formula along with several other native Sonoran Desert plants, e.g., ragweed, brittlebush, and estafiate ("the grandmother herb" or women's sage). The wolfberry fruit might also serve as a yin tonic (similar to its relatives in Chinese medicine), capable of nourishing and lubricating fluids of the body, a valuable attribute for those living in a dry climate. Consider adding small handfuls of wolfberries to teas or soups to help offset night sweats or excessive dryness, and during periods of excessive sexual activity.

CHOLLA (*CYLINDROPUNTIA* SPP.)

Medicinally, our focus is on the fruit and the root of cholla cactus. Various species of cholla fruit have been used medicinally by indigenous peoples. The fruit pulp's main attribute is its cooling energy. Simply gather the fruit, peel, and mash. The mashed pulp (including seeds is fine) can be applied to burns, bites, stings, or heat rash with a thin cloth or directly poulticed onto the skin. Diluted in water (1:3) it can be sipped to alleviate heat stroke. The root, *raíz de cholla* as it's known in Sonora, is often gathered from *Cylindropuntia fulgida*, or jumping cholla, and can be used in all cases of urinary tract irritation, infection, or calculi (stones) development in the bladder or kidneys.

PRICKLY PEAR (*OPUNTIA SPP.*)

Found abundantly throughout the Sonoran desert (and all North American deserts), prickly pear beautifully bridges the gap between food and medicine. The flower, fruit, and pad of *Opuntia* species all offer medicinal uses. Although there is overlap in their applications, each has distinct attributes.

Flowers: Prickly pear will flower in the early to mid-spring, depending on elevation. The flowers, comprised of inner and outer tepals, range in color from yellow, salmon, pink, beige, to deep red, all of which can be used. It is best to allow them to dry on the cactus before gathering. Once dry, simply pick the crispy flower cluster up carefully from the green fruit (or ovary) below. Be aware that tiny glochids from the green fruit may have penetrated the flower and remain stuck in the tepals. Flowers can be used whole or ground to make tea. Infuse in hot water and let stand several minutes. The flower tea has antioxidant and anti-inflammatory properties and is specific for the prostate (combine with damiana). Prostatic hypertrophy (swelling) may be quickly reduced through regular use of the tea (the fruit juice may be beneficial, also). It is also useful in urinary tract infections and mild cases of acid reflux due to its cooling and moistening nature. This tea will aid in any situation where tissue repair is needed.

Fruit: Delicious, varied in its taste, and a first-rate medicine. Traditionally various North American tribes

applied both fruits (roasted and mashed) and pads (roasted and filleted) to bruises, sprains, and wounds. Both the fruits and pads are known for their effects on insulin resistance (improving fasting glucose, triglycerides, and high blood pressure). Drinking the fully ripened fruit juice is an excellent remedy for sore, inflamed muscles, tendons, and ligaments. It also helps bring fluidity and springy responsiveness back to beleaguered joints. As little as one-half ounce of the juice per day may be effective. For some, the juice is very soothing to esophageal irritation such as in acid reflux.

Pads: Nopal pads (roasted or raw) make an excellent drawing agent for venomous bites, stings, and abraded tissue, or as a soothing agent for bruises, sprains, and breaks.

BARREL CACTUS (*FEROCACTUS WISLIZENI*)

The stout and humble barrel cactus offers much in the way of food and medicine. The sour fruits are mucilaginous when fresh and are used in Sonora as a drink to treat acid reflux. To make a drink, slice open the ripened yellow fruit and remove the seeds. Chop and mash the fruit slightly before adding to a cup of water. Let sit for 15 to 30 minutes, strain, and drink. The water should be slimy and soothing. Barrel cactus root is used similarly to cholla root in treating an irritated and infected urinary tract. You can gather exposed lateral roots from knocked-down barrel cactus, which are often easy to find.

SAGUARO (*CARNEGIEA GIGANTEA*)

The fruits of the inimitable saguaro are relished by nearly all creatures amidst the dry heat of early summer, and at no other time of the year. Before the introduction of European fruit tree cultivars, honey, sugar—and the advent of air conditioning—the saguaro fruit served as the prime sweet treat and cooling and moistening medicine to the indigenous of the Sonoran Desert at the hottest and driest time of year. According to records left by the colonial missionaries, indigenous peoples would suddenly disappear for weeks at a time during cactus fruiting season, and return to the mission nearly unrecognizable for all the weight they had put on by eating nothing but cactus fruit while they were away. This is a testament to the nourishing properties of saguaro fruit and also supports findings from traditional Chinese medicine suggesting that sweet flavors help develop bodily flesh. Saguaro seeds, often kept in storage throughout the year, were mashed in water and given to nursing mothers to drink to improve their milk flow. The flesh of the saguaro has been used to apply to painful, rheumatic joints, as well as breaks and sprains.

I suggest you refrain from this application unless you've encountered a healthy portion of a fallen, dying saguaro from which to cut the flesh. The saguaro, after all, is a protected species in our desert. Unless a member of the Tohono O'odham Nation, you can only harvest saguaro on private land.

Foraging for (and growing) medicine offers inhabitants of the Sonoran Desert an opportunity to view their beautiful homeland with new eyes and participate in its bounty in new ways. I encourage all readers to seek out the highly valued, traditional edible and medicinal plants of their own region or homeland and those who are practiced in the usage of these plants.

BENEFICIAL WILDLIFE NEIGHBORS IN NATIVE FOOD FORESTS
- just a tiny sample of what's possible

ALL PHOTOS BY DORIS EVANS, UNLESS OTHERWISE NOTED

1. Desert tortoise digs a basin just before a rainstorm, in which it hopes to capture rainwater. If it fills, the tortoise will drink its fill. Photo and research: Phil Medica, U.S. Geological Survey

2. Desert spiny lizard

3. Young screech owls

4. Javelina

5. Female Costa's hummingbird feasts from a chuparosa flower.

6. Texas horned lizard harvests rain falling on its back. Its semi-tubular hinges, deeply indented between all of its scales, have rough internal surfaces that enhance capillary transport of the captured water to its mouth. Photo and research: Wade C. Sherbrooke

7. Spadefoot toad voices its "love call" after big summer storms.

8. Bobcat

9. Queen butterfly feeds on the flower of a climbing milkweed vine.

10. The Wilson's Warbler and other small neotropical songbirds migrate from Central America through the Sonoran Desert and up into Canada and back each year. Along its journey this warbler must refuel and seeks out flowering native mesquite trees to feast on the bounty of insects they attract. Photo and research: Charles van Riper III, U.S. Geological Survey

11. Cholla cactus, such as this chain fruit cholla, make excellent nesting sites as they are cat proof. Photo: Jill Lorenzini

12. Cottontail

13. The sight of a spotted skimmer dragonfly indicates that water is nearby.

14. Mexican free-tailed bats set out at dusk to consume enormous amounts of insects.

15. A tarantula (here in its burrow) has a diet consisting mostly of insects.

16. Zebra-tailed lizard wags its tail.

17. Family of Gambel's quail

18. Roadrunner

19. Mule deer

20. Native bee pollinating a staghorn cholla cactus bloom within a water-harvesting, traffic-calming chicane. Photo: Brad Lancaster

21. Young Cooper's hawk

22. Desert iguana hunting creosote flowers to eat. Photo: Jill Lorenzini

23. This young, non-venomous gopher snake helps control rodent populations.

24. The Sonora suckerfish was once abundant and fished from the Santa Cruz River when it flowed through Tucson. By 1937, the fish were extinct in this area, as the river's flows had subsided due to both overpumping of groundwater and the mismanagement of the river and its watershed. Like the horned lizard and desert tortoise, we can harvest or plant (not drain) the rain to irrigate native food-plants for free, which decreases the pumping of groundwater while increasing its recharge. If enough of us do so there is a chance we can bring back the river, the fish, and the Great Mesquite Bosque we lost.
Photo: George Andrejko, Arizona Game and Fish

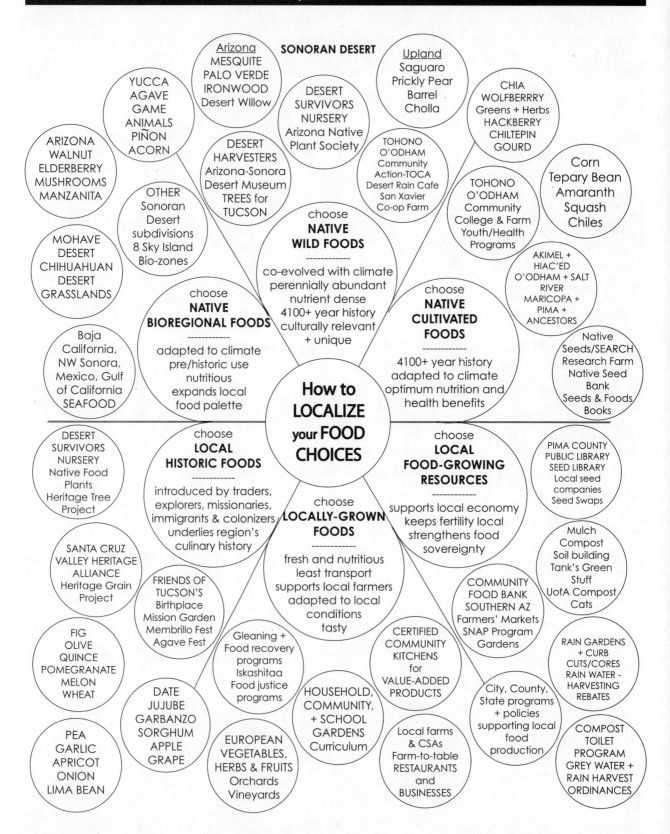

How to LOCALIZE your FOOD CHOICES

SONORAN DESERT

Arizona
MESQUITE
PALO VERDE
IRONWOOD
Desert Willow

Upland
Saguaro
Prickly Pear
Barrel
Cholla

YUCCA
AGAVE
GAME
ANIMALS
PIÑON
ACORN

CHIA
WOLFBERRRY
Greens + Herbs
HACKBERRY
CHILTEPIN
GOURD

ARIZONA
WALNUT
ELDERBERRY
MUSHROOMS
MANZANITA

DESERT
SURVIVORS
NURSERY
Arizona Native
Plant Society

DESERT
HARVESTERS
Arizona-Sonora
Desert Museum
TREES for
TUCSON

TOHONO
O'ODHAM
Community
Action-TOCA
Desert Rain Cafe
San Xavier
Co-op Farm

TOHONO
O'ODHAM
Community
College & Farm
Youth/Health
Programs

Corn
Tepary Bean
Amaranth
Squash
Chiles

OTHER
Sonoran
Desert
subdivisions
8 Sky Island
Bio-zones

choose
**NATIVE
WILD FOODS**
----
co-evolved with climate
perennially abundant
nutrient dense
4100+ year history
culturally relevant
+ unique

choose
**NATIVE
CULTIVATED
FOODS**

4100+ year history
adapted to climate
optimum nutrition and
health benefits

AKIMEL +
HIAC'ED
O'ODHAM + SALT
RIVER
MARICOPA +
PIMA +
ANCESTORS

MOHAVE
DESERT
CHIHUAHUAN
DESERT
GRASSLANDS

choose
**NATIVE
BIOREGIONAL FOODS**
----
adapted to climate
pre/historic use
nutritious
expands local
food palette

Native
Seeds/SEARCH
Research Farm
Native Seed
Bank
Seeds & Foods
Books

Baja
California,
NW Sonora,
Mexico, Gulf
of California
SEAFOOD

DESERT
SURVIVORS
NURSERY
Native Food
Plants
Heritage Tree
Project

choose
**LOCAL
HISTORIC FOODS**
----
introduced by traders,
explorers, missionaries,
immigrants & colonizers
underlies region's
culinary history

choose
**LOCAL
FOOD-GROWING
RESOURCES**
----
supports local economy
keeps fertility local
strengthens food
sovereignty

PIMA COUNTY
PUBLIC LIBRARY
SEED LIBRARY
Local seed
companies
Seed Swaps

SANTA CRUZ
VALLEY HERITAGE
ALLIANCE
Heritage Grain
Project

FRIENDS OF
TUCSON'S
Birthplace
Mission Garden
Membrillo Fest
Agave Fest

choose
**LOCALLY-GROWN
FOODS**
----
fresh and nutritious
least transport
supports local farmers
adapted to local
conditions
tasty

Mulch
Compost
Soil building
Tank's Green
Stuff
UofA Compost
Cats

FIG
OLIVE
QUINCE
POMEGRANATE
MELON
WHEAT

COMMUNITY
FOOD BANK
SOUTHERN AZ
Farmers' Markets
SNAP Program
Gardens

Gleaning +
Food recovery
programs
Iskashitaa
Food justice
programs

CERTIFIED
COMMUNITY
KITCHENS
for
VALUE-ADDED
PRODUCTS

RAIN GARDENS
+ CURB
CUTS/CORES
RAIN WATER -
HARVESTING
REBATES

PEA
GARLIC
APRICOT
ONION
LIMA BEAN

DATE
JUJUBE
GARBANZO
SORGHUM
APPLE
GRAPE

HOUSEHOLD,
COMMUNITY,
+ SCHOOL
GARDENS
Curriculum

City, County,
State programs
+ policies
supporting local
food
production

EUROPEAN
VEGETABLES,
HERBS & FRUITS
Orchards
Vineyards

Local farms
& CSAs
Farm-to-table
RESTAURANTS
and
BUSINESSES

COMPOST
TOILET
PROGRAM
GREY WATER +
RAIN HARVEST
ORDINANCES

RESOURCES

ETHNOBOTANY

At the Desert's Green Edge: An Ethnobotany of the Gila River Pima by Amadeo M. Rea. University of Arizona Press, 1997.

The Desert Smells Like Rain by Gary Paul Nabhan. North Point Press, 1987.

Food Plants of the Sonoran Desert by Wendy C. Hodgson. University of Arizona Press, 2001.

From I'Itoi's Garden: Tohono O'odham Food Traditions. Tohono O'odham Community Action (TOCA) with Mary Paganelli Votto and Frances Manuel. 2010.

Native Foodways magazine. Tohono O'odham Community Action (TOCA).

People of the Desert and Sea: Ethnobotany of the Seri Indians by Richard Stephen Felger and Mary Beck Moser. University of Arizona Press, 1985.

Southwest Foraging: 117 Wild and Flavorful Edibles from Barrel Cactus to Wild Oregano by John Slattery. Timber Press, 2016.

Tending the Wild: Native American Knowledge and the Management of California's Natural Resources by M. Kat Anderson. University of California Press, 2005.

COOKING WITH NATIVE PLANTS

Cooking the Wild Southwest: Delicious Recipes for Desert Plants by Carolyn Niethammer. University of Arizona Press, 2011.

Eat Mesquite: A Cookbook! by Desert Harvesters. 2011.

From I'Itoi's Garden: Tohono O'odham Food Traditions. Tohono O'odham Community Action (TOCA) with Mary Paganelli Votto and Frances Manuel. 2010.

Wild Recipes: Seasonal Samplings by Barbara Rose and Jill Lorenzini. Self-published, 2008. (BeanTreeFarm@ gmail.com)

CREATING/STEWARDING WILDLIFE HABITAT AT HOME

Search "Habitat at Home" at TucsonAudubon.org

EDIBLE INSECTS

Man Eating Bugs: The Art and Science of Eating Insects by Peter Menzel and Faith D'Aluisio. Material World, 1998.

MEDICINAL USES OF NATIVE PLANTS

Medicinal Plants of the American Southwest by Charles W. Kane. Lincoln Town Press, 2011.

Medicinal Plants of the Desert and Canyon West by Michael Moore. Museum of New Mexico Press, 1989.

PLANT IDENTIFICATION

Botany in a Day: The Patterns Method of Plant Identification, 6th Edition, by Thomas Elpel. HOPS Press, 2013.

Native Plants for Southwestern Landscapes by Judy Mielke. University of Texas Press, 1993.

Plants of Arizona by Anne Epple and John Weins. Falcon Press, 2012.

Shrubs and Trees of the Southwest Deserts by Janice Emily Bowers. Southwest Parks and Monuments Association, 1993.

Shrubs and Trees of the Southwest Uplands by Francis H. Elmore. Southwest Parks and Monuments Association, 1976.

FireFlyForest.com/flowers

SWbiodiversity.org

NATURAL HISTORY OF SONORAN DESERT

Growing Native with Petey Mesquitey radio show and podcast on KXCI.org

A Natural History of the Sonoran Desert, 2nd Edition, edited by S. J. Phillips, P. W. Comus, M. A. Dimmitt, and L. M. Brewer. Arizona-Sonora Desert Museum Press/ University of California Press, 2015.

Requiem for the Santa Cruz: An Environmental History of an Arizona River by Robert H. Webb, Julio L. Betancourt, R. Roy Johnson, and Raymond M. Turner. University of Arizona Press, 2014.

Southern Arizona Nature Almanac by Roseanne Beggy Hanson and Jonathan Hanson. University of Arizona Press, 2003.

DesertMuseum.org

PLANNING FOR SONORAN DESERT CONSERVATION

Pima County's Sonoran Desert Conservation Plan

SOLAR COOKING

The Sunny Side of Cooking: Solar Cooking and Other Ecologically Friendly Cooking Methods for the 21st Century by Lisa Rayner. Lifeweaver LLC, 2007.

WATER HARVESTING

Rainwater Harvesting for Drylands and Beyond: Guiding Principles to Welcome Rain into Your Life and Landscape, Volume 1, 2nd Edition, by Brad Lancaster. Rainsource Press, 2013.

Rainwater Harvesting for Drylands and Beyond: Water-Harvesting Earthworks, Volume 2, by Brad Lancaster. Rainsource Press, 2008.

WORKSHOPS AND HOW-TO

AZnps.org

BeanTreeFarm.com

CommunityFoodBank.org

DesertHarvesters.org

HarvestingRainwater.com

LorenziniWorks.com

SonoranPermaculture.org

Tierra y Libertad

TOCAonline.org

SUPPLIERS OF SONORAN DESERT WILD FOOD INGREDIENTS AND PRODUCTS

ArizonaCactusRanch.com

BeanTreeFarm.org

DesertForager.com

FoodConspiracy.coop

MesquiteFlour.com

NativeSeeds.org

SanXavierCoop.org

TOCAonline.org

SUPPLIERS OF SONORAN DESERT WILD FOOD PLANTS AND SEED

DesertSurvivors.org

DrylandSeeds.com

TucsonCactus.org

Wildlands Restoration

MULCH AND COMPOST

TanksGreenStuff.com

See DesertHarvesters.org for additional resources.

AUTHOR BIOS

AMANDA BRAMBLE is the director of Ampersand Sustainable Learning Center, a living demonstration site near Cerrillos/Madrid, New Mexico, for permaculture, appropriate technologies, and sustainable practices. Amanda and her husband, Andy, live and work at the Center, hosting workshops and community events, retreats, residencies, and internships "for everyday folks wanting to respond intelligently to the state of the Earth." Learn more at AmpersandProject.org.

KIMI EISELE is a writer and multidisciplinary artist in Tucson. Her work is grounded in exploration of place and environment, creating opportunities for community collaborations, civic participation, and deeper discovery of our connection to nature. She is the writer/editor of *BorderLore*, the e-journal of the Southwest Folklife Alliance. Her novel, *The Lightest Object in the Universe*, is forthcoming (Spring 2019) from Algonquin Press. Learn more at KimiEisele.com.

RICHARD FELGER is an associated researcher at the University of Arizona Herbarium and School of Plant Sciences. He has written or co-authored more than 100 peer-reviewed publications in addition to books and numerous popular writings in botany, ethnobiology, new food crops, and other fields.

BRAD LANCASTER is co-founder of Desert Harvesters and the author of *Rainwater Harvesting for Drylands and Beyond*, Volumes 1 and 2 (Rainsource Press). He teaches and lectures nationally and internationally on how to partner with living systems through the reciprocal harvests of water, sun, shade, wind, and more to grow healthy communities. Learn more at HarvestingRainwater.com.

NEIL LOGAN is an applied ethnobotanist and agroforestry systems designer in Hawaii and co-directs the FARM Center. He and Richard Felger are collaborating with other scientists in the development of mesquite and nipa (a salt-tolerant grain) as global food crops.

JILL LORENZINI is a writer, visual artist, educator, natural builder, and desert harvester. She regularly offers workshops and demonstrations on desert harvesting, cooking, and natural building. Learn more at LorenziniWorks.com.

JOHN SLATTERY enjoys foraging for wild foods and medicines of the greater Southwest region with his daughter Ofelia and their various companions. He founded Desert Tortoise Botanicals, a handcrafted herbal products company, in 2005, and began the Sonoran Herbalist Apprenticeship Program in 2010, in Tucson, where he resides. Learn more about John at johnjslattery.com and discover more about desert plants and how to harvest them in his book, *Southwest Foraging* (Timber Press, 2016).

ACKNOWLEDGMENTS

Any meal is the product of countless actions and efforts, from planting and tending to harvesting and processing to experimenting, preparing, and cooking, and finally to sharing the flavors and sustenance of these efforts. The same is true of *Eat Mesquite and More*.

First and foremost, we offer endless gratitude to the Tohono O'odham, Akimel and Hia C-ed O'odham, Yaqui/Yoeme, and Apache peoples, and their predecessors, along with early settlers and long-time desert dwellers for their discoveries and use of mesquite pods and other edible native plants, and for their willingness to share harvest and culinary traditions. We are indebted to those who first inspired Desert Harvesters to provide community mesquite millings and other efforts to connect people to the wild food abundance of this place: Clifford Pablo and the San Xavier Co-op Farm for early and continued offerings of locally grown and milled mesquite flour and other native, wild foods; Carlos Nagel for early marketing of mesquite flour to the masses; and David Omick and Pearl Mast and the Cascabel Conservation Association for the original and ongoing celebration of mesquite through community mesquite millings, pancake breakfasts, and wild food feasts in rural southeastern Arizona.

We extend sincere gratitude to the generous cooks who shared their recipes with us and the many volunteer testers and tasters who sampled them—your culinary gifts will now reach many. Endless gratitude to those who helped plan and raise funds for *Eat Mesquite*, the precursor and foundation for this new volume. Many thanks to those who carried through the vision for this revised and expanded cookbook: Brad Lancaster for writing, coordinating, editing, and photography; Jill Lorenzini for writing, photography, illustration, and recipe coordination and review; Julie Burguiere for spearheading early efforts to help secure critical grant funding; Mikaela Jones for recipe coordination, organization, reviews, and testing; Kimi Eisele for writing, editing, organizing, and content decision-making; Lori Adkison for recipe reviews and coordinating recipe photography; Christian Timmerman, Ian Fritz, Barbara Rose, Kathleen Dreier, Jim Martin Harris, Josh Schachter, and Ben Johnson, Doris Evans, Steven Meckler, Charles van Riper III, Phil Medica, and Wade Sherbrooke for photography; Bill Mackey and Kay Sather for illustrations; Barbara Seyda and Debra Makay for copyediting; Jane Lorenzini for technical help; Teri Bingham for design and layout; and Janet Perlman for indexing.

Huge appreciation to all Desert Harvesters volunteers for their help testing, tasting, reviewing, revising, and selecting recipes: Chris Cowen, Deb DiBiasie, Kathy Della Penta, Vickie Everitte, Margot Garcia, Jim Harris, Harmony Hazard, Cameron Jones, Philip Keuper, Ellie Kirkwood, Kim Knebel, Max Yue Li, Terry Lim, Jamie Madden, Aaron Martz, Daniel Moss, Kathy Paul, Andy Pieper, Alexandra Rosenburg, Emily Rockey, Madeline Ryder, Aspen Samuelson, Elizabeth Smith, Caitlin Stern, Anna Tyler, Lori VanBuggenum, and Aaron Wright. Additional thanks to cooks Raven Bolas, Aaron Flesch, Sara Jones, and Kara Jones.

Special thanks to core Desert Harvesters staff, past and present: Jeau Allen, Julie Burguiere, Megan Hartman, Nick Garber, Dana Helfer, Brad Lancaster, Jill Lorenzini, Anastasia Rabin, Barbara Rose, Amy Valdés Schwemm, and Linda Wood. Your passion, time, and efforts are an incredible gift to this community and the world. We cannot thank you enough.

Many thanks go to the following individuals and organizations for their contributions: Dunbar/Spring Community Garden and Neighborhood Forest, along with its gardeners and foresters; Barbara Rose and interns Alex Rosenberg, Aspen Samuelson, and Aaron

Martz of Bean Tree Farm; Richard Felger and Neil Logan; Ofelia Zepeda; Peter Gierlach and Spadefoot Nursery; Gary Paul Nabhan; Clifford Pablo and the Tohono O'odham Community College Agriculture Extension Program; Stella and Tanisha Tucker; Terrol Dew Johnson and Tohono O'odham Community Action (TOCA); Barbara Eiswerth and the Iskashitaa Refugee Network; Jeau Allen of Desert Seeds, the Mesquitery, and Aravaipa Heirlooms; David Omick and Pearl Mast; John Slattery and Desert Tortoise Botanicals; Amanda Bramble of Ampersand Sustainable Learning Center; Audra Chrisophel, Kara Jones, and Abigail Plano of Community Food Bank of Southern Arizona's Santa Cruz River Farmers Market; Elena Ortiz and Las Milpitas Farm; Jim Verrier and Desert Survivors Native Plant Nursery; Bernie Jilka and Nighthawk Natives Nursery; Gene Joseph and Plants for the Southwest; Miles Anderson; the Mesquite Harvest Working Group (Nick Garber, Jeau Allen, Martha Ames Burgess, Blake Gentry, Mike Gray, Brad Lancaster, Gail Loveland, Laurie Melrood, Meghan Mix, Valerie McCaffrey, Mark and Lee Moody, and Amy Valdés Schwemm) for researching safe harvesting practices of mesquite; Mercado San Augustín; Kelly Watters and the Food Conspiracy Co-op; Mike A. Mayer and the Cooper Center for Environmental Learning; the San Xavier Co-op Farm; Amy and Doug Smith of EXO Roast Co; Lia Griesser and Mikaela Jones of EXO Kitchen; Jo Schneider and La Cocina Bar, Food, and Music; John Adkisson and Iron John Brewery; Rebecca Safford and Tap and Bottle; Doug Biggers and Megan Kimble and *Edible Baja Arizona Magazine*; *Edible Baja Arizona's* Baja Brews and all participating Tucson craft brewers; and the San Pedro Mesquite Company.

Eat Mesquite and More was made possible with funding from LUSH Cosmetics Sustainable Lush Fund, the Community Food Bank of Southern Arizona's Punch Woods Endowment Grant, Southwest Folklife Alliance, Technicians for Sustainability, Mary Ann Clark, Time Market, The B-Line, Desert Forager, and all those who donated to our Generosity by Indiegogo campaign. Many thanks to Julie Burguiere, Megan Hartman, Nick Garber, Brad Lancaster, Linda Wood, Debbie Bringhurst, and Shannon Scott for helping acquire and/or manage those funds.

And finally, deep bows of gratitude to the unique plants and animals that help sustain, enliven, beautify, nourish, and enchant our human lives in the Sonoran Desert.

INDEX

Note: Illustrations are shown by italic page numbers